BLACK PROFILES IN COURAGE

BLACK PROFILES IN COURAGE

A Legacy of African-American Achievement

Kareem Abdul-Jabbar

and Alan Steinberg

FOREWORD BY HENRY LOUIS GATES, JR.

Perennial

An Imprint of HarperCollinsPublishers

First published in hardcover in 1996 by William Morrow and Company, Inc.

BLACK PROFILES IN COURAGE. Copyright © 1996 Kareem Abdul-Jabbar. All rights reserved. Printed in the United States of America. No part of this book may be used or reproduced in any manner whatsoever without written permission except in the case of brief quotations embodied in critical articles and reviews. For information address HarperCollins Publishers Inc., 10 East 53rd Street, New York, NY 10022.

HarperCollins books may be purchased for educational, business, or sales promotional use. For information please write: Special Markets Department, HarperCollins Publishers Inc., 10 East 53rd Street, New York, NY 10022.

First Perennial edition published 2000.

Library of Congress Cataloguing-in-Publication Data is available.

ISBN 0-380-81341-6

07 08 09 ❖/RRD H 20 19 18 17 16 15 14 13 12 11

———∞———

This book is dedicated to all Americans who seek
to embrace their heritage. It is especially dedicated to
young Americans, who most need a heritage to embrace.
I write to inform, encourage, inspire.

A life is not important except in the impact
it has on other lives.
JACKIE ROBINSON

Sticks in a bundle are unbreakable.
BONDEI PROVERB

When the music changes, so does the dance.
HAUSA PROVERB

FOREWORD

BY HENRY LOUIS GATES, JR.

I was always bound for college, it seems, if memory serves me correctly. My mother, Pauline Coleman Gates, wanted both of her boys to become doctors. For her, a *doctor* signified both dignity and security: a combination of the scaling the pinnacle of knowledge and of intellectual discipline as well as the capacity to command respect and a comfortable, secure standard of living within one's community. The mastery of medical arts also entailed a certain nobility: the ability to fend for one's self, as independently as the possession of a highly valued skill allows almost anyone in our society, and the ability to relocate quickly if the level of racism where one lived ever escalated beyond one's capacities to preserve one's dignity, livelihood, and self-respect.

College bound as I was, early on, even in late elementary school, I began to collect college catalogs. These I would devour cover to cover, determined to master even the smallest details of the premedical requirements at schools such as Michigan State, UCLA, and my own state university, West Virginia University. I chose these schools for one reason alone: the strength and history of their basketball programs. The "final four'' playoff in the NCAA championship was for me an opportunity to refine my shortlist, to add or subtract a university from my own final four. Without a doubt, my number-one choice throughout the sixties was—by such a long shot that number two couldn't even come close—UCLA.

What did I, a colored boy growing up in the Allegheny Mountains two hours west of Washington, D.C., know about the academic strengths and weaknesses of UCLA? Very, very little. But I did know—like every other schoolgirl or -boy in America—that UCLA was the home of an unrivaled dynasty in college basketball; moreover, the black and shining prince of that kingdom was a Roman Catholic honors student named Lewis Alcindor.

Lew Alcindor was an inspiration for me, but most certainly not on the basketball court. I never was very skilled at athletics but I was an avid spectator, priding myself on being able to remember statistics and to memorize patterns of set plays. In part because I had not been blessed with athletic abilities and in part because I had been born into a family of bookworms, my interests in sports were intellectual, the pleasures I derived from play vicarious. For me, sports, including basketball, assuming pride of place among the athletic arts, were a pleasant diversion, an avocation rather than a vocation. While my childhood friends would fantasize about becoming Wilt Chamberlain, Willie Mays, or Jackie Robinson, I had thoughts of Albert Schweitzer, George Washington Carver, or Dr. Charles Drew. I envied our star athletes their uncanny court prowess, but I relished their nickname for me: the professor. I became our varsity team's statistician, enabling me to be close to the action without having to play and sharpening a skill that could help me to understand even more about the deeper logic of this seemingly helter-skelter game. And maybe, just maybe, I thought, I could perform such a task at my beloved UCLA.

One day, I was devouring the pages of *Ebony* magazine, as was my wont, hungry to encounter the profiles of our leaders in culture, in politics, in the performing arts. I dare say, *Ebony* has done more to distribute knowledge about the black community, current and historical, and thereby to cement the bonds of communities, than any other single agency or institution in African-American history. Leafing through on this day, in the middle of my high school years, I came upon a profile of my beloved Mr. Alcindor, as I set out to learn whatever I could from this timely story of this compelling man.

Alcindor had captured my attention not so much because of his size or his considerable skills in the lanes, but because he was so obviously an intellectual, so obviously a thoughtful person who read *books*. He was also articulate—"Well spoken, that boy," my own father would say on those all too infrequent occasions when "Big Lew" (soon to metamorphose himself into Kareem Abdul-Jabbar)—would enter our lives through an interview, usually following one of his triumphantly devastating athletic performances.

(This "Abdul-Jabbar" business took awhile to get used to, up in the hills of Appalachia, where I grew up, as did his dome-shaped Afro. At first, his fans among us resisted, calling Abdul-Jabbar "Alcindor" or "Big Lew." This resistance arose in part out of fear of his chosen religion and in part out of an uncertainty about how to pronounce it correctly. "Abdul-Jab-bár" never did become "Abdul-Jab-bár" in my home town;

"Abdul-Jábbar," as in talking incessantly, was just about the best that the older folks could do. "Cream Abdul-Jabbar" was the brilliant center who blocked an unprecedented number of shots, dominated offensive and defensive rebounds, and perfected a deadly weapon known far and wide as the sky hook.)

But he was also the person who introduced me, at least, to *The Autobiography of Malcolm X*. Read this book, Alcindor said in that *Ebony* profile; all Americans, white and black, should read this book. And so I did.

I sat up all night reading that book, just as my father would the following night. I went on to read other books by black authors referred to in Malcolm's pages and reviewed, of course, in the pages of *Ebony*. Slowly, gradually, inevitably, I became engulfed in reading books about the Black Experience and, simultaneously, I began to reshape my own list of the "final four" schools and what I wanted to study, selecting them now for what they promised to offer me by way of the life of the mind.

Kareem Abdul-Jabbar, for as long as I can remember, has always championed the role of the scholar-athlete, of the nurturing of the mind as well as the body. In this he has forced us to reexamine the stereotype of the black athlete, the highly endowed physical specimen, passed along from one exploitative coach and athletic system to another and cursed by an "education" perhaps best defined as "majoring in basketball." No, Kareem Abdul-Jabbar exemplifies a conception of the athlete that is more Athenian than American: the person of letters is also a master of the physical arts.

Black Profiles in Courage, ranging as it does over four full centuries, focuses on the life and times of a small group of individual African Americans who are truly *American* heroes yet who are exemplary of the larger historical saga that persons of African descent have created in the New World, between the bold explorations of Estevanico and the quiet yet still-life determination of Miss Rosa Parks. And what a wondrous saga it has been! Mr. Abdul-Jabbar selected, as John Kennedy did three decades ago, a group of people whose sacrifices were for the common good, whose will was unbending, whose individual ambitions and endowments they put in the service of a cause greater than personal wealth or fame— and that is the triumph over slavery, first, and, second, over antiblack racist segregation between the founding of this great republic and the birth of Dr. Martin Luther King's great civil rights movement in the middle of this century. From Harriet Tubman, the pioneering leader of the Underground Railroad who *walked* so many of our people to freedom, furtively and by night, to the thoughtful Rosa Parks, well trained as a civil rights official, well chosen to make the symbolic gesture that would ignite the protest movement that would bury legal segregation forever; from Frederick Douglass, certainly the most widely known and respected African American through the second half of the nineteenth century, a man as popular as an orator as many pop stars are today; from Joseph Cinque, the prototypical black revolutionary, determined at all cost to lead a mutiny of his fellows against the madness that is human chattel slavery, to the collective courage and determination of black soldiers to boldly defend this country abroad despite that very country's deepest ambivalence about these citizens' status at home—from all of these tales to the sublime scientific (and still unheralded) achievements of Lewis H. Latimer, who played a critical role in the invention of both the telephone and the incandescent light bulb. *Black Profiles in Courage* is a highly readable and engaging record of the triumph of the human spirit over seemingly insur-mountable odds. It is essential reading for all who long for an accessible introduction to African-American history.

But *Black Profiles in Courage* is more than this: It is the testimony of a great athlete to the importance of scholarship, study, and intellectual reflection—the crucial importance of the life of the mind. At a time when so many of our own children believe that it is easier to become *Michael* Jordan rather than *Vernon* Jordan, easier to become a professional athlete than a lawyer or a physician, more important to be a ''b-boy'' than an A student, testaments by African-American athletes to the importance of the work of scholarship and learning are even more important today than they were when I stumbled upon Lew Alcindor urging me and my fellows to read the great autobiography of Malcolm X. By his example, Kareem Abdul-Jabbar has in the writing of this book performed a service for our youth far greater even than the remarkable triumph he achieved on the court. He has shown us that even while the life of the body inevitably fades, the life of the mind triumphs forever—as long as one can read and write. A scholar-athlete himself and a *deeply moral person*, Kareem Abdul-Jabbar's achievement can find no greater home than in the pages of this splendidly researched and written book.

Harvard University
Cambridge, Massachusetts

ACKNOWLEDGMENTS

I would like to acknowledge, with gratitude, scholars who came before me and inspired this work. A particular thanks to editor, writer, historian, Dr. John Henrik Clarke, who was instrumental in developing the Harlem Youth Action Project (HARYOU) in the 1960s, where I apprenticed in a journalism workshop. HARYOU provided summer programs in art, music, and journalism and sought to inspire Harlem youngsters to participate in community activities. To research several of my journalism articles, I was directed down the street to the Schomburg Center for Research in Black Culture, which I came to call a "revelation warehouse." In fact, some of the research for this book was done at the Schomburg Library. For all the knowledge I absorbed through HARYOU and the Schomburg Center, and for giving me a glimpse of what was possible so I could one day write this book, I owe a debt I can never repay to Dr. Clarke.

For further development of my passion for scholarship, I wish to particularly acknowledge Dr. Albert Hoxie of the Department of History at UCLA. When I was his student, Dr. Hoxie's brilliant lectures on western civilization fired my imagination, inspired me to explore the true heritage of my own people, and taught me that authentic history was not dry, lifeless facts but rather the living legacies of real human beings.

Last, a special acknowledgment to my UCLA basketball mentor and coach, John Wooden. A former English teacher, Coach Wooden taught me grammar, punctuation, even some diction to go along with my layups and hook shots. More than anyone, he inspired me to understand that being both a scholar and an athlete was certainly within my grasp.

To Dr. Clarke, Dr. Hoxie, and Coach Wooden, I offer my heartfelt thanks.

Alan wishes to thank the following for their help, guidance, and support throughout the long haul: Debra Constantini, Steve and Sharon Fiffer, George Colburn, Ruth Wiener, Wally Egebergh, Bob Shekter. And always, in spirit, Jack and Estelle Steinberg.

We both extend special acknowledgment to the following authors and books for providing particularly useful road maps on our journey for the truth: Professor Ivan Van Sertima, author of *They Came Before Columbus*; William Loren Katz, author of *The Black West*; Art T. Burton, author of *Black, Red, and Deadly*; Glennette Tilley Turner, author of *Lewis Howard Latimer*; and Howard Jones, author of *Mutiny on the Amistad*.

Special thanks to our agent, Jay Acton, who laid the groundwork years ago and brought us together for this mutual labor of love; to our editor, Paul Bresnick, and his assistant, Jon Moskowitz; to Steven Diamond for helping us find the best photographs to illustrate our text; and last, but clearly not least, to Lorin Pullman and Gabrielle Palay for their professionalism, guidance, humor, and plain hard work above and beyond the call of duty.

Thank you one and all.

CONTENTS

xvii

INTRODUCTION

When I played my last professional basketball game on June 13, 1989, I began my passage from one kind of life to another. At forty-two, it was a scary transport. Even though I had a farewell year to prepare myself emotionally, I still felt strange when it ended. It was like saying good-bye forever to someone you loved; it felt like a death. But it was also a rebirth. Because for the first time since I was eight, I was free to explore my other interests. I immediately started addressing myself to young people more often, at basketball clinics and camps, after speeches, sometimes just out and about in my daily life. It has disturbed me for years that so many youngsters seem indifferent and adrift. Even though the seventies, eighties, and nineties were so different from the fifties when I grew up, kids I talked to kept reminding me of the beat generation of my youth: alienated and lacking direction, a moral center, or goals. And yet, like kids of every era, they still looked up to their idols. Some even looked up to me.

That made me wonder: "Who are kids' heroes today? What lessons do they have to teach?" When I asked this of kids, I was not surprised to learn that their heroes were mainly high-profile athletes and entertainers. Virtually none I spoke to knew anything about African

Americans of other eras or the history of our people in this country. They knew their favorite athlete's statistics, or a movie star's films, or a rock star's latest hit song. None knew the names or contributions of true African-American heroes like Crispus Attucks, Lewis Latimer, and Bass Reeves, never mind anything in depth about more traditional historical figures like Frederick Douglass and Harriet Tubman. Few recognized the name of Rosa Parks.

A few years ago, I felt compelled to write a book about heroic, significant African Americans, if for no other reason than to make important information available to these kinds of kids. I wanted to reemphasize the importance of developing a moral center and character, and the fact that we are *all* connected to each other in this country and that we should be busy reaffirming our connections, not our differences.

I am forty-nine now; most of my heroes are gone. But what they stood for still seems heroic to me. And even though today's culture promotes lower standards—self-indulgence, celebrity worship, ignorance, irresponsibility, certainly vulgarity—I still see my parents' values as beacons in the fog. I wish I could say that I think young people today see those beacons, too. But I can't. And that was the main reason for this book. I want to shine a brighter light, especially for them.

As a schoolkid, I remember feeling confused about the role of black people in American history. They didn't seem to have one. My history lessons presented blacks as ignorant savages brought here in subservient roles who contributed nothing to American life. And they came from a people who contributed nothing to the history of the world. It was like the TV shows I watched in the fifties. Occasionally, you'd see a black actor, but rarely in a speaking role. The message was: We know you're here, but you don't matter.

That is one reason why it's important for people to understand their own worth at an early age. Too many youngsters today, particularly African Americans, feel disconnected from their country. They feel America is about things that happened in the eighteenth century to people they can't identify with; and between now and then, who cares? They sense they have no stake in things and that participation in government, commerce, and cultural life is beyond their grasp. In other words, our children feel this country is not for them.

We have to change that. We have to empower our young people—especially African Americans who are largely unaware that other African Americans played key roles in *creating* this nation. We need to help them feel they are part of this country and will always *want* to be part of it. One way to do that is to provide better information about our common heritage as Americans. That is one thing I try to do in this book. By spotlighting black people whose contributions to American history have been distorted, stereotyped, or ignored, I am saying, "Take a closer look at the history we *share*. It isn't mine, it isn't yours, it isn't theirs, it's *ours*." Most black people don't get this information at home or in school. Much of it isn't in the culture anymore. I wanted to put a little bit of it back into the culture. In providing my personal view of these people and the events surrounding their lives, I am saying to everyone, not just blacks, "Take a closer look at these courageous African Americans. In many ways, they were just like you. They could have been you. You could have been them.''

My parents taught me that knowledge is power. A good way to exercise that power is to understand your heritage: where your people came from, how they got here, what their hardships were, what they accomplished. That is why I think it is especially important for young African Americans to understand how their ancestors contributed to making this country great. African contributions to the history of the New World were quite significant; they just haven't been conveyed to the people who need to know about them.

Part of the problem is our history books. The ones we used in school focused on white people's concerns: what white people wanted, what white people said, what white people did. Basically, the only things they said about black people were: *Negroes were slaves* and *Lincoln freed the slaves*. That was our purpose: We were brought here to tote that barge and lift that bale—and without any reward. This undertone carries through to today, because history books still don't convey black people as fundamentally ''American.'' We have been traditionally presented as insignificant bystanders to American history, not major participants. No wonder that when Colin Powell was first named chairman of the Joint Chiefs of Staff so many white people I know reacted with astonishment. Here we had an exceptionally bright, capable, powerful black man, yet most people knew nothing about him. Who was he? Where did he come from? How did he get to be such an important military figure? Whites were surprised because it is not yet common to hear about a black person in a position of power and influence; this is still perceived as a threat. Later, of course, when Powell became a hero in the Gulf War, whites granted him the respect he had already earned before his involvement in that war.

There is plenty of historical precedent for the diminishment of black accomplishment. It is a subject I emphasize throughout this book, and the attitude behind it is the same one that fueled Southern resistance to Reconstruction. The idea was simple: Marginalize black people so they don't count. Repress them so they can't achieve political or economic power. Confine them to permanent underclass status as servants and slaves to keep them from rising equal to or above the white ruling class. Southern white supremacists assured that black participation in American life would always seem illegitimate and irrelevant. And this is a process that has continued, with history as part of that process. In fact, history has helped perpetuate negative stereotypes and images of black people that many *blacks* have come to accept.

Fortunately, I went through a cultural change growing up because I am West Indian. And West Indians don't see the bars; they see the spaces between the bars. Maybe that's because they haven't absorbed defeat as thoroughly as African Americans. Here, it is grilled into us, whereas in the West Indies, no one has his foot on your neck, so to speak. Jim Crow is not part of life down there. So I eventually developed a sense of being able to *accomplish* in America, which many native blacks did not grow up with.

But like every other youngster, every so often I needed some outside guidance. Something extra to help me get through. I always looked to my family first. The most important lesson they taught me was the value of developing character, an ideal we don't hear much about in our society anymore. They instilled in me the touchstones of character: pride, honor, discipline, dignity, and courage of conviction or moral backbone. I found out later that courage was not simply having the guts to take a stand, physically, if challenged, but also something internal, a moral core.

I also learned important lessons from my other personal heroes: Jackie Robinson, Thelonious Monk, Malcolm X, to name a few. Jackie's pride, courage, and fierce determination left an imprint on my soul. One way or another, with his bat or his glove, or his legs, or his mind, he kept trying to beat you. I wanted a touch of that in me. And the first time I heard Monk play so soulfully at the Village Vanguard, I was inspired by his wild, creative cool. I thought, "I wish I could do *anything* like he plays his music." Then Malcolm X came along, and his boldness, personal commitment, and intelligence impressed me. More than anyone else, he made me realize that life was broader than basketball, and that it was my responsibility to learn as much as possible about my world, especially my own people.

I remember something else I learned in my UCLA days from reading *The Autobiography of Malcolm X*: the idea that to live a meaningful life, a person needs both character and a core philosophy. Today, I ask myself, "Who's teaching our kids *that* anymore?" And, "If people think of *me* as a hero, how can I influence their character in some positive way, other than just teaching them basketball?"

In John F. Kennedy's book *Profiles in Courage*, which he wrote as a young senator, he termed courage "the most admirable of human virtues." I define courage as recognizing when something needs to be done and doing it, even when there are easier choices. Courage should also be motivated by intelligence and moral understanding. The attempt to do the right thing, despite adverse consequences, is the type of courage that I most admire. To me, that is the true measure of character.

And that is what I write about in *Black Profiles in Courage*: people of courage and character who affected our world. Maybe it will make a difference.

CHAPTER 1

EXPLORATION

Estevanico

W hen you think of the great explorers, who comes to mind? Marco Polo, Columbus, Magellan, Drake, Balboa, Coronado, de Soto, Ponce de León, Cortés. Maybe a few others.

No one thinks of Estevanico.

Yet Estevanico was one of a kind. He was the first black person mentioned by name in American history. The only black in the first party to cross the North American continent. The first non-Indian to discover the Old World Southwest. The first to set foot in Arizona and New Mexico. His courage and ingenuity opened the Southwest to civilization. So Estevanico wasn't just an explorer; he was a pioneer.

But bring up this subject and people look at you funny: "Black explorers? What are you talking about?" The idea of black people involved in the discovery of this continent is still shocking news to most white people. I can understand that; it was shocking news to *me*. Because, for the most part, history ignored it. Along with the amazing fact that black people were involved in virtually every European exploration of the Americas. The reality is:

- Between 1492–1503, blacks sailed with Columbus on all four of his voyages to the New World.

- In 1513, thirty blacks accompanied Balboa across the Isthmus of Darien (Panama) and to the summit of Sierra de Quarequa, where he discovered the Pacific Ocean.

- In 1519, three hundred blacks hauled Cortés's big cannons through Mexico and helped him defeat the Aztecs (Cortés insisted that Negroes were worth their weight in gold to expeditioners), including one African black who stayed behind to sow and reap the first wheat crop in North America.

- Blacks were with Ponce de León in Florida.

- They helped Pizarro conquer the Incas in Peru.

- They marched with Coronado in New Mexico and de Soto in modern-day Alabama, where an African became the first Old World settler in the New World.

And there's more shocking news: Despite what mainstream history teaches us, even those Africans with the early explorers were not the first blacks on this continent. In 1975, incredible new archaeological evidence documented that blacks were present in Central, South, and

North Americas, B.C.—and that isn't just "before Columbus."

—∞∞—

Before I ever heard of Estevanico, I was intrigued by the idea of an African presence in the Americas, pre-Columbus. In history class as a kid, we got very little about blacks, period, but I do remember being taught that the first blacks in the Americas came to Jamestown as slaves in 1619. That is still taught in schools today—and it is totally false.

I did not find that out, though, until I started investigating the truth on my own. My first step was reading two books recommended by a friend: *They Came Before Columbus* and *African Presence in Early America*. Professor Ivan Van Sertima, a pioneer in linguistics and anthropology, wrote the first and edited the second. When I read them, I was so galvanized by the material that I started looking for someone to argue with. I tried to get people to say something ignorant that was generally assumed to be true, and then I referred to Van Sertima's books: "Did you know this? And this? And this?" They couldn't refute it: "Where did you *get* that? I never *heard* that before." The information hit them like revelations.

One reason is the continued presumption of white supremacy on this continent—the belief that black people have no legitimacy here because they were brought over as slaves by superior cultures. African Americans have never escaped the stigma of inferiority perpetrated by this myth. And we know now that it *is* a myth. That's why it is so important for both blacks and whites to learn the truth: that black people were not only an early presence on the continent, they actually preceded whites by at least *twenty-five hundred years*. And *those* early visitors came freely, on their own.

To understand the full significance of this, we need to digress a little more. It has been documented that Stone Age negroid people were central to the development of the first civilizations in the Nile Valley. Also that negroids were most likely the first to paint human portraits on rocks, to use fire and tools, and to cultivate seeds and grains. Through twenty ancient Egyptian dynasties, at least 40 percent of the population was negroid, including many of the famous pharaohs, Queen Nefertiti, and, almost certainly, Cleopatra. For hundreds of years, black Ethiopians and Egyptians were regaled throughout the ancient world. And Africans, especially Egyptians, were not only not landlocked, they navigated the Atlantic well before Christ. The Phoenician navy had the boats and they used Egyptians—who were mostly mulatto—as sailors. Great historians, including Homer and Herodotus, spoke repeatedly of negroid cultures in the ancient world.

But blacks weren't just in ancient Africa, as we always thought. For example, pre-Columbian South American Indians were used to finding blacks living near them in small, isolated communities. They knew about the powerful equatorial currents that swept boats across the mid-Atlantic to the Americas—each year, they kept finding shipwrecks on their northern coasts.

King Don Juan of Portugal knew about these currents too. When he secretly conducted trade with the Guinea coast in West Africa, his mariners told him of lucrative African excursions on these currents for gold, silver, and spices in an unexplored world west and south—the South American continent. In his lust for power and wealth, Don Juan kept this information to himself. But after Columbus's Caribbean discoveries (present-day Cuba, the Dominican Republic, Haiti, Puerto Rico), Don Juan wanted to prevent Spain from claiming more islands and also from discovering the southern continent. So he proposed that Portugal and Spain partition the world into exclusive exploration zones. Based on his Guinea intelligence, he drew a north-south line between the poles, establishing Portugal's zone of influence as everything east, including Europe and Africa; and Spain's as everything west, including the Americas. The Spanish agreed, mainly because they believed Columbus's assurances that nothing but water lay to the east of the line.

But Columbus probably lied. He was known to be egotistical and greedy. Most likely, he cut a separate deal with King Don Juan to share in the future bounties of the unexplored southern continent.

On June 7, 1494, Spain and Portugal signed the Treaty of Tordesillas, which certified Don Juan's line. Don Juan must have felt like he won the lottery. He didn't care about the Caribbean discoveries; he just wanted the rich new world to the south for Portugal. But he and Columbus miscalculated: Relying only on the Guinea reports (Don Juan never sent a fleet to check it out), they believed most of the southern continent lay on Portugal's side of the Tordesillas line. But, in fact, all but two hundred miles of Brazil lay on Spain's side.

A year later, Don Juan died and the treaty went unenforced. By then, Columbus had been back to the Americas. And while he was in Hispaniola (today Haiti and the Dominican Republic), the Indians showed him spear points made of a metal the Africans called *guanin*, which Columbus later assayed at eighteen parts gold, eight copper, and six silver. When he asked where the Indians got them, they said, ''From black merchants that came to us from the Southeast.'' This tended to confirm the Guinea reports: Black Africans were on the new continent.

Spain decided to trace their route from Africa. On May 30, 1498, Columbus sailed six ships along the route. They ended up riding the north equatorial current to a Caribbean island with three huge rocks, which Columbus named Trinidad for the Holy Trinity. Though he could see the mainland, Columbus never went there. But on August 7, 1498, some of his men visited an Indian settlement and returned to the ship with African headdresses and loincloths—convincing proof of the presence of African blacks.

According to Ivan Van Sertima, those Spaniards also found African settlements and artifacts, but history ignored or suppressed their discoveries—right through the twentieth century.

―∞∞―

Fifteen years later, when Balboa explored the Isthmus of Darien, he and his men heard Indian tales of gold to the south. Peter Martyr, Balboa's historian, reported that after one day's march south they stumbled onto an Indian village and found not gold but fierce black captives—the first blacks that whites actually saw in the Indies. It turned out they were spoils of wars between aborigines and groups of immigrant blacks. The Indians considered them foreign invaders and fought them continually. Centuries later, this fact helped modern anthropologists determine that there was a sizable black population on the continent, or there wouldn't have *been* any wars. Or many traces of their existence.

The fact is, there were significant traces. And they dated to well before the arrival of whites. When archaeologists and anthropologists came up with this evidence, it blew the roof off the old, accepted, prejudiced view in art and history that Europeans were the first to reach the New World. The discoveries started in 1862, when enormous stone heads of Negroes were uncovered at a pre-Columbian Olmec Indian site in Mexico. Because of scientific dating techniques, we know now what they could not have fathomed then: Some of the heads date to 800–700 B.C. Other finds were realistic portraits of African blacks in clay, stone, and gold, and pre-Columbian negroid skeletons in South, Central, and North Americas. The distinctive negroid features on the stone heads and clay sculptures are irrefutable: full lips, high cheekbones, wide fleshy nose, curly dark hair, goatee beard, even African tribal earrings and hats. The size of some of the stone heads—six to nine feet high, weighing forty tons each—and the placement near sacred altars indicate that some ancient Indian cultures actually worshipped the negroid people among them as gods.

What all this says to me is that we belong here as much as, if not more than, any other ethnic group and that white people would not be here at all if early black mariners and explorers had not done *their* thing to open up the Americas for civilization.

———

Which brings us back to Estevanico and his phenomenal journey to America in the early sixteenth century. And how his personal courage in a situation not of his own design nevertheless made him one of the greatest black heroes in American history.

Estevanico was born into slavery in Azamor, Morocco, at the end of the fifteenth century. In 1513, he was captured by Spanish conquistadors and became the manservant of nobleman Don Andrés Dorantes. In June 1527, Dorantes and his thirty-year-old servant became part of a historic quest when Spanish Emperor Charles V ordered his governor of Florida, Pánfilo de Narváez, on an expedition to the New World. Seven years before, Narváez was sent to Mexico to seize Hernándo Cortés for disobeying orders. But Cortés put out Narváez's eye and imprisoned him for four years. Now Narváez had his second big mission: to settle and find gold in the Gulf Coast region, from Florida to the River of Palms (a river in present-day Mexico).

On April 14, 1528, a gale forced Narváez to anchor his five ships near modern-day Tampa. According to the expedition's royal treasurer, Álvar Núñez Cabeza de Vaca—the only survivor to record the events (in his *Relación* published in 1542)—Narváez's first mistake was to divide his four-hundred-man force, a typical Spanish strategy. He ordered about three hundred of his soldiers to follow the Gulf shore by land while the rest of the fleet would sail parallel, until they met again at the nearest suitable harbor. He made his next mistake on shore when he stumbled onto a strange ritual: Indians wrapping their dead in painted deerskins with traces of gold, and burying them in wooden cargo boxes. In sign language, Narváez asked where the gold came from and they answered "Apalachee" (a region near present-day Tallahassee, Florida). Narváez had seen the riches of Mexico firsthand, and he wanted some of Cortés's glory and wealth for himself. So he made his next mistake: He ordered the cargo boxes burned, forced some of the Indians to act as guides, and started a march to Apalachee. From then on, the expedition was in constant peril.

Over the next two months, Indian massacres, desertions, malaria, typhoid, and starvation whittled down the force. When the rest reached Apalachee, Cabeza de Vaca wrote: "We believed what had been told us of this land and that there would be an end to our great hardships. . . . Having come to where we had been informed there was much food and gold, we already felt recovered in part from our sufferings and fatigue." But then Narváez made another mistake: When he entered the village the men were away, so he imprisoned the women and children. Later, of course, the men attacked. The Apalachees were more than a match: They were tall and valiant and extraordinary archers. According to Cabeza de Vaca: "There were men who swore they had seen two oak trees, each as thick as the calf of a leg, shot through by arrows." They also saw their comrades and horses shot through that way—the Apalachees put their arrows through the seams of the Spanish armor, literally in one side and out the other.

The survivors—including Estevanico, who fought loyally beside his master's horse—retreated to a swampy inlet at Apalachee Bay. Trapped there, they were forced to eat one of their horses every third day to survive. Finally, they realized their only hope of escape was by sea. They devised a bellows out of deerskins and then melted their stirrups, crossbows, even their spurs into tools and nails. In six weeks, using pitch pine as resin, palmetto leaves as caulk, and horse tails and manes as ropes, they jury-rigged five thirty-three-foot scows. Juniper branches were fashioned into oars; stitched-together shirts were hoisted as sails. But by the day they left, September 22, 1528, eighteen men had been killed by Indians and forty more had died of illness and starvation.

Estevanico acted as chief guide as they sailed west along the Gulf, praying they would reach a Spanish outpost in Mexico. But they had no idea how far it was. Meantime, Indians attacked from shore and kept them from getting fresh water. When they crossed the Mississippi River around New Orleans, men were washed overboard and winds marooned the survivors on a desolate island for six days. Some were so thirsty and starved, they drank salt water, which cost five lives. When the group set sail again, a storm destroyed two boats and drowned more men. Estevanico helped steer and bail his boat, trying to hook up by rope with the other boats so they could ride out the storm together. But Narváez called out from his boat that he was no longer responsible, and that everyone should save his own life. Then his boat disappeared. They never saw him again.

On November 6, another storm deposited Cabeza de Vaca's boat on La Isla de Mal Hado (Misfortune Island) off Galveston, Texas. The next morning, a group of Karankawa Indians closed in. Fortunately, they were friendly; they accepted beads and small bell trinkets in exchange for fish, water, and roots. The following day, the Spaniards tried to sail but huge rollers swamped them ashore again, drowning three men. The Karankawas arrived at sunset and took the survivors in for winter. Later that same day, a second boatload of forty-eight Spaniards showed up, including Estevanico and his master, Dorantes. They had washed ashore earlier. Now, only eighty expeditioners were left.

When winter hit, food was scarce and more men died. Some survivors became so delirious due to starvation, they cannibalized the bodies of their comrades. Then a plague wiped out all but fifteen. When it spread to the Indians, they accused the Spaniards of sorcery and made them slaves—a double irony for Estevanico. When Karankawas kept dying, the chief commanded his new slaves to end the plague. No one knew what to do.

Estevanico invented a plan. He remembered some incantations from their travels, so he recited them over the sick. Dorantes started signing the cross and chanting Christian prayers, probably as much for themselves as the Indians. A third Spaniard, Alonso del Castillo Maldonado, the son of a Salamanca doctor, performed some minor surgeries. Everything worked; Indians kept saying they were cured. Since Estevanico initiated most of the ''healing,'' he became known as a great medicine man and priest.

Within weeks, only four Spaniards remained: Dorantes, Estevanico, Maldonado, Cabeza de Vaca. For six years, they were kept apart most of the time, but still managed to plan an escape. Finally, in September 1534, at a semiannual Indian meet to gather their favorite seasonal fruit, the prickly pear, the four Spaniards slipped away and headed west to the mountains. On the way, they met other Indians who persuaded them to cure their sick. Estevanico was guide, medicine man, and spokesman—he had taught himself to speak Indian dialects. By now, he was revered not only for his healing powers but also for his exotic blackness. It may have been the only time in American history that a slave's blackness actually helped him escape.

For eight months, Estevanico guided the group all the way to northern Mexico, bartering beads and healings with Indians for safe passage. Cabeza de Vaca wrote that Estevanico ''was our go-between. He informed himself

about the ways we wished to take, what towns there
were, and the matters we desired to know.'' They even
accumulated groupies—hundreds of Indians trailing
them in worship and fear. They called the four Spaniards
''children of the sun'' for their godlike powers to cure
or kill.

In the spring of 1536, the four encountered Indians in
the Sonora Valley who mentioned the legendary Seven
Cities of Cíbola to the north, a fabulous empire suppos-
edly full of jewels and gold. So they trekked north to
see for themselves. On the way, they passed through
villages that were deserted and burned. Stragglers in the
cliffs told them bands of Spanish Christians had raided
the villages and taken the women, boys, and half the men
for slaves. Estevanico sympathized openly; the other
three Spaniards were also repulsed because they, the former slaveholders, had learned what it meant to be a
slave. Estevanico volunteered to find the Spaniards, hoping to finally end his long ordeal.

In March at the Sinaloa River, Estevanico finally met
his countrymen again. He described his eight-year journey of six thousand miles over land and sea. He also
mentioned the Seven Cities of Cíbola. The Spaniards
knew of the legendary towns built on golden sands. They
retrieved the other three men and escorted them back to
Spanish headquarters in Mexico. There, the men told
their story to Viceroy Antonio de Mendoza, who believed they knew the way to the fabled Seven Cities. So
Mendoza purchased Estevanico from Dorantes and
started planning a major expedition.

Three years later, Franciscan Friar Marcos de Niza
was appointed expedition leader. Mexican Indians were
granted freedom to haul goods to trade for jewels; Estevanico, still a slave, was ordered to guide. On March

7, 1539, the group headed north from the frontier province of New Galicia. Friar Marcos wore a gray robe; Estevanico brightly colored linens, ankle bells, and a ceremonial gourd rattle with red and white feathers—an Indian gift from years before. He also took two greyhounds to help with tracking.

Friar Marcos kept a detailed record of the journey. Northern Indians, who had never seen Christians, spoke of more northerly towns where people who lived in houses, not huts, had golden jewelry and pots, jars of gold, and even golden blades to wipe sweat from their bodies. The friar decided to rest until Easter in the town of Vacapa, but sent Estevanico ahead with Indian carriers to find these towns. Estevanico was instructed that if he found moderate wealth, he was to send back a sign with a runner: a cross as wide as a hand with fingers spread. If greater wealth, a cross two hands wide. If wealth greater than that of New Spain (Mexico), a large cross commensurate with the potential amount.

Four days after Estevanico left, a messenger returned to Friar Marcos with a cross "as high as a man." He told the friar that the Seven Golden Cities lay ahead just thirty days, and the people there lived in houses of lime and stone with turquoise-lined doorways. He also said a large entourage of Opata Indians had joined Estevanico— they revered the great black medicine man but they also planned to share in the spoils. Over the next week, Estevanico sent crosses back from Arizona and New Mexico, each one larger than the last. He urged the friar to hurry.

Each time Estevanico approached a town, he sent an Indian ahead with the feathered gourd rattle as a sign of his prestige. That had always made him welcome before. But this time, when he sent the gourd rattle into Hawikuh, a Zuni pueblo considered to be the first of the Seven Cities, it came back from the chief with a warning that if they came ahead, they would all be killed. What Estevanico didn't know was that the gourd rattle originally belonged to mortal enemies of the Zunis, and it enraged them.

Days later an exhausted messenger from Estevanico found the friar on the road to Cíbola. The messenger "came in a great fright, having his face and body all covered with sweat, and showing great sadness." He explained that Estevanico tried to enter the pueblo despite the chief's warning. But Zunis seized the party of three hundred and imprisoned them in a large adobe house, without food or water. The next morning, the messenger snuck out to drink from a nearby river when he heard a commotion behind him. He saw Estevanico and the others running from the house, with Zunis chasing them and killing them with arrows. Before escaping upstream, the messenger watched his companions die, and he was certain Estevanico was among them.

This version was confirmed when two more survivors showed up. They had pretended to be dead by lying among the corpses before finally running away. Friar Marcos decided to ride to a hill outside Cíbola just to glimpse the great city. Even though he only saw dull adobe buildings in the distance, he knew if he took his party in and all were killed, no one in New Spain would know he had found the Seven Cities. So he turned back.

No one ever found the Seven Golden Cities. But Estevanico's search for them transformed him into the immortal "Black Mexican" of Zuni myth. And it was Estevanico's bold quest to find the Seven Cities that kept its legend alive, which led to Coronado's and de Soto's fateful explorations of the Southwest.

That is how an obscure black African slave became an extraordinary agent of history and a memorable hero, *in fact* as well as in myth.

CHAPTER 2

REVOLUTION

The First Rhode Island • Peter Salem
Salem Poor • James Armistead Lafayette
Crispus Attucks

Black people don't know enough about their own history in America. Most don't know that blacks were
instrumental in founding this country. Until I found that
out on my own, I didn't know it either.

When I was in college at the University of California
at Los Angeles (UCLA), I wanted to know more about
blacks in American history. So I started asking questions
and buying books. I accumulated a varied library on African-American history and just kept adding to it. During
my National Basketball Association (NBA) career, especially the last half, one of my favorite ways to relax
was reading these books and learning more about black
participation in American history. I was surprised at how
much I did not know. In 1983, a fire destroyed my home
and I lost hundreds of books, including most of my fa-

vorites on African Americans. So I started showing up
at the Aquarius Bookstore in Los Angeles to replenish
my library a few books at a time. One day while I was
browsing, a book cover caught my eye. It was a painting
of a black youngster on horseback firing a pistol at a
mounted British officer. The book was Burke Davis's
Black Heroes of the American Revolution. It looked like
it was for kids because it was a thin hardback with large
type. But when I started reading, the material drew me
in and held me. I was not only intrigued by the stories,
but I was also startled by how much of it I didn't know.

That one thin book was mind-boggling. It started to
change my sense of my heritage. I was astonished to
learn that blacks had fought in the Revolutionary War.
In 1770, *one fifth* of the population of the Colonies was
African-American. Most were slaves, so they had nothing to lose by joining up. Anything that could free them
from degradation and suffering was worth pursuing. So
they joined local and state militias and, for the first eight
months of the war, they were openly accepted in the
Continental Army. African-Americans fought in the
opening salvos at Lexington, Concord, and Bunker Hill.
The truth is, they not only fought well, but many were
bonafide heroes.

I never heard any of this in school.

I kept on reading. I discovered that as many as five
thousand African Americans served in the three-
hundred-thousand-man Continental Army during the
Revolutionary War; that bigoted Southern politicians ob-
jected to black participation because they didn't think
blacks would be good soldiers and were afraid to have
them armed with guns; that on November 12, 1775,
George Washington was forced to ban all blacks from
service; and that when the war dragged into its third

year, and the Continental Line was down to six thousand volunteers, Washington caved in and allowed blacks to enlist en masse—and they saved the cause.

I was excited by all these new facts. But I was also outraged—I couldn't understand why I didn't know it before. So I started reading every book I could find on black contributions to the Revolution: *The Negro in the American Revolution, The Black Presence in the Era of the American Revolution, Before the Mayflower, The Negro in the Making of America, History of the Negro Race in America.* All this fresh information made me reflect seriously on how black Americans had been continually denied their basic rights on the basis of race and ethnic features. And how we are still battling to gain those rights, 220 years after the first Independence Day.

When I learned that five thousand African Americans served the patriot cause, I wanted to hit something. Why hadn't I known about this? But it really wasn't so amazing. It turns out that Colonial blacks had already fought in four European conflicts in the Americas: King William's War (1689–1697); Queen Anne's War (1701–1713); King George's War (1744–1748); and the French and Indian War (1756–1763). They had also served as Minutemen, the local volunteers who pledged to defend their towns on a minute's notice. All this made me understand, for the first time, that America was really our country, too—and in more ways than most people know.

Early in my research, I discovered what might have been our first government cover-up: the absence of black people's names on war documents. If thousands of blacks served in the war, why were only a handful identified? I had to dig to find the reason: Whites deliberately left black names off military rolls; or listed them only by their common "slave" names; or simply dismissed them in demeaning, anonymous categories like "A Negro man," "Negro, name unknown," and "Mulatto waiting boy."

In his meticulously detailed book, *The Negro in the American Revolution*, Benjamin Quarles points out that because whites denied blacks access to a formal education, very few blacks recorded their thoughts. Although some *five hundred thousand* African Americans were an integral part of our fledgling nation, incredibly we know almost nothing about them. Which is why Quarles suggests that the only way to understand blacks of that era is to study what they *did*.

But even that is difficult. White historians kept revising history to diminish the contributions of people of color. European immigrants believed they had the sole right to rule and benefit from the riches of the New World. Therefore, everything, including history, had to support their sense of entitlement. By denying blacks and other people of color any credit for the expansion of civilization, they effectively legitimized a legacy of white preeminence. It was a knee-jerk reaction that, unfortunately, persists today: *Keep American history white*.

An early example was the memorial treatment of two heroes of the Battle of Groton Heights. On September 6, 1781, British troops under the American traitor Benedict Arnold tried to divert George Washington from confronting Lord Cornwallis, commander of British forces in the South, at Yorktown by burning the towns of New London and Groton, Connecticut. A white farmer, William Latham, and his black slave, Lambert, were tending cattle when they saw the British arrive in boats. They volunteered on the spot. Sprinting across a field into a small earthwork called Fort Griswold, they reported to patriot commander Lieutenant Colonel William Ledyard.

When the British attacked, Lambert Latham (slaves rarely used their real last names; they usually adopted their master's) suffered a disabling bullet wound to his right hand. But he kept loading and firing his musket with his left. The outnumbered Americans held out longer than expected and inflicted heavy casualties. So when the Redcoats finally breached the walls, a bitter British officer yelled, "Who commands this fort?" Ledyard replied, "I did once. You do now." But when he gallantly handed over his sword, the officer ran it through Ledyard to the hilt. Lambert Latham was incensed; he immediately killed the British officer with his bayonet. Redcoats then slaughtered Lambert, stabbing him thirty-three times. Then they murdered the surrendered Americans. One was Ledyard's orderly, Jordan Freeman, the only other black man present. Earlier, Freeman and a white officer had killed British officer William Montgomery by impaling him with pikes as he scaled the wall.

Witnesses praised Jordan Freeman for his bravery. Accounts stated that Lambert Latham "fought manfully by his master's side" and fell "nobly avenging the death of his commander." The fact that the actions of blacks were reported at all tends to confirm the accounts.

Yet fifty years later, these two heroes were memorialized with typical insults. In 1831, when Connecticut dedicated a marble tablet honoring the eighty-four patriots killed at Groton Heights, Colonel Ledyard's name was carved across the top, followed by the names of eighty-one white soldiers. Jordan Freeman and Lambert

Latham were segregated below, as "Colored Men." That might have been custom then. But it was not custom to misinscribe Lambert's familiar nickname of Lambo as *Sambo*, so it read "*Sambo* Latham." That was an obvious racial slur.

This kind of deceit continued for centuries. One subtle example is the altering of reproductions of John Trumbull's famous 1786 painting, *The Battle of Bunker Hill*. I have seen the painting in numerous history books; in each one, the black man prominent in the lower right corner of the original, fighting by his master, a Lieutenant Grosvenor, is missing, cropped off. Apparently no one cared; the affront went uncorrected until 1968 when the government featured Lieutenant Grosvenor and his fighting black slave, ironically, on a national stamp.

I believe that some racial attitudes are unconscious. But cropping a painting is not one of them. That was done deliberately to keep black people irrelevant, on the edges, out of the mainstream.

History is filled with these devious omissions. Like the little-known incident in the critical Battle of Cowpens during the war. In late 1780, George Washington assigned the southern command to Rhode Island blacksmith Nathanael Greene. Greene devised a strategy to confuse his enemy in the Carolinas, Lord Cornwallis, and also to conserve American lives. He divided his forces into small skirmish units that struck from cover and quickly dispersed. Hit and run, live to fight another day.

On the cold, damp evening of January 17, 1781, Greene's men sprang an ambush at Hannah's Cowpens, a Carolina cow field named for the man whose cattle grazed there. This engagement pitted some seven hundred Continental soldiers under General Daniel Morgan and Lieutenant Colonel William Washington against nearly twelve hundred of General Banistre Tarleton's crack British dragoons. Tarleton had been sent to the Carolinas to wipe out Greene's skirmishers once and for all. Instead, it was Tarleton who got wiped out.

The arrogant Tarleton sent his superior mounted forces headlong into Morgan's two thin lines of riflemen. The Continentals beat them back and quickly withdrew. Tarleton pursued, unaware that Washington's cavalry-men were waiting in the rear. Suddenly, Morgan's men emerged from the woods and attacked Tarleton's left flank while Washington's boys pinched in on the right. The vaunted dragoons broke in panic and ran. During the thirty-minute fight, the Continentals lost just 12 men. The British lost more than 100, including 1 major, 13 captains, 14 lieutenants, and 9 ensigns. General Morgan took an astonishing 830 prisoners, including 230 wounded (to our 60). In all, Tarleton lost nearly his en-tire force—one fourth of Cornwallis's field army.

The once-fearless dragoons were so demoralized that months later they limped into Yorktown and were easily encircled by Washington, thus ending the war. Corn-wallis admitted then that the rout at Cowpens was "a very unexpected and severe blow." Major understate-ment; that loss decimated him and cost Britain the war.

But another significant event occurred at Cowpens that was barely noted. Toward the end of the humiliating British retreat, Tarleton impulsively charged Lieutenant Colonel Washington on his horse. It was almost per-sonal: *You disgraced me, so I will kill you myself.* Tar-leton swiped his saber at Washington, who swiped back. Both missed. Suddenly, another British officer charged Washington with saber raised. But just as he was poised to slash, Washington's bugler rode up and shot the British officer with a pistol. Years later, a biographer of George Washington (the president was William Washington's cousin) indicated that the brave bugler was a black teenager "too small to wield a sword," making him, at least for me, doubly heroic. Yet we will never know his name; it was not recorded. I only discovered him myself because the cover of Burke Davis's *Black Heroes of the American Revolution*—the book that attracted me in the Aquarius Bookstore—is a reproduction of the distinguished 1845 William Ranney oil painting, *The Battle of Cowpens*, depicting this incident.

So here is an extraordinary black teenage slave who becomes a hero in a turning-point battle of the American Revolution, and is so significant that one of the finest portrait artists of the eighteenth century features him in a painting that ends up on the cover of an important twentieth-century history book—and yet *we don't know who he is*.

————

What aggravates me is *why*. Why were white historians so intent on denying black people credit for being at the forefront of historic events, particularly in our first war? My own belief is that it was too much of a contradiction to enlist blacks in the fight for freedom and then deny them those rights on the basis of their skin color. So the denial reflex took over: *Hide all the dark faces*. It is a major theme throughout our history.

For example, in my library at home I have an October 1891 issue of *Century* magazine that features one of Frederic Remington's famous paintings and sketches of the black Buffalo Soldiers in action after the Civil War. Remington was fascinated by the Buffalo Soldiers—he even rode with them during the summer of 1888 in Arizona to draw them in person. This particular portrait titled *Captain Dodge and His Colored Troops to the Rescue* immortalizes a daring rescue by the Ninth Cavalry during a Ute revolt in 1879.

Here are the facts: On September 29, a group of usually peaceful Utes, enraged at the brutal policies of Indian agent Nathan Meeker, murdered him and nine employees of the White River Agency at Milk Creek, Colorado. When Major T. T. Thornburgh led three cavalry companies to the scene, he and a dozen of his men were killed, 50 were wounded, and the rest pinned down. A soldier who went for help happened upon Captain Francis S. Dodge, D Company, Ninth Cavalry, on a routine scouting patrol 70 miles away. Dodge and his black troopers rode twenty-six hours to the scene and had to fight their way in with food and ammunition. The Ninth fought ferociously. Sergeant Henry Johnson, who repeatedly risked his life by filling thirty canteens with creek water for the wounded, eventually received the Congressional Medal of Honor. So did Captain Dodge. Yet later, most public credit went to General Wesley Merritt, who arrived, late by train, at Fort Rawlins, Wyoming, with 200 cavalrymen and 150 infantrymen. He led his all-white detail, mostly in wagons, 170 miles in three days, but they did not arrive at Milk Creek until October 5. By then, the fighting was over. The silence was so stark Merritt thought everyone was dead. Only when the Ninth responded to a bugle call did he lead his troops in. Of course, neither Merritt nor his men received any medals for this mop-up action.

Frederic Remington knew the facts. That was why he titled this famous portrait *Captain Dodge and His Colored Troops to the Rescue*. Nevertheless, the magazine's editor, Harold McCracken, *re*titled it *Captain Dodge's Troopers to the Rescue*. The reason he could get away with this was because the picture shows troopers on horseback whose faces are obscured—for example, one by a horse; another by a rifle. If you don't look closely, it is easy to assume the troopers are white. Why wouldn't they be? Weren't they *always* white? The point is, by deleting the word "Colored," McCracken intentionally distorted Remington's subject: the courageous action of the *black* troopers of the Ninth Cavalry. In other words, once again: *Keep American history white*.

There is intentional distortion today, too. The 1950 movie *Tomahawk* was based on the life of ex-slave and legendary black frontiersman, hunter, trailblazer Jim Beckwourth. In his own day, he was regarded as the fiercest Indian fighter of his generation. And that included his famous white contemporaries Jim Bridger and Kit Carson (Beckwourth was actually called the "black Kit Carson"). During the Gold Rush, on April 26, 1850, Beckwourth made the historic discovery of a pass through the Sierra Nevada to the Yuba and Truckee rivers. He also led the first party of seventeen wagons through. It is still called Beckwourth Pass today. There is also a town named Beckwourth, California. We know all about Bridger and Carson, but how many people have even *heard* of Jim Beckwourth? One reason he is so obscure is that he is rarely mentioned in mainstream history books. Another reason is the continuing policy of *hiding all the dark faces*. For example, when they cast Beckwourth's role in *Tomahawk*, the actor who played the part—Jack Oakie—was lily white.

More recently, Clint Eastwood's movie *Hang 'Em High* was based on the life of a remarkable black marshal named Bass Reeves, who worked the Oklahoma

Territory for the infamous Judge Parker. But the film-makers fictionalized the character by renaming him and then casting Eastwood in the lead.

The truth is, color consciousness is deeply embedded in the American psyche. I remember when I was in college, somebody said, "Why do they separate the eggs at the supermarket? You have the brown eggs over here and the white eggs over there." The brown eggs were always cheaper, even though they came from the same hens. The implication was clear. Just last year, film critic Roger Ebert concluded his TV review of the animated feature *The Penguin and the Pebble* with another clear observation. He said, "Why is it, in cartoons, evil characters are always depicted with dark faces, either brown or black? While the good characters, the heroes and heroines, always have light or white faces?" I thought, "Well, I know why. It's the same bias that leaves black names off military rolls, and crops black heroes from paintings, and transforms blacks into whites in movies."

The inferiority of darkness is reinforced by our whole popular culture. Whites *and* blacks have absorbed it.

That is why it is important for all Americans—especially African Americans—to know about specific black heroes of the American Revolution: brave, mostly invisible men who rose above oppression, abuse, and undeserved indignities to play key roles in establishing our common American heritage.

Great heroes like the First Rhode Island, Peter Salem, Salem Poor, James Armistead Lafayette, and particularly Crispus Attucks.

⊸⊷⊷

The First Rhode Island

For the first three years of the Revolutionary War, slaves were banned from General Washington's Continental Army. Only freed blacks who had fought in the early campaigns were allowed to reenlist. The prevailing fears were that slaves would turn cowardly in the heat of battle and that arming slaves would invite rebellions, especially down South. So, in October 1775, Washington convened a conference on the issue. Though blacks had proven their valor, skill, and patriotism in wars numerous times the previous seventy years, whites still perceived them as incapable and untrustworthy. Finally, on October 13, 1775, Washington made a hasty and foolish decision to include freed blacks in the military ban. That opened the door for a shrewd British ploy. On November 7, 1775, John Murray, Earl of Dunmore, the recently deposed royal governor of Virginia, issued a proclamation from a British man-of-war summoning American bondsmen to the British cause in exchange for their freedom:

> I do hereby . . . declare all indented servants, Negroes, or others (appertaining to Rebels) free, that are able and willing to bear arms, they joining His Majesty's Troops, as soon as may be, for the more speedily reducing the colony to a proper sense of their duty, to His Majesty's crown and dignity.

The response was immediate; more than a thousand slaves flooded British camps. They were ready to serve *anyone* offering freedom. By December, the British had hundreds of runaway blacks in uniform with emblems saying LIBERTY TO SLAVES sewn on their tunics. Lord Dunmore called them his "Ethiopian Regiment." (This rally of slaves seemed like a British coup until they were routed in their first fight with Virginia militia, causing Dunmore to hastily withdraw his ships from Virginian waters.)

Lord Dunmore's stratagem of enlisting Southern slaves to fight against their own country was so predictable, it might seem odd to us today that men like Jefferson and Washington did not foresee it. But the reason was simple: They owned slaves themselves and it clouded their judgment. Though both later repudiated slavery, ultimately they were of their times and of their race. Another stinging irony was that many of their own slaves defected to the British. That turned out to be smart because neither Jefferson nor Washington (a slave owner since age eleven, when his father died) ever completely shed his heritage. Washington did not free any of his three hundred slaves until after his death; Jefferson freed just three of his four hundred slaves in his lifetime (two were believed to be his daughters by his teenage slave mistress, Sally Hemings).

I always speak highly of Thomas Jefferson. Even though he owned slaves, he regarded slavery as immoral and he worked against it his whole life. In 1769, when he was elected to the Virginia House of Burgesses, he tried to ease the process by which slaves could be freed by their masters. As a young lawyer in the early 1770s, he defended slaves in court and insisted on their "natural right" to freedom. In 1774—when he owned 187 slaves, mainly as an economic necessity—he wrote the pamphlet *A Summary View of the Rights of British America*, attacking King George III for his perpetuation of the "detestable" institution of slavery in the Americas.

When Jefferson wrote his original draft of the Declaration of Independence, he included an unqualified condemnation of King George for waging "cruel war against human nature itself, violating the most sacred right of life and liberty in the persons of a distant people who never offended him, captivating and carrying them into slavery in another hemisphere, or to incur miserable death in their transportation thither."

To me, this bold statement was an example of remarkable personal courage. Here was a complex public figure doing what he could, pragmatically, within the limits of his power, to undermine a popular American institution on which his own wealth depended. Unfortunately, he was swimming up a waterfall. Congress deleted the passage to mollify Northern slave traders and Southern slave owners who opposed it.

In Jefferson's time, slavery was a given; it was the way things were. He understood that no one could change it singlehandedly. Yet he never gave up; he always took public stands against it; he never let the issue die. In 1782, when he realized the war had not really been the *American* Revolution so much as the *white* American Revolution, he protested the immorality of the master-slave relationship again in his *Notes on Virginia*:

The whole commerce between master and slave is a perpetual exercise of the most boisterous passions, the most unremitting despotism on the one part, and degrading submission on the other. Our children see this and learn to imitate it. . . . The parent storms, the child looks on . . . gives a loose to his worst of passions, and thus nursed, educated, and daily exercised in tyranny, cannot but be stamped by it with odious peculiarities. The man must be a prodigy who can retain his manners and morals undepraved by such circumstances.

Though Jefferson was the most distinguished American opposing slavery in the era that shaped our history, black people today don't mention him when they consider how far we've come. They don't seem to know that every step forward actually started with Thomas Jefferson.

When word of mass slave defections spread, Southern slave owners tried to coerce their remaining slaves through threatening ads, like this one in the *Virginia Gazette*:

> Be not then, ye Negroes, tempted by [Lord Dunmore's] proclamation to ruin yourselves . . . whether we suffer or not, if you desert us, you most certainly will.

Meantime, the British were busy employing runaway slaves as mostly laborers, carpenters, and blacksmiths, but also some as shock troops, guides, and spies. This threatened the American brain trust. As the war dragged on, individual states started embracing the idea of black enlistees, especially states permitting slaves to serve as substitutes for their masters. By January 1776, when it became clear the war would drag on and white enlistees would be increasingly hard to find, Washington lifted his ban. The decision was critical: Black manpower provided not only essential reinforcement but also some of the fiercest fighting men in the Continental Line. Frederick Douglass would conclude a half century later that African Americans fought this war hoping against hope for a new life "based upon human brotherhood and the self-evident truths of liberty and equality.'' Whites already enjoyed these privileges; they had less at stake. This special incentive inspired blacks to unexpected heights of courage and glory, and the same incentive would continue to push them, in every war for the next two hundred years, to play increasingly significant roles in the American military.

Among the most instructive and inspiring examples of black pride, patriotism, skill, and courage during the Revolution are the little-known triumphs of Rhode Island's black battalion. One of only two all-black regiments in the Continental Line, Colonel Christopher Greene's First Rhode Island of ninety-five slaves and thirty freedmen quickly established itself as the most respected in the army. In their first action, the August 29, 1778 Battle of Rhode Island, these raw recruits heroically covered a decisive, four-hour retreat of six American brigades. In that time, they withstood three ferocious assaults of crack Hessian-British regiments who underestimated the ragtag-looking blacks firing muskets in their shirtsleeves. Their fighting was so effective (they inflicted casualties at an incredible 6 to 1 ratio) that General Lafayette proclaimed this battle ''the best fought action of the war.'' The First Rhode Islanders were not just intrepid; they were staunchly loyal— one of the only American units to stay the course of the war. They continued to fight until disbanding at Saratoga, June 13, 1783, when they were publicly praised by Lieutenant Colonel Jeremiah Olney for ''faithfully persevering in the best of causes, in every stage of service, with unexampled fortitude and patience through all the dangers and toils of a long and severe war.'' For their exceptional service, every slave in the regiment was granted his freedom.

The First Rhode Island held up a standard of courage and excellence that black soldiers continued to uphold. In fact, they fought notably in every major battle of the war, and mostly in integrated units. Oddly, however, blacks would not experience integrated service again for some 170 years. That was partly because history white-washed or ignored so many other significant examples of African-American accomplishment in the Revolutionary War. For example:

- Slave Prince Whipple, a bodyguard to General Washington's aide, and slave Oliver Cromwell were among the 2,400 hand-picked men to cross the Delaware with Washington and rout the Hessians at Trenton (Cromwell rowed stroke oar in Washington's boat).

- A patriot slave named Pompey engineered Colonel Anthony Wayne's critical seizure of Stony Point, New York, by acquiring the password to the British fort.

- Black sailor Caesar Tarrant was cited for his extraordinarily gallant piloting of the Virginia schooner *Patriot*.

- Numerous blacks served under Virginian John Paul Jones on September 23, 1779 aboard the *Bonhomme Richard* when it defeated the British frigate *Serapis* in a duel at sea.

- Freedman Prince Hall fought at Bunker Hill and in other key battles, and became the most vocal African-American protester of discrimination in Boston. It was Hall's impetus that produced the most famous

slave petition of his time, presented to the General
Court of Massachusetts on January 13, 1777. It requested, in part:

. . . That your petitioners apprehend that they have,
in common with all other men, a natural and inalienable right to that freedom, which the great Parent of the universe hath bestowed equally on all
mankind, and which they have never forfeited by
any compact or agreement whatever.

The petition suggested a legislative act freeing the
slaves. While it was not granted, courageous public
stands of African-American freedom fighters like Prince
Hall speeded the death of slavery in the North. Unfortunately, despite the paper gains, at war's end most
blacks were drummed out of service and relegated to
their previous lives. This cold formula set a traditional
pattern for the treatment of African Americans in the
military: The government bars them until they are desperately needed; praises them as first-class heroes when
they succeed in battle; then dismisses them back to their
lives as second-class citizens.

PETER SALEM

Here is Peter Salem—a slave, a blacksmith, a crack shot
with a rifle—and along comes a group of white patriots
with *their* belief in the dignity of man, and they say,
"Come and fight the British with us. You can earn your
freedom that way." His owners, the Belknaps, grant him
his freedom to go and fight. All of a sudden, he goes
from bondage and inconsequence to becoming a key par-

ticipant in the destruction of the British order in America.

Two months after he fights with distinction at Lexington and Concord, Salem becomes a hero by helping repel two British assaults at Bunker Hill. The first published account of the battle, and also later diaries, all document Peter Salem's action that day. The highlight was when Major John Pitcairn, a commander of the British Royal Marines, tried to rally his troops for a last desperate charge. The moment Pitcairn stood up and yelled "The day is ours!" Peter Salem put a musket ball through Pitcairn's head. The rally collapsed and the British withdrew in confusion.

So here we have a recently freed slave joining a score of other blacks who fought that day, and distinguishing himself from everyone, black and white, in the first patriot victory over the British. I think that is significant. So did the Continental Army, because Salem was presented to General Washington as the man who not only killed Major Pitcairn but who also carried the most important day in American military history.

Peter Salem went on to fight in other major battles, including Stony Point and Saratoga. After the war, he took up cane weaving and built his own cabin near Leicester, Massachusetts. He was the frequent subject of engravers and painters, and his rifle was put on permanent display at the Bunker Hill Monument. Yet he died in 1816 in a Framingham poorhouse.

The full circle of black anonymity.

SALEM POOR

Salem Poor was a twenty-eight-year-old freedman who left his wife behind to enlist in Benjamin Ames's militia company to fight for liberty. He did not have to join; he had freedom already. But he fought in battle after battle defending Boston, and he eventually killed a key British officer, Lieutenant Colonel James Abercrombie. Afterward, fourteen of Salem Poor's fellow officers submitted a petition to the general court, praising him for his extraordinary valor. That rare December 5, 1775 document was preserved. It read:

> The Subscribers begg leave to Report to your Honorable House, (which Wee do in justice to the Caracter of so Brave a Man) that under Our Own observation, We declare that A Negro Man Called Salem Poor of Col. Frye's Regiment—Capt. Ames. Company, in the late Battle at Charlestown, behaved like an Experienced officer, as Well as an Excellent Soldier, to Set forth Particulars of his Conduct Would be Tedious. Wee Would Only begg leave to say in the Person of this sd. Negro Centers a Brave & gallant Soldier. The reward due to so great and Distinguished a Caracter, wee submit to the Congress.

An interesting side note: Although volunteer soldier Salem Poor survived the battles of White Plains and Valley Forge, and stayed in the army after the Revolution, Congress never offered him a reward.

His only reward was that history forgot him.

James Armistead Lafayette

If there was ever a paragon of selfless heroism it was certainly James Armistead Lafayette. As a slave of William Armistead in Virginia, James got his master's permission to serve our French ally, the Marquis de Lafayette. The French nobleman who had joined up with General Washington in 1777 came to Williamsburg in 1781 to stop Cornwallis and end the harassment of Benedict Arnold, who was leading troops on raids in Virginia. At first, the marquis used James to carry communications between French units. Eventually, he decided to have James infiltrate Arnold's camp. James was so convincing in his pose as a runaway slave that Arnold used him to guide his raiders along the local roads. When Arnold was dispatched back North, James worked for Cornwallis himself who, ironically, soon instructed him to spy on Lafayette.

So James snuck back and forth between the camps, though serving only Lafayette. As a Virginia native, James traveled the back routes without map or guide, where others could not go. He would sometimes spy on the British camp in the morning (officers freely discussed their raids in front of him, ignoring James as just another irrelevant Negro), deliver letters to other American spies in the afternoon, and return to Cornwallis the same night. It was information from James that tipped Washington to the location of Cornwallis's camp at Yorktown, where he was quickly forced to surrender. Shortly afterward, Cornwallis presented himself at the marquis's headquarters and was astonished to find James there—the man he considered and trusted as *his* personal spy.

James Armistead Lafayette performed amazing feats in the South where blacks rarely received acknowledgment for anything. But *Lafayette* praised him. And maybe because of that, James adopted his surname, call-

ing himself for the rest of his life James Armistead Lafayette.

In 1784, the French marquis met James once again in
Richmond, and was dismayed to find he was still a slave.
So Lafayette wrote James a testimonial—the only one
by a foreign general on behalf of a slave—proclaiming
that James Armistead had rendered

> services to me while I had the honor to command
> in this state. His intelligence from the enemy's
> camp were industriously collected and more faith-
> fully delivered. He properly acquitted himself with
> some important commissions I gave him and ap-
> pears to me entitled to every reward his situation
> can admit of.

Two years later, the Virginia General Assembly com-
mended James Armistead Lafayette who, ''at the peril
of his life found means to frequent the British camp, and
thereby faithfully executed important commissions en-
trusted to him by the marquis,'' and granted his emancipation, ordering the treasurer to pay William
Armistead the same price a slave of James's caliber
would command at auction.

Despite all this, just as it was for so many black heroes
of the Revolution, James saw little else come his way.
It took until 1819—twenty-seven years after the war—
for the Virginia legislature to grant the now poor and
infirm James his petition for relief. They voted him a
sixty-dollar-a-year pension. Five years later, he experienced one last moment of grace when his old
commander, the marquis, visited him on his final trip to
America.

CRISPUS ATTUCKS

To me, the most significant African-American hero in the eighteenth century was Crispus Attucks.

Crispus Attucks first came into my consciousness when I started playing pro ball in 1970 with Oscar Robertson, a Crispus Attucks High School grad. I understood that in the midfifties Crispus Attucks was the first black high school to win the state championship in Indiana. So I asked Oscar, ''Who was Crispus Attucks?'' He said, ''Most people don't know.'' He explained that Attucks was with the group of patriots that died in the Boston Massacre—and he was *black*. That stunned me. I had prided myself on my knowledge of history—I had switched my major to history at UCLA and read voraciously—so I could not believe I had never heard of him. Nothing came of it until years later when I started looking into black contributions in the Revolutionary War. I had heard about a man called Black Sam, who owned old New York's Fraunces Tavern where George Washington bid farewell to his men in December 1783. He was thought to be a patriot spy, but no one knew for certain if he was black in anything but name. I did more reading and was amazed to discover that it was a black man who ignited the confrontation that led to the war.

Here was the first real American martyr, and he was black, and I knew nothing about him. I remember telling myself I would never get caught short about the history of my people again. I started reading everything about Attucks that I could find. At the start of my Crispus Attucks education, I imagined him as larger than life: leader of men, noble freedom fighter, combination of

Jefferson, Washington, Paine. The classic American hero, only black. But history recorded only fragments of his life, and portrayed him as an ordinary eighteenth-century black man. In some ways, even unsavory. It turned out that twenty years before the Boston Massacre, Attucks had been a slave in a provincial Boston suburb. We know this because after the Boston Massacre, on March 5, 1770, someone dug up an old ad that ran in the Boston *Gazette* on October 2, 1750. The ad began:

> Ran away from his master William Brown of Framingham, on the 30th of Sept. last, a Molatto Fellow, about 27 Years of Age, named Crispus, 6 Feet two Inches high, short curl'd Hair, his Knees nearer together than common: had on a light colour'd Bearskin Coat . . .

It included a ten-pound reward—which, of course, no one would ever collect. Because the next time the name Crispus Attucks appeared in public was the day after he passed into history at the Custom House square.

To me, Attucks's enslavement and ordinariness made him seem all the more courageous. I was so fascinated with his story, it mattered more to me at the time than winning an NBA championship. Suddenly, I was obsessed with finding out all I could about that freezing March night in 1770 when a runaway black slave incited the riot that led to the war that founded our nation.

What *did* happen that night? And how did an obscure black man find himself at the forefront of those historic events?

First, some context. The Boston Massacre did not happen in a vacuum, it was provoked by King George III and British Parliament. In the mid-1760s, the Crown tried to tighten its grip on her rebellious American colonies. It started when Britain imposed the Sugar Act, cutting our sugar trade with the West Indies. Then came the Currency Act, forbidding us from printing our own paper money. Next, the Mutiny Act, forcing us to provide for British troops stationed among us. Last, but certainly not least, the hated Stamp Act, requiring us to purchase stamps for all legal documents, including ship's papers, tavern licenses, newspapers, almanacs, pamphlets, decks of cards, even dice. The colonists finally realized: "Hey, maybe belonging to the Empire is not in our best interests anymore." That was when agitators calling themselves the "Sons of Liberty" started terrorizing the British. They assaulted so many stamp agents and burned so many stamps, almost none got sold.

Five years later, King George III imposed more harsh duties, stationed a thousand British soldiers in Boston (population fifteen thousand), and created a board of customs commissioners to end colonial smuggling. In response, colonial merchants boycotted British goods. Finally, British Prime Minister Lord North repealed all new duties except for the tea tax. But it was too late. For seventeen months, Bostonians had resisted the troops, baiting and insulting them, calling them "Oppressors! Trespassers!" At one point, the customs commissioners were so scared, they retreated to Castle William out in the harbor. It took two British regiments to protect them every day as they came back to work at the Custom House.

Meantime, patriot rabble-rouser Samuel Adams started circulating stories of soldiers raping and committing other crimes against citizens. Most of this was invented, along with the explosive rumor that British soldiers planned to attack the city. Citizens panicked; mobs prowled the streets and taverns and started brawls with soldiers. Heads got cracked, weapons were brandished; Boston was a tinderbox.

On the clear, frigid night of March 5, the fuse got lit. Nobody knows who lit it. We do know that around 8 P.M. soldiers from Murray's Barracks in the center of town traded insults with a rowdy group of sailors led by tall, brawny, forty-seven-year-old Crispus Attucks. Like Peter Salem, Attucks was originally from Framingham, though for twenty years he had been working cargo ships out of the Bahamas and whalers off New England. He was known on the lower Boston docks as a tough customer: part African, part Natick Indian ("Attuck" was the Natick word for "deer"). As a slave, he had suffered oppression at the hands of his own countrymen, so he certainly would have resented the British yolk. Maybe more than most, he was primed for a fight.

Attucks's loud, drunken mob drove the soldiers back to their barracks gate. But the soldiers regrouped and loaded their muskets and threatened to shoot. A citizen rang the fire bell in the Old Brick Meeting House and crowds poured into the streets, hauling buckets and fire bags, guns and clubs. Nobody knew what was happening. That was when a young barber's apprentice ran through the crowd, holding his bloodied head and crying, "Murder! Murder!" He claimed the Custom House sentry bashed him with a musket for cursing a soldier.

Three groups formed up and marched on the Custom House. The largest—about thirty sailors with cudgels and sticks—followed Crispus Attucks. Somewhere along King Street, Attucks grabbed a big piece of cordwood from a butcher's stall and flourished it over his head as his followers cheered. When they reached the Custom House square, they joined a bigger, angrier crowd. As the injured apprentice pointed out the sentry who hit him, people screamed, "Kill him! Knock his head off! Burn the sentry box!" They tossed stones, ice balls, sticks. The sentry was scared for his life. He backed up the steps, stuffed shot in his musket, and yelled for help. Almost instantly, a squad of the Twenty-ninth Regiment came at the trot, flashing their bayonets. They formed a half circle around the sentry box, and Captain Thomas Preston ordered them to load. Attucks stepped forward, practically leaning into a soldier's bayonet, and yelled, "You lobsters! Bloody backs! Cowards!" People started throwing things at the Redcoats as they aimed their guns, chest-high, at the crowd.

No one knows exactly what happened next.

One account offered at the soldiers' trial was that Crispus Attucks inflamed the mob by yelling, "Don't be afraid. They dare not fire." When others cried, "Fire! Fire and be damned!", Attucks allegedly threw a stick at Private Hugh Montgomery, who stumbled back and fired his musket, the ball striking Attucks in the chest. Then all hell broke loose. The mob surged forward and other soldiers fired. Attucks took a second ball in the chest, crumpled to the gutter, and died. In all, eleven were shot and five died.

Ironically, the most widely accepted version of events was that of a slave named Andrew who was near the soldiers when they fired. He told the Court of Inquiry in no uncertain terms:

> The People seemed to be leaving the soldiers, and
> to turn from them when there came down a number
> from Jackson's corner, huzzahing and crying, damn
> them, they dare not fire, we are not afraid of them.
> One of these people, a stout man with a long cord

wood stick, threw himself in, and made a blow at
the officer; I saw the officer try to ward off the
stroke; whether he struck him or not I do not know;
the stout man then turned around, and struck the
grenadier's gun at the captain's right hand, and immediately fell in with his club, and knocked his gun
away, and struck him over the head; the blow came
either on the soldier's cheek or hat. This stout man
held the bayonet with his left hand, and twitched it
and cried, ''Kill the dogs. Knock them over.'' This
was the general cry; the people then crowded in.

Andrew insisted the ''stout'' man (meaning, most
likely, ''brave'' or ''resolute'') was ''the Molatto who
was shot.'' Crispus Attucks. To the colonists, Attucks
was now a martyr. But not to John Adams. As a lawyer
for the Crown, our future second president had to discredit his own countrymen. Since key witnesses all
named Attucks as the chief instigator, Adams went after
him with a vengeance. He slandered Attucks by calling
him the leader of ''a motley rabble of saucy boys, negroes and molattoes, Irish teagues and outlandish jack
tars.'' In other words: a low-life thug. In his final ar-
gument, Adams poured on the melodrama. He argued
that Attucks was so dangerous, his ''very looks was
enough to terrify any person.'' Implying, obviously, that
any soldier confronted by Attucks was justified in shooting. Adams then urged the court to conclude it was Crispus Attucks ''to whose mad behavior, in all probability,
the dreadful carnage of that night is chiefly to be as-
cribed.''

It does make you wonder: Was Crispus Attucks nothing more than a dockside thug spoiling for a fight? Or

was he a true American hero ready to die for the cause of freedom?

What we know for sure is that Crispus Attucks was a hard man who led a hard life. He escaped slavery at twenty-seven, went to sea, associated with unscrupulous types, and had a reputation on the docks as a shady character. And on the night of March 5, 1770, he was down there agitating; it was a riot, not a peaceful demonstration. They were throwing sticks and glass; they were trying to *hurt* people. If you read John Adams's defense of the British officers, it sounds like he's defending the Los Angeles Police Department. He says, in effect, "Your Honor, these gentlemen were performing their duties to uphold the law and trying to keep public peace. And these thugs were agitating against the orders of Her Majesty, and had to be silenced." It sounds familiar.

This was not a classic confrontation between oppressor and oppressed. The troops of the Twenty-ninth Regiment were not battle-hardened vets. They were scared recruits, an ocean away from home. They just wanted to do their tour of duty and sail back. On the other hand, the rioters were not exactly protesting "taxation without representation." They were there to get the British boot off their necks.

Maybe Crispus Attucks had no business being in that square. Maybe he didn't care about taxes or the British boot. He was not politically active; we don't know if he could even read. But coming from Boston, he certainly shared in the resentment of the British. Any demonstration against them would have been fine with him—a chance to vent his spleen and maybe crack a British skull or two. He did tag a grenadier. And he was probably looking to hurt somebody else when he got shot.

We don't know his motives—there will be no news

at eleven. But Crispus Attucks will always be an American hero. Say he *was* engaged in thuggery. Fortunately for him, it was thuggery *for the right side*. Also, and this is important: Here was an escaped slave with no education and very little stake in anything—he did not own land; he worked odd jobs—and yet he was the first to risk his skin for a way of life, and maybe for a better life.

What counts is, a black man was in the first group of patriots to bite the dust, for *whatever* reason. If you read about the scoundrels that fought at the Alamo or the Spanish-American War, you will find some were cowards who shot at people over their shoulders while running away. Not every hero is Audie Murphy, taking prisoners for country and God. So even if Crispus Attucks was not motivated by noble thoughts on the dignity of man, he nevertheless aligned himself with the downtrodden, because he knew the *British* were the worst of all evils. To me—and to history—that makes him a hero.

I am not alone in this belief. On Crispus Attucks Day in Boston seventy-five years after the Revolution, the famous white orator, Wendell Phillips, said Ralph Waldo Emerson believed the Boston Massacre was the spark that ignited Americans to fight for liberty. And Crispus Attucks was its first hero. He quoted Emerson:

Who set the example of the guns? Who taught the British soldier that he might be defeated? Who first dared look into his eyes? Those five men! The fifth of March was the baptism of blood. . . . I place, therefore, this Crispus Attucks in the foremost rank of the men that dared. When we talk of courage he rises, with his dark face, in the clothes of the laborer, his head uncovered, his arm raised above

him defying bayonets. . . . When the proper sym-
bols are placed around the base of the statue of
Washington, one corner will be filled by the colored men defying the British muskets.

About twenty-five years later, Harriet Beecher Stowe,
who wrote *Uncle Tom's Cabin*, said Crispus Attucks and
the others who died in the Boston Massacre were more
than ordinary heroes:

It was not for their own land they fought, not even
for a land which had adopted them, but for a land
which had enslaved them, and whose laws, even in
freedom, oftener oppressed than protected. Bravery, under such circumstances, has a peculiar beau-
ty and merit.

No one questions John Adams as a foundation rock
of this country. Well, Crispus Attucks was his equal. He
did what had to be done, too. Without one, there could
not have been the other.

—✸—

What lessons did I learn from the First Rhode Island,
Peter Salem, Salem Poor, James Armistead Lafayette,
Crispus Attucks? First: It is typically American to believe that things can get better and to be willing to sacrifice for that possibility. Peter Salem and Salem Poor
died free men. James Armistead Lafayette was honored
and lived a free life after the war. Crispus Attucks stood
up and was counted when it mattered. Second: I will
always remember these men with respect because they
directly confronted authority, believing they were right.

They made the American dream possible—and all they had were the shirts on their backs.

Still, it's strange to think of these heroic African Americans risking their lives for a society that oppressed them for 150 years. Whenever I talk of this, I always think of something else Harriet Beecher Stowe said about the black patriots. She said we should consider them "magnanimous" because they served a nation that didn't acknowledge them as citizens or equals.

That is an understatement. The sad reality was that freedom was not forthcoming for black people after the war. Although sixty thousand gained freedom by serving the military and almost one hundred thousand left for Spanish Florida, Indian camps, Britain, Canada, Nova Scotia, even Africa, the vast majority were returned to slavery. In fact, most black patriots did not benefit *in their lifetimes* from the noble principle of equality that Jefferson espoused in the Declaration of Independence. When I first realized this, it struck me as outrageous. As America strived to model itself on the high ideals of "inalienable" rights, it deliberately allowed slavery to pick up where it left off. And slavery lasted, legally, another eighty-one years.

That is why I still find it tough to accept that freedom and equality was what the Revolution, the Declaration, and the original United States of America were really all about.

CHAPTER 3

RESISTANCE

Joseph Cinque

H uman bondage has always been part of civilization. The ancient Egyptians enslaved the people they conquered. So did the ancient Romans and Greeks. Moslem traders of the eleventh century exported their North African captives to other Moslem countries. Long before Europeans came on the scene, a small percentage of black Africans enslaved fellow black Africans. But there was a difference between ancient and modern slavery. In ancient times, slavery was not about race. Most victims were convicted criminals or captives in wars and religious feuds. They usually remained in the same geographic area or at least on the same continent.

The global economy did not impact the African slave trade until Spain and Portugal discovered the New World. Even then, the Spanish first tried to enslave Indians. They failed because Indians were nomadic hunters, not laborers or farmers, and fiercely independent. As forced laborers, they tended to sicken and die. In fact, so many died that in 1517 a missionary named Bishop Bartolomé de las Casas suggested substituting African blacks instead. And that's what happened.

African blacks were better suited. Most lived in settled villages, towns, and cities. They were expert farmers who grew permanent crops, and the men were used to laboring in the fields. Also, Africans understood that anyone could become a slave at any time. And once enslaved, epecially in a different culture, they knew they could not escape and hide in the crowd. In a Caucasian society, where could a black person hide? This was an important consideration for white American slave owners.

So African blacks quickly became the slaves of choice. In the early 1500s, Portugal started exporting blacks by the thousands across the Atlantic in exchange for material goods. Buyers would then sell these slaves in the Indies or Americas for money, cotton, sugar, tobacco, or rice. Then they would trade those commodities in Europe for manufactured goods. This slave-trading cycle generated enormous wealth and new industries worldwide. In fact, black African slavery played a key role in stimulating the Industrial Revolution.

For three centuries, millions of black Africans were kidnapped from their homeland and sold overseas as chattel, other people's property. It was not until the early 1800s that the climate started to change. In 1807, Britain took the moral lead by becoming the first European nation to ban the slave trade. That was ironic because Britain had already prospered for two hundred years from its own slave-trading ventures. The fact is, the slave trade boosted the British economy so that Britain could *afford* to quit the trade, and then, sanctimoniously, condemn it.

In the spring of 1839, a twenty-five-year-old Mende rice farmer named Joseph Cinque was working on a road in Sierra Leone, West Africa, when four black strangers overpowered him and chained him to other blacks. He must have known instantly he would never see his wife and three children again. He knew of others who were taken from West Africa, and of the horrors of the Middle Passage. (The trip to procure slaves was usually triangular: the first leg from home base to Africa; the Middle Passage leg from Africa to the West Indies—at least fifty days, during which one of every eight black captives died; and the last leg from the West Indies back to home base again.) Cinque also knew that none of those kidnapped ever returned home.

For three days, he and the other blacks were force marched to Lomboko where white men herded them into the cramped hold of the *Tecora*, a Portuguese slaver headed to Cuba. On the grueling two-month Middle Passage, more than a third of the blacks died. When the *Tecora* arrived at Cuba, the captain anchored offshore and waited for nightfall before unloading his human ''cargo.'' That was because they were in violation of the 1817 British-Spanish slave trade ban. But there was a bizarre catch to the ban that aided the slaver. The penalty for delivering slaves to Cuba was death—unless you could sneak them ashore. Once actually *in* Cuba, there was no enforcement. Then the blacks automatically became slaves who could be shipped, legally, anywhere in the Spanish domain. Naturally, the shrewdest slavers operated under cover of night.

Following a three-mile march into the jungle, Joseph Cinque found himself in a crowded holding pen where he and the other blacks lived for two weeks. Finally, in June, they made another long march to Havana where they were warehoused in the infamous barracoons. These were long roofless buildings that served as slave markets and prisons where Africans waited to be sold like animals. After ten days, Cinque and forty-nine other young African males were purchased by a young Spaniard named José Ruiz. His partner, Pedro Montés, also purchased four African children, three female and one male. On June 28, the fifty-three slaves were marched through Havana to a schooner named the *Amistad* (ironically, Spanish for "friendship"), ready to transport them to plantations up the coast at Puerto Principe. On board with them would be the *Amistad* owner and captain, Ramon Ferrer, a mulatto cook called Celestino, a sixteen-year-old cabin boy named Antonio, and two Spanish crewmen. The slaves would stay in the hold, chained together in crude iron collars.

At sea the weather was tropically hot, so Captain Ferrer brought his mattress up on deck. The Africans were permitted breathers on deck for their meager daily rations of one banana, two potatoes, and a cup of water. The winds kept shifting, so the usually short voyage lengthened and tempers flared. Celestino flogged a black named Burnah for sipping extra water. Cinque was worried; none of the Africans spoke Spanish, so they had no idea where they were going or why. Then an insignificant incident set fateful wheels in motion.

While on deck, Cinque asked the cook in sign language what would happen to him and the others. Teasing, or maybe just being sadistic, Celestino pointed at barrels of beef and gestured that the Spaniards would slit their throats, slice them up, salt them, and eat them like the barreled beef. This petrified Cinque; he hid a rusty nail under his arm and retreated below. Over the next few days Celestino whipped several more blacks, including Cinque. After that, Cinque began plotting a revolt with a fellow captive named Grabeau. One night, Cinque used the rusty nail to pick the padlock releasing the chain connecting the iron collars. The freed blacks then scrounged some sugarcane knives with two-foot blades and planned their next move.

At 4 A.M., during a storm, Cinque led the others up the hatchway. The lone Spaniard at the wheel screamed, "Murder! Murder!" and there was a scuffle in the dark. Ruiz and Montés rushed up from their bunks to find their two crewmen trying to stop Cinque and several other blacks from beating Captain Ferrer. Ferrer got to his feet with a dagger and killed one of his attackers before Cinque struck him down. Then others stabbed and strangled him. Celestino had already been hacked to death as he slept in a lifeboat.

One crewman either jumped or was killed and then tossed overboard. Antonio, the cabin boy, begged for mercy and was shackled to the anchor. Ruiz, Montés, and the second crewman tried to stave off the mob. But when they slashed their attackers, the blood turned some of the wounded hysterical. The crewman grabbed an oar but was disarmed, beaten, and stabbed to death. Ruiz surrendered meekly. Montés was dazed and bleeding but managed to slip below and hide behind a barrel by wrapping himself in an old sail. Meantime, Cinque, Burnah, and Grabeau assumed command of the *Amistad*.

The following morning, Montés was discovered. But

Cinque spared him to sail the ship. He had remembered that on the way to Cuba the ship sailed away from the sun, so he gestured at Montés to sail toward the sun. In other words: Take us back to Africa or die. But Montés and Ruiz conspired to sail deliberately slowly toward the sun during the day, then steer back north at night. Their hope was that a British ship patrolling for slavers would rescue them.

For the next two months, the *Amistad* zigzagged across the sea, heading mainly northwest toward America. When supplies and water dwindled, eight men died from drinking medicines they mistook for extra water. Several vessels spotted the *Amistad* and a few came alongside. But the disheveled black crew, looking like sinister pirates with their long sugarcane knives, scared everyone off. The U.S. Navy quickly learned about the strange, wandering ship.

On August 25, 1839, Cinque had to order the *Amistad* close to shore for resupply. Only Ruiz and Montés knew they were actually off Culloden Point at Long Island, New York. Cinque and eight others gathered some Spanish doubloons they found in a trunk and rowed ashore for water and food. They managed to buy potatoes, gin, and two dogs for food from secluded islanders. That afternoon, as they prepared to return to the ship, five white seamen approached Cinque and his men on the beach. In sign language, Cinque offered them gold doubloons to take the ship back to Sierra Leone, and they agreed. But, apparently, the seamen thought there was more treasure on the *Amistad*, and they planned only to seize the ship for themselves.

The next day an American naval schooner, the USS *Washington*, beat them to it. Oddly, though, instead of escorting the *Amistad* to the nearby Brooklyn Navy

Yard, two *Washington* lieutenants named Meade and Gedney steered to New London, Connecticut—probably because slavery was still legal there, and they knew this would facilitate their own salvage claim on the ship. The press was waiting at the dock. Rumors had circulated that black pirates had murdered the captain and crew of the *Amistad* and then preyed on American merchant ships along the coast. Some newspapers sided with the blacks, claiming that since slavery was illegal in New York, where they were originally seized, the captives were entitled to go free. The New York *Evening Star* even praised the handsome Cinque for his regal bearing and "sagacity and courage."

The following morning, a federal district judge held an inquiry aboard the *Washington*. He examined the *Amistad*'s papers—which had been falsified in Havana—and they seemed to support Ruiz and Montés's story that the *Amistad* was a Spanish slaver transporting "ladinos" (legal Spanish subjects) to their new owners in Cuba. Ruiz, Montés, and Antonio testified that these ladino slaves revolted at sea and committed piracy and murder. So the judge decided to hold them in the New Haven jail until the next meeting of the circuit court grand jury at Hartford, in September. Meantime, Lieutenant Gedney filed a salvage suit for the *Amistad*, its cargo, and all its slaves.

As the story deepened, the press spread it across the nation. It struck a nerve with Abolitionists. They realized that this case could help them publicize the immorality and cruelty of slavery. So they planned their strategy to use the *Amistad* case to remind the nation of the ideals in the Declaration of Independence and the hypocrisy of condoning human slavery in a nation founded on the individual's natural right to liberty and equality.

To fully understand the impact of Joseph Cinque's courageous revolt, we must consider some historical context; specifically, the climate for slavery in America at the time.

Emancipation bills had been introduced in Massachusetts in 1776 and 1777, based on the notion that slavery was "contrary to the laws of nature" and to "the natural and inalienable rights" cited in the Declaration. In 1793, the first antislavery petition was presented to Congress and signed by Benjamin Franklin. It reaffirmed that "equal liberty was the portion, and is still the birthright, of all men." Eight states subsequently abolished the slave trade and emancipated their imported slaves.

But that same year, something unexpected shifted the tide again: Eli Whitney invented the cotton gin. Now, one slave working the "gin" (slang for "engine") could clean more cotton in a few hours than several slaves could clean in a week by hand. As a result, cotton was king and slavery revived and became fixed in the South. When cotton and sugar plantations expanded, so did the demand for slaves. Despite the Embargo Act of 1808 banning the slave trade in America, the big plantationers violated it regularly. And they argued forcefully that slavery was an irreplaceable source of wealth and prosperity that must be considered "necessary, right, and a positive good."

After the War of 1812, overcultivation of cotton depleted the soil in some Southern states. So farmers and planters migrated southwest to Alabama and Mississippi where they could replant. This expanded the cotton industry and the need for slaves. But voices for freedom continued to protest. In 1817, the American Colonization Society was founded to promote the buying of slaves in order to resettle them as free men in Africa. Its most vocal sponsors were prominent Americans like Henry Clay, Daniel Webster, and James Madison. But free blacks and white Abolitionists claimed that colonization was wrong because it implied that blacks were undesirable and inferior. Nevertheless, the American Colonization Society spent millions on their plan. But over ten years they managed to resettle only fifteen thousand blacks in Africa. Meantime, the black birthrate in America surpassed that number every three months. In fact, by the 1830s, despite all legal reforms, the U.S. population of thirteen million included at least three million black slaves.

Then a courageous white man appeared on history's stage to help blacks fight for freedom. In 1831, former indentured servant William Lloyd Garrison published the first issue of his Abolitionist newspaper, *The Liberator*, in Boston. He changed his mind about colonization, partly because of the success of a British plan that granted immediate emancipation to its West Indian slaves. Garrison now advocated immediate abolition without compensation for slave owners. To that end, he established the New England Anti-Slavery Society in 1832 and the American Anti-Slavery Society the next year. He was so passionate and confrontational, most people assumed he was black. Almost in tears, he would tell white crowds, "I never rise before a colored audience without feeling ashamed of my race."

He meant it. In the first *Liberator*, he wrote, "I am in earnest—I will not equivocate—I will not excuse—I will not retreat a single inch—AND I WILL BE HEARD." He *was* heard. Addressing the World Antislavery Convention in London in 1833, Garrison boldly told a supportive white crowd at Exeter Hall:

> I accuse the land of my nativity of insulting the majesty of Heaven with the grossest mockery that was ever exhibited to man . . . of giving open, deliberate, and base denial to her boasted Declaration of Independence . . . suffering a large portion of her population to be lacerated, starved, plundered . . . trafficking in the bodies and souls of men, of legalizing on an enormous scale licentiousness, fraud, cruelty, and murder.

In other tirades, he denounced the Constitution as ''a covenant with death and an agreement with hell,'' and he called orthodox churches ''disgraces to Christianity . . . heathenish, filled with apologies for sin and sinners of the worst sort . . . predominantly corrupt and servile.'' He attacked American Christianity as ''the main pillar of American slavery.''

These sentiments resonated across the nation. They helped establish two hundred antislavery societies with over two hundred thousand members. Millions supported the cause silently, even in the South.

While *The Liberator* gathered steam in Boston, thirty-one-year-old Nat Turner edged onto the stage in Southampton, Virginia. Turner had believed since childhood, when he told inspired prophecies, that he was born for ''some great purpose.'' In his twenties, he declared himself a preacher on a divine mission. One day he told his followers he foresaw ''white spirits and black spirits engaged in battle, and the sun was darkened, the thunder rolled in the Heavens, and blood flowed in streams.'' He started preaching that the Holy Ghost had told him,

"The great day of judgment is at hand." Everywhere Nat Turner preached, he mentioned recurring visions of blood on the ground, blood on the leaves, blood on the corn. When the earth eclipsed the sun on February 12, 1831, Turner proclaimed it a sign. He announced that "as the black spot had passed over the sun, so would the blacks pass over the earth."

From that day on, Turner plotted insurrection with seven other slaves. He said their mission was not robbery or revenge but to deliver all blacks from slavery. The violence began Sunday, August 21, when one of Turner's henchmen murdered Turner's master, Joseph Travis, with a broad ax blow to the head. Afterward, the insurgents murdered families at three neighboring farms. Within twenty-four hours, Turner's small band had expanded to fifteen slaves. They picked up guns, horses, and money along the way, butchering homestead to homestead. By midday, Turner's bloodthirsty group numbered sixty.

When the first bodies were found, citizens thought the British were invading America again. So they hid in the woods or retreated home to hide. By the time they learned it was a slave rebellion, Turner's mounted army—which he led with an ivory-handled, silver-tipped sword—had murdered thirty whites. But strangely, in what appeared to be a frenzied, random massacre, Turner's mob exercised some restraint: They killed only slave owners and their families, sparing poor whites who happened to be on the scene.

When President Andrew Jackson learned of the spree, he sent three companies of artillerymen together with U.S. sailors and marines. Eventually, three thousand federal, state, and county militia organized to suppress Nat Turner's bloody revolt. But before they were stopped,

Turner's army had taken fifty-seven lives. Interestingly, Nat Turner killed only one person himself.

The hysteria and the presence of troops led to the maiming, torture, and murder of innocent blacks. Turner's own wife was whipped, tortured, and forced to turn over her slave papers. Some outraged whites murdered innocent blacks and impaled their decapitated heads on road posts as a warning to other blacks. Within ten days, all the insurgents were killed or jailed, except for Nat Turner. On August 31, juryless trials got under way. The judges consisted of a panel of local slaveholders or their associates. There was no cross-examination and no testimony by the accused. By mid-September, twenty-nine were convicted. Most were hung, others sent to prisons out of state. The trials continued through October.

Sunday, October 30, an armed farmer discovered fugitive Nat Turner hiding in a muddy hole beneath a fallen tree, near his owner's farm. He was taken to the little town of Jerusalem where for three days Turner dictated a lengthy "confession" to Thomas Gray, a lawyer and frustrated writer. Gray wanted to write a book about the events from Turner's point of view, and Turner wanted to send his message to the nation, so they made a deal. The result was a pamphlet entitled *The Confession of Nat Turner—The Negro Insurgent*. It was an important document about the dehumanization of slavery and how it pushed men over the edge. The document revealed not so much Turner's religious fanaticism as his surprising intelligence and even his courage. In fact, he refused to implicate fellow conspirators who were killed or convicted, or to name a single supporter. Not one slave was tried based on anything Turner revealed in his pamphlet.

Nat Turner's trial took place on Saturday, November 5, 1831. He pleaded not guilty "... because I do not feel so." But the case was so overwhelming, Turner's lawyer declined to conduct a defense. The court quickly ruled guilty and Judge Jeremiah Cobb issued the sentence: Turner would be hanged on Friday, November 11, until he was "Dead! Dead! Dead!" Moments before hanging, the calm, remorseless Turner made his final prophecy: He predicted a terrible storm after his death. Oddly enough, shortly after he died, a violent thunderstorm actually erupted over Southampton.

Following Nat Turner's revolt, William Lloyd Garrison was accused of inciting bloodshed in the South through his *Liberator* articles. From then on, there was a concerted Southern effort to discredit Garrison and his paper. He was publicly branded a "murdering hound," "infamous wretch," and "incendiary plotter." Threats were made on his life. But he refused to stop publishing his Abolitionist assaults. Almost overnight, this once obscure reformer became a national symbol of antislavery sentiment. He was a hero to blacks and the devil to most whites.

At that time, the North was thought to be a safe haven for slaves where they could find equality and justice. But anti-Negro sentiment was widespread there, too—especially after Nat Turner's revolt. For example, when Prudence Crandall attempted to admit Negro children into her private school in Connecticut, the community protested and sued, and the state supreme court ruled against her. In 1835, a mob attacked Garrison in Boston for speaking about abolition and he barely escaped by climbing out a window and spending a night, voluntarily, in jail. That night, he penciled a satirical note on his cell wall:

William Lloyd Garrison was put in this jail on Wednesday afternoon, October 21, 1835 to save him from the violence of a "respectable and influential mob," who sought to destroy him for preaching the abominable and dangerous doctrine that "all men are created equal" and that all oppression is odious in the sight of God.

Shortly after this incident, another mob shot to death Abolitionist editor Elijah Lovejoy in Alton, Illinois. The same year, little-known Illinois legislator Abraham Lincoln signed a memorandum proclaiming that slavery was "both injustice and bad policy" but also that the "promulgation of abolition doctrines tends rather to increase than to abate its evils." So it is clear that white Abolitionists like William Lloyd Garrison were essential to the black cause. And it is important for black people to remember that extraordinarily courageous white people risked their reputations, livelihoods, property, even their lives to help blacks gain freedom, without recognition or reward beyond the personal satisfaction of doing the right thing. And that they—along with brave black Abolitionists like Charles Lenox Remond, Samuel Ringgold Ward, Henry Highland Garland, William Wells Brown, Sojourner Truth, Harriet Tubman, and, above all, Frederick Douglass—were in the moral forefront of their time.

Even more so than the man who would, decades later, become known as America's Great Emancipator.

⸙

But now back to Joseph Cinque.

Just after the *Amistad* captives were jailed, Connecticut Abolitionist Dwight Janes told his supporters that during the inquiry aboard the USS *Washington*, José Ruiz admitted to him that the *Amistad* blacks were, in fact, Africans that he and Montés kidnapped into Havana as slaves. Janes informed two prominent Abolitionists in particular: Reverend Joshua Leavitt in New York and renowned New Haven lawyer Roger Baldwin. He urged Baldwin to take the case and find someone who could speak the Africans' language to get their version. Janes feared that the Spanish government would cut a deal with President Martin Van Buren for the return of the ship and its blacks to Cuba. The notion was that since Van Buren was up for reelection in 1840, he would want to avoid a diplomatic scandal over African blacks.

Roger Baldwin was an inspired choice. He had been a governor and U.S. senator. His mother was the daughter of Roger Sherman, an original signer of the Declaration of Independence. And on one of Baldwin's first cases, he had won freedom for a fugitive slave by boldly applying for a writ of habeas corpus. (Habeas corpus—Latin for "having the body"—appears in the original U.S. Constitution and is one of the oldest concepts in Anglo-American law. It provides for a hearing before a judge to determine the legality of any person's detention or imprisonment.) In other words, according to habeas corpus you may not legally detain or imprison someone without first proving cause. Yet that is what appeared to have happened to the *Amistad* blacks.

Baldwin accepted the case. He was joined by brothers Lewis and Arthur Tappan, fellow Abolitionists and respected descendants of Benjamin Franklin. Lewis had once written that slavery was "the worm at the root of the tree of Liberty. Unless killed the tree will die." Shortly, the *Amistad* Committee was formed to raise money for the defense and provide for the blacks while in jail. The defense posture was that the blacks should be freed on the basis of the natural law, American and Spanish laws banning the slave trade, and "the voice of humanity and liberty."

The Abolitionists visited the jail often, but communication with their clients was difficult. Finally, the jailer allowed a visit by Yale linguistics professor Josiah Gibbs. He memorized some Mende words and then stalked the New York docks chanting those words. Amazingly, Gibbs found two Africans who knew the language: James Covey, a former slave from Sierra Leone, and Charles Pratt, a Mende native who seven years earlier had been seized, like Joseph Cinque, by Spanish slavers. Gibbs brought Covey and Pratt to the New Haven jail, where they conversed with Cinque and the others and translated their story. The lawyers then shrewdly leaked details to the newspapers whose subsequent articles generated sympathy for the blacks nationwide. Connecticut residents were so intrigued, some four thousand visited the jail to view the Africans, as though they were on display in a museum. Since many of the blacks were sick and malnourished, and one had just died, these visits further rallied public support.

It was obvious that the public and the captives themselves regarded Joseph Cinque as the leader. He was portrayed in newspaper articles as the son of a prominent Mende family, courageous, gentle, intelligent, proud. Lewis Tappan said Cinque portrayed the dignity and grace of Othello. A noted phrenologist (a pseudopsychologist who believes in the relationship between mental capacity, character, and the shape of a person's skull) declared that Cinque's "cerebral organization" was "superior to the majority of negroes" in the United

States. All this publicity promoted Cinque as noble victim and his Spanish captors as despicable villains.

On September 6, the Spanish minister in Washington demanded the return of the *Amistad* and its human "cargo" for a mutiny trial in Cuba. He insisted that the United States had no right to interfere with Spanish officials enforcing Spanish laws. Meantime, American Southerners applied pressure on the White House to return the blacks to Spain. President Van Buren's concerns were strictly political. He refused to study the legal issues or the facts of the case because he did not want to risk losing reelection by becoming embroiled in a complicated slavery issue.

In the circuit court trial, the Abolitionists immediately launched their habeas corpus strategy. In a brilliant move designed to stoke public sympathy, they requested the writ on the three young African girls. This would force the Spaniards to show cause for imprisoning three helpless females who were obviously too young to have been born into slavery, which would portray the Spaniards as perjurers as well as brutal and cruel slavers. It would also open the way for the Abolitionists to publicly debate the key issue of whether human beings could legally be considered property. They calculated that even if they failed on the writ, they would still manage to publicize that the African blacks were people, not property, and entitled to freedom like anyone else.

The main problem was that writs of habeas corpus in federal cases were rarely granted before the Civil War. In the 1830s, this particular law was still too vague. In fact, there was little clearly defined criminal law, period. Also, it was clear that by granting the writ the court would be moving toward the implication that *all* slaves were people, not property, and therefore "naturally" free. It certainly did not want to fall into that trap—and the prosecution knew it. They argued that according to international treaties and American law, the blacks were slaves belonging to Ruiz and Montés and should be immediately remanded to their owners. It sounded reasonable. Yet U.S. Supreme Court Associate Justice Smith Thompson ruled that arguments on a writ of habeas corpus would be heard—a small victory for the defense.

Every day the case grew more complex and generated more publicity. Once Spain had officially requested the ship's return under the 1795 Pinckney Treaty with the United States, the case became an international drama. The U.S. attorney reiterated Spain's rights, but Roger Baldwin argued that the real issue was neither legal rights nor treaty laws, but rather the color of the Africans' skin. He declared, ''It is only when men come here with a black skin that we look upon them in a condition in which they may by any means be made slaves. But when we find them here from the coast of Africa, the same rule must apply to the black as to the white man.'' He also argued that in Connecticut, unlike other parts of the country and the world, every colored person is presumed free until proven otherwise. So the case snowballed into political, legal, and moral issues; national and international laws and treaties; and opposing interpretations of what constituted slaves, property, and human beings.

It took months to sort out in court. But what happened over those months permanently altered America's legal view of slavery and expanded the writ of habeas corpus into one of our most effective legal guardians of freedom.

Basically, in circuit court Judge Thompson ruled that:

- Salvage claims against the Africans were invalid because, in Connecticut, only claims against property were valid, and Connecticut did not consider blacks as property.

- Since Lieutenant Gedney had seized the ship in New York, and because there was not enough evidence of murder and piracy, Connecticut did not have jurisdiction to conduct a murder-piracy trial.

- The court would not grant the writ of habeas corpus to immediately release the prisoners. That decision, along with the decision of whether the Spanish had legal property rights to the blacks, would fall to the U.S. district court.

While each side argued its briefs, the White House suddenly shifted position. Swayed by national sympathy for the African captives, and probably sensing a backlash at election time, the Van Buren administration now recognized the Africans as free men brought into U.S. jurisdiction illegally, and stated that if they were truly African, the government would send them home.

The defense was relieved there would be no trial for piracy and murder. But they were disappointed with the habeas corpus denial because it meant the Africans must stay confined. The opposition kept playing the race card. Every chance they got, they stirred the obvious public fears. They proclaimed that if the blacks were to ultimately go free under habeas corpus—a legal term that few laymen even understood—the South would collapse. Also, their release would imply that *all* slaves had a right to commit murder, which would trigger slave rebellions around the world, along with a massive influx of fugitive blacks into the United States. And what about the fact that the U.S. Constitution recognized the property rights of slave owners over their slaves?

The case moved to district court before Judge Andrew T. Judson, an anti-Abolitionist with known racist views. The Abolitionists had a daunting task: demonstrating the evils of the slave trade while emphasizing the humanity of blacks and challenging the constitutionally protected custom of treating slaves as property. Wisely, the defense accepted the legal advice of former President John Quincy Adams. Though not an Abolitionist, Adams staunchly opposed slavery as inhumane and an indefensible contradiction of the Declaration of Independence.

On November 19, the defense opened by raising habeas corpus with renewed zeal. Ellis Gray Loring, an Abolitionist who also served as the Tappans' attorney, made an undeniable point when he asked, "Can anyone believe that Judge Thompson would have remanded white men to prison, there to lie for months, or years perhaps, till the question of their freedom had been regularly adjudicated by the court of highest appeal?" Loring raised another intriguing point, provided to him by Adams: Even if it was conceded—which it was not— that the *Amistad* blacks were legal Spanish slaves, they would no longer have been slaves at the time of capture by Lieutenant Gedney because they had already committed an act of "self-emancipation."

Uphill fight. Constitutional law opposed them; and newspaper pieces and public protests demonstrated that racial hatred was still deeply entrenched. President Van Buren was so certain of a prosecution victory, returning the ship and blacks to Cuba for trial, that he arranged for a U.S. Navy ship to facilitate. He wanted to bury the issue by hustling the blacks away as fast as possible. Out of sight, out of mind.

On January 8, Joseph Cinque finally took the stand. Wrapped in a blanket, he looked distinguished and proud. James Covey translated. Understanding that he was under oath, Cinque spoke movingly about his capture: being chained and ''packed'' on the slave ship (he demonstrated being manacled by sitting on the floor and holding his hands and feet together); the cruel treatment aboard the *Amistad* ordered by Ruiz and carried out by Celestino, the cook; the arrival in New York and seizure of the ship by Gedney. Later, Grabeau and another captive corroborated this story. Cinque appeared bright, dignified, sincere—the press said he had the bearing of a prince.

Finally, on January 13, 1840, Judge Judson ruled that:

- Connecticut did have lawful jurisdiction.

- The salvage claims of the white men Cinque met on the beach were dismissed on the grounds that these men never took possession of the *Amistad*.

- Customary salvage was awarded to Lieutenant Gedney and his associates at the rate of one-third of the appraised value.

- The *Amistad* and its nonhuman cargo must be returned to its Spanish owners.

- The cabin boy, Antonio, was legally a Spanish slave and must be returned to Spain.

- Since the murders were committed aboard a Spanish-owned ship, America had no jurisdiction in that matter.

Judson remanded the Africans to President Van Buren who would provide their passage back to Africa. On the key issue of whether the Africans were the property of Ruiz and Montés, the court ruled that slaves *were* property, and if Spain had proved ownership the Africans would have been returned under treaty law. However, since Spain failed to prove ownership, the court declared that Cinque and his fellow black captives "were born free" as natives of Africa, and kidnapped illegally, and that therefore they "have been and still of right are free and not slaves." Further, they committed murder in self-defense and only out of "desire of winning their liberty and returning to their families and kindred."

At first, the defense and Abolitionists around the country were jubilant. It was an unprecedented victory. (Rumor was that the defense was so sure they would lose, and the Africans returned to Spain, they arranged an elaborate escape on the Underground Railroad. Co-incidentally, after the court ruled that the *Amistad* cabin boy, Antonio, must be returned to Spain as a slave, he disappeared. Eventually, he ended up living free and working in Montreal.) Even though they won the central battle, the defense felt that by virtue of the Antonio ruling they had failed in their larger mission to prove all slaves were, by "natural" law, free people and not property. Also, the ruling returning the captives to Africa seemed another victory of legal over "natural" law. And, unfortunately, the vicious public expressions of racism throughout the trial meant the institution of American slavery was still intact.

Immediately after the verdicts, the U.S. district attorney filed an appeal. Eventually, John Quincy Adams defended before the U.S. Supreme Court under Chief Justice Roger B. Taney. This was ironic because, in 1770, Adams's father had defended the British soldiers who fired on Crispus Attucks; and here, seventy years later, the son was defending other black victims under the white oppressor's boot. "Oh," Adams wrote in his journal at the time, "how shall I do justice to this case and to these men?" He decided to accomplish that by constantly reminding the court of the principles in the Declaration of Independence and America's commitment to human rights. Adams won. The appeal was denied.

When the final verdict was communicated to the Africans, Cinque replied with simple dignity, "Me glad—me thank the American men—me glad." He then translated to his people that they were free. They laughed and spoke in Mende but were more subdued than expected. When the jailer asked if they were eager to get home to Africa, Cinque replied cautiously, "I don't know. I think one or two days—then say—we all talk—think of it—then me say." They were distrustful; what if their return was a trick? What if they were to be enslaved again when they stepped off the boat?

Assurances were made; the blacks were moved to Farmington until passage could be arranged; and Cinque's mood lightened—he made speeches and performed tribal dances and was widely admired as "The Black Prince." In August 1841, while the Abolitionists struggled to raise funds for commissioning a ship, one of the Africans drowned in a canal. It was thought to be a suicide brought on by severe depression over the long delay. Appeals were made to the government for aid, but neither Congress nor the president acted.

Finally, using money from private donations, on November 27, 1841, the thirty-five survivors of the original fifty-three blacks sailed back to Africa. The voyage took fifty days; they had been away three years. Ten males and the three females remained in Sierra Leone to do missionary work. Joseph Cinque and the others returned to Mende. Cinque later worked at Kaw-Mende as an interpreter for the American Missionary Association. He died a free man around 1879.

Months before the district trial concluded, Martin Van Buren lost reelection to William Henry Harrison. Many believed that the unpopularity of his position on the *Amistad* blacks contributed to his defeat.

Throughout America, the slavery debate was enlivened by the *Amistad* affair. At trial, it had been the aim of the defense and their Abolitionist supporters to draw the connection publicly between the illegal capture of these few African blacks and the terrible strictures of American slavery. And that is what Americans were now debating—right up until the eve of the Civil War. So Joseph Cinque's revolt for freedom at sea found logical expression in America's bloodiest internal conflict.

Since the *Amistad* case was followed closely across the nation, for many Americans Joseph Cinque's name became associated with courage, dignity, and the struggle from oppression. At the time, blacks considered it a great triumph of spirit. Another major triumph associated with the case was the expansion of the legal application of habeas corpus. The Abolitionists and the lawyers who took up Cinque's cause established for the future a solid basis for applying habeas corpus in cases involving slavery and fugitive slaves. By relentlessly raising the habeas corpus issue, they hammered it into the American consciousness that people cannot be imprisoned without legal cause. In accomplishing that, they also established the concept that a human being's dignity transcends any commercial arrangement forced upon him. The commitment to these concepts gave Abolitionist supporters across America a big dose of encouragement that they *could* succeed.

To me, Joseph Cinque's courageous rebellion typifies the story of blacks trying to get home. I think millions of black people in this country today have a nagging sense of having been kidnapped. We know we were removed from our ancestral homelands against our will and brought to a strange land, and forced to work for the pleasure and profit of others. So it is very easy to see ourselves in the story of someone in that actual situation who rebelled in self-defense. When I think of the battle for civil rights in America in my time, it is clear to me that Joseph Cinque was the root and Thurgood Marshall—pioneer of school desegregation—was the branch and the fruit and the flower.

I learned one other important lesson from Joseph Cinque's amazing story: Never underestimate the power of an individual act of courage. When one person takes a stand, despite background, status, or even intent, it may one day affect many other lives. Joseph Cinque's personal act of revolt rippled outward on a choppy sea where it might have dissolved and been forgotten. Yet look where it finally touched shore. His isolated act eventually resulted in a wider application of the habeas corpus concept of justice for millions of oppressed Americans. He did not intend that; it just happened.

It is an important, inspiring, and remarkable example of the noble true sentiment that if you stand up for what you know to be right, even though you might consider yourself just a ripple in the sea, you *can* make a world of difference.

CHAPTER 4

INCITEMENT

Frederick Douglass

O nly thirty years after the civil rights "revolution" of the 1960s, race relations in America keep deteriorating. African Americans still live separate and unequal—not just in the South, but in Boston, New York, Chicago, Dallas, Denver, Los Angeles. Despite all our legal victories over discrimination, blacks and whites seem to understand each other less today and fear each other more. The problems affect both sides. The O. J. Simpson trial showed that black people still experience America very differently than white people; 131 years after the Civil War, old racial stereotypes still shape race relations; offensive relics like Strom Thurmond and Jesse Helms still get reelected behind Old South bigotry while slicker racists like David Duke stand in the wings; too many blacks still don't see the need for education and maintaining their families; and there is still too much rage in our ghettos, built like prisons in the sixties and

seventies to isolate African Americans from "respectable" society.

I think one reason for the backslide in race relations
is that most Americans have lost touch with our legacy
of slavery. To me, slavery has always been the defining
event of American society—in the same way that the
Holocaust is the defining issue of Judaism. Fairly or not,
most black people's first impressions of white people
have something to do with prejudice and associations
with slavery—and vice versa. This dates back to the
country's birth. Certainly it was no accident that slavery
was the major moral issue the signers of the Declaration
failed to address when they proclaimed liberty, equality,
and justice for all, and went home to oversee their slaves.
Just as it is no accident that our public dialogue on race
today is more a monologue of frustration and rage. And
the message this sends to African Americans is: White
people still don't want to acknowledge the real roots of
our estrangement.

In *The Negro in the Making of America*, Benjamin
Quarles was right when he pointed out that slavery was
"both a labor system and a social order." It was about
two things: economics *and* white supremacy. On the sur-
face, economics was the primary engine. Early last century, a steady demand for cotton, tobacco, sugar, and rice
created a steady need for slaves. After the U.S. ban on
the foreign slave trade in 1808, American traders just
shifted gears and took the business interstate. Older,
slave-rich states of the upper South, like Virginia, Maryland, and Kentucky, sold their surplus slaves to newer,
shorthanded states, like Alabama and Mississippi. Bro-

kers also started leasing slaves daily, weekly, monthly, and seasonally to factories, railroads, and worker-intensive trades. For forty years before the Civil War, 750,000 African Americans were merchandised this way; it was the South's most lucrative interstate commerce. In 1830, slaves produced 1 million bales of cotton; by 1860 it was up to 4 million, worth $191 million in European markets—almost two thirds of the total U.S. export trade. Right up to the eve of the Civil War, slaves were harvesting three quarters of the *world's* cotton—in effect, justifying their own enslavement.

But something else drove this vicious cycle of misery: *white supremacist racism.* A major reason for its longevity is the willingness of white people to believe black stereotypes. That started with the colonial slave codes as white society switched from equal opportunity indentured servitude to black-only slavery. It was reinforced by Southern extremists—including the majority of nonslave owners—who did a thorough job of demonizing black people.

But we don't much talk about this today in our schools, as though it is taboo. For example, we don't learn anymore about people like the Virginia attorney George Fitzhugh. Yet pre-Civil War, George Fitzhugh was the archetypal Southern white supremacist. His name was almost as well known as those of Andrew Jackson and John C. Calhoun, the two most influential Old South politicos of their day. (Calhoun vehemently disputed the notion that all men were created equal. He once said, "A Negro, being socially, mentally, and anthropologically inferior to a white man, had no natural rights, deserved none, and could not make responsible use of them.") During 1854, as an editor of the *Richmond Examiner*, the South's largest circulating newspaper, Fitzhugh used the paper as a bully pulpit for his pro-slavery propaganda, which then circulated in the Northern press. Under attack from antislavers, he wrote: "We should indignantly hurl back upon our assailants the charge that there is something wrong and rotten in our system. From their own mouths we can show free society to be a monstrous abortion, and slavery society to be the healthy, beautiful and natural being which they are trying, unconsciously, to adopt." Obviously, he was in denial. The "monstrous abortion" was *slavery*—and all the George Fitzhughs.

The same year, in his book *Sociology for the South* (one of the strongest pro-slavery documents of the antebellum South), Fitzhugh drew on his knowledge of history, economics, and popular views of the day to attack Jeffersonian ideals and justify the superiority of whites to govern. Some excerpts of his most widely shared views:

. . . [The negro] is but a grown up child, and must be governed as a child. . . . The master occupies towards him the place of parent or guardian . . .

. . . the negro race is inferior to the white race, and . . . would be far outstripped or outwitted in the chase for free competition. Gradual but certain extermination would be their fate . . .

. . . Men are not "born and entitled to equal rights!" It would be far nearer the truth to say, "that some were born with saddles on their backs, and others booted and spurred to ride them,"—and the riding does them good.

These crackpot ideas made lasting impressions on white people who had no firsthand knowledge of blacks. Three years later in his second book, *Cannibals All! or Slaves Without Masters*, Fitzhugh represented the preposterous myth of the contented slave:

> The negro slaves of the south are the happiest and, in some sense, the freest people in the world. The children and the aged and infirm work not at all, and yet have all the comforts and necessaries of life provided for them. They enjoy liberty, because they are oppressed neither by care nor labor.

Concurrent with whites demonizing and mythologizing blacks, they sanctified themselves by excusing slavery as a benevolent favor, saving blacks from lives of failure or savagery; or they justified slavery as the natural expansion of the realm of Christianity. The real reasons for slavery were simpler: ego gratification, power, comfort, wealth. The slave owner could accomplish all of this by forcing ignorant blacks into his combination prison and plantation and by working them to death while growing rich off their sweat and blood.

So George Fitzhugh knew he was lying; he was a cunning, educated, political snake. But he spewed his venom anyway because it was what white America wanted to hear, what Southerners needed to hear. His kind of stereotyping lent credibility to the popular belief that whites were superior to blacks, genetically, intellectually, morally, spiritually, racially. It is interesting to me that while Fitzhugh was hawking this mythology, the South stood virtually alone in the world community on the issue of white supremacy. By 1840, slavery was under global condemnation and already illegal in Latin

America and the British Empire. Nevertheless, in 1850 the 1.7 million whites with slaveholding interests were able to dominate the other 4 million whites in Southern society. The South was like South Africa under apartheid: a depraved culture clinging to self-serving myths masquerading as custom. This nonnation, this small *section* of a nation, kept defying the forward march of not just the Union, but Western civilization.

This was the complicated South into which Frederick Douglass was born. An island of bondage and white mumbo jumbo that nothing and no one had been able to reform—not the Bible, the Declaration of Independence, the Bill of Rights, the Constitution, the president, or even a catastrophic war the South brought on itself.

Of all the heroic African Americans who had the courage and fortitude to escape from slavery, how many do we know about today? Once free, who stood up to be counted for all African Americans? Who met with and influenced eight presidents? Who left an indelible mark on history and the nation?

Only one African American truly fills this bill: Frederick Douglass.

Here was the son of a black slave and white slave owner, starting life at the bottom: a constant affront to his master's white wife; albatross to his master's black mistress; seed of the immorality of Christians who sold their own children into slavery. Frederick the mulatto, enduring extra hardships as a member of a growing new group of outcasts lower on humanity's scale than even the original slaves brought over from Africa. First just trying to survive; then resisting; finally escaping; somehow arriving on the world stage, analyzing the status of *all* blacks and trying to find political means of changing their circumstances.

Here was a man whose adult life spanned fifteen different presidents and fifty years of change, yet he remained the one black constant in the sociopolitical landscape. Orator par excellence whose speeches were a rare combination of uncommon courage and brilliant political thought. Founding father of the first civil rights and black protest movements. The most visible, persuasive, influential African American of the nineteenth century. A life, ironically, that could have happened only in America.

Yet history has underestimated him. To fully appreciate the scope of his courage and accomplishment, we must look past the familiar, white, banal versions of his life. Because his greatness was not just in what he did, but also in how and why; it was in his trademark frontal attacks on oppression, using *words*, and their emotional power, to sway.

The source of that power was the unique life behind the words.

He was not born a Douglass. He was born Frederick Augustus Washington Bailey in February 1818 on a Maryland plantation. He never knew his white father and, like most slave children, was separated early from his mother. At six, he was removed from his grandmother's care to the plantation where he slept in a corn sack on a clay floor, ate gruel from a wooden trough, and witnessed other slaves being beaten and murdered. His mother saw him only a few times, at night, when she would walk twelve miles to watch him sleep and then hike back by sunrise to work in the fields. When Harriet Bailey died, Frederick missed her funeral; no one

told him about it. He was alone at seven—like millions
of other children of slaves.

(In this country, white people tend to berate blacks for
the breakdown of black families, but they habitually
deny their history of suppressing these bonds, starting
with the kind of slavery Frederick Douglass endured. It
is a major problem in the black community. But we all
need to ask why this weed still grows. Its roots are slavery; it flourishes today on prejudice, injustice, and white
supremacy. Deal with the roots and the weed dies, and
maybe flowers will grow.)

The annihilation of black families was one of slavery's vilest offenses, and it affected Frederick Douglass
profoundly. Years later, he still insisted that the worst
cruelty of slavery was that it "abolished fatherhood and
motherhood." The hollowness he felt over his mother's
death tormented him; he continually sought reconnection
to something bigger than himself. I believe it also fed
his driving need to become a protector of his race.

In 1826, eight-year-old Frederick was sent to live with
Hugh Auld, manager of a shipbuilding firm in Baltimore,
and his wife, Sophia. Since Sophia had never owned a
slave, she did not know the protocol. Warm and humane,
she did not expect from Frederick the servile behavior
that masters normally elicited from slaves. She taught
him to stand dignified and straight and look her in the
eye, and follow the "Do Unto Others" rule. Her kind-
ness lowered his guard. For example, when Sophia read
him stories from the Bible, he boldly asked her to teach
him to read. She did; but when she boasted about his
progress to her husband, Hugh, he exploded in rage: "A
nigger should know nothing but to obey his master—to
do as he is told to do . . . Now, if you teach that nigger

how to read, there would be no keeping him. It would forever unfit him for being a slave.''

Prophetic words: *Once they've seen Paris, how do you keep them down on the farm?*

Sophia abruptly turned cold and cruel, and she terminated the reading lessons. It devastated Frederick; she had treated him with pure Christian decency and then, suddenly feeling her power, she started treating him like a disobedient dog. It taught Frederick a key lesson: that the power and privilege generated in an intimate relationship with people whose humanity you refuse to recognize turns you depraved. Overhearing Hugh Auld's outburst taught him an even more important lesson: *The power white men have over blacks comes from keeping blacks ignorant.* He perceived that education really meant equality—and this showed him the path to freedom. He figured if reading made you ''unfit'' for slavery, then he must work harder, on his own, to master the language and set *himself* free.

Knowledge is power. Words are weapons.

Hugh and Sophia tried to deny Frederick access to newspapers and books. But it was too late; he outwitted his captors by devising clever strategies to continue learning. First, while out doing errands, he converted the white street kids he met into substitute teachers. He would bring bread to trade these hungry kids for on-the-spot lessons. It was typical Our Gang stuff—American ingenuity at its most basic level: kids in the street figuring out how they will do X, Y, Z. Frederick is saying, ''Listen, I got some bread. And maybe we can get some jam here. . . . And, by the way, what about those books?'' Then he would challenge the kids to games to see if they could write more letters of the alphabet than him, just so he could learn what *they* knew. (Interestingly, when Douglass wrote his first autobiography in 1845, he withheld the kids' names to protect them from reprisals—an early sign of his magnanimous soul.)

Another strategy was sneaking peeks at newspapers and books when Sophia was out, and copying down words to study in private. This was how he discovered an intriguing new word: *abolition.* Once he learned its meaning, he was always drawn to any mention of it as somehow relevant to him. One day, he bought *The Columbian Orator*, a collection of essays on freedom, democracy, and courage. In it was a dialogue between slave and master, ending with the master freeing his slave. For Frederick, it was potent reinforcement of: *Knowledge is power* and *Words are weapons.*

Next, he taught himself to write by watching ship carpenters print letters on timbers, then learning the words from the letters. The process exhilarated him. But it caused a crisis. The more he read, the more he strained in the yoke. Hugh Auld's fears materialized in Frederick, who knew too much now to accept his condition.

What impressed me also was Douglass's mature perception that Sophia's transformation had destroyed her character. He could not have articulated it then, but he certainly saw how a slave owner's sense of entitlement and absolute power over another person's life corrupted him. (We see this all through history with dominant white cultures denying the humanity of their victims and then using that as rationale to oppress and destroy them. Victims of the Nazi Holocaust will say there was never a group of people more diabolically clever and cruel than the Nazis. African Americans will say slaveholders are in that same slot. They run neck and neck.) The fact that young Frederick could perceive the degenerate values of the upper echelons of white society was evidence of his exceptional intellect. And his courage and ability, later, to share these insights in the cause of freedom separated him from other Abolitionists, and most human beings.

——— ✤ ———

Not long after Nat Turner's rampage, Frederick Douglass was sent to serve Hugh Auld's sadistic brother, Thomas, who starved his slaves and beat them (including Frederick several times) when they stole food to survive. Yet Auld professed piety and righteous Christian virtue. One day, Frederick personally witnessed another example of Christian virtue, Thomas Auld-style, when Thomas tied up a lame slave woman and, while whipping her bloody, quoted from scripture: "He that knoweth his master's will, and doeth it not, shall be beaten with many stripes."

Frederick was incensed; the world seemed upside down. He became so unruly, Thomas thought he might become another Nat Turner. So he put Frederick out to Edward Covey, the local "Negro breaker." For a fee, Covey "broke" disobedient slaves with notorious brutality. In the first six months, he flogged Frederick every week and worked him mercilessly, dawn to midnight. The torture chipped away his soul. Even twelve years later, Frederick remembered sorrowfully:

> Mr. Covey succeeded in breaking me—in body, soul and spirit. My natural elasticity was crushed; my intellect languished; the disposition to read departed; the cheerful spark that lingered about my eye dried out; the dark night of slavery closed in upon me, and behold a man transformed into a brute!

He considered murder, even suicide. But before he could act, on a stifling August afternoon he collapsed from sunstroke in the wheat fanning yard. When he couldn't get up, Covey kicked him and gashed his head with a stick and left him to bleed. Later, Frederick managed to drag himself to Thomas Auld's farm, but Auld sent him back. When Frederick returned in despair and Covey tried to tie him to a post for another whipping, he grabbed Covey's throat and they wrestled fiercely in the dirt. Frederick fought only defensively—he knew the penalty for striking a white man. Covey was stunned and scared; when other slaves refused to help him for two hours, he finally gave up, muttering threats. But he never raised a hand to Frederick again. And he told no one about it; he thought it would ruin his reputation.

Frederick considered this bout "the turning point in my career as a slave." It revived his self-respect and his drive to be free. He learned another truth that would later become a motto: *Men are whipped oftenest who are whipped easiest*. He promised himself he would never again submit to a whipping—in *any* form.

On January 1, 1834, Frederick Bailey was leased to farmer William Freeland, a kindly Southern gentleman. Frederick immediately started teaching a sabbath school—an illegal school for blacks. He was committed now to educating his own people. Meantime, he was planning to escape by canoe with five other slaves, all posing as fishermen. He forged papers and prepared to die rather than return. Once he accepted that he would either be free or dead, his new sense of purpose was clearly defined, and he started making long-range plans for his freedom.

But the day of the escape, someone betrayed them. Frederick spent a week in jail and ended up back with

Hugh and Sophia in Baltimore. He was eighteen, anguished, defiant, a ticking black time bomb.

Hugh Auld let Frederick work as an apprentice caulker at a shipyard where he had to endure abuse from up to seventy-five white carpenters all giving him orders: "Haloo, nigger, come turn this grindstone!" "I say, darky . . . heat up some pitch!" One day, four of his coworkers, who resented blacks taking jobs from poor Northern whites, beat Frederick with bricks, spikes, and fists. He fought back but was overmatched while fifty others watched, some of them yelling, "He struck a white man! Kill him!"—which they could do legally. This conflict revealed to Frederick the spectrum of black-white relations. They had all worked well together until jobs grew scarce. Then, like Sophia Auld, the whites reverted to the exclusivity of their skin color, and ran the blacks out. Knee-jerk reaction.

Hugh Auld tried to press charges because his "property" had been damaged. But blacks could not charge whites in court unless a white person testified on their behalf—and none would. After Frederick recovered, Auld let him seek employment and collect his own wages, but took most of his nine dollars a week. Frederick resented it as "robbery." In the meantime, though still a slave, he was admitted into an educational association for free blacks called the East Baltimore Mental Improvement Society where he sharpened his debating skills. But he could not shake his resentment over the fact that a black man could not get justice. There was chattel slavery and now he knew there was caste slavery, too. For a black to get justice in America, he figured, he would have to make his own or change society.

He resolved to do both. On September 3, 1838, after three weeks planning, with a friend's sailor outfit and a document stamped with an American eagle, he posed as a free seaman on a train to Delaware and a steamboat to free-soil Philadelphia. But he knew he still wasn't safe from roving slave catchers, so he continued on ferries and trains to New York. There he stayed with David Ruggles, African-American head of the Vigilance Committee that directed hundreds of runaway slaves to safety via the Underground Railroad.

Only then did he finally relax, free at twenty-one, for the first time in his life.

When Frederick Bailey left New York for safer New Bedford, Massachussetts, he assumed a new name to avoid identification. He chose Douglass, after the heroic character in Sir Walter Scott's novel *Lady of the Lake*. Just six months free, instead of laying low like other runaway slaves, Frederick subscribed to William Lloyd Garrison's Abolitionist paper, *The Liberator*. He would later explain: "The paper became my meat and my drink. My soul was set all on fire. Its sympathy for my brethren in bonds—its scathing denunciations of slaveholders—its faithful exposures of slavery—and its powerful attacks upon the upholders of the institution—sent a thrill of joy through my soul, such as I had never felt before!" Douglass also joined the mostly white, confrontational American Anti-Slavery Society and attended risky Abolitionist meetings. In order to live, he shoveled coal, cut wood, dug cellars, loaded boats on the wharves, and worked in an oil refinery.

On March 12, 1839, at a church meeting, Douglass made an impromptu speech criticizing the colonization concept of shipping American blacks to Africa. It earned a notice in *The Liberator*. At another meeting, he related his own experiences as a slave for the first time. He sensed this was a way to embrace the cause. But it wasn't until August 16, 1841, in Nantucket—home of the fiercely Abolitionist Quakers—that he delivered his first great public speech. He recounted his life as a slave, just as he had relived it a thousand times in his head. He dramatized the sights, sounds, emotions—the cracking whip; the doleful songs of brutalized field hands; the screams of a starving child—how it *felt* in slavery's chains. Methodically and poetically, he engaged the all-white audience with a litany of insufferable wrongs:

> . . . In law, the slave has no wife, no children, no country, and no home. He can own nothing, possess nothing, acquire nothing. . . . He toils that another may reap the fruit; he eats unbolted meal, that another may eat the bread of fine flour; he labors in chains at home, under a burning sun and biting lash, that another may ride in ease and splendor abroad. . . . he is sheltered by the wretched hovel, that a master may dwell in a magnificent mansion . . .

> . . . Where are his newspapers? Where is his right of petition? Where is his freedom of speech? his liberty of the press? and his right of locomotion? He is said to be happy; happy men can speak. But ask the slave—*what* is his condition? . . . and you had as well address your inquiries to the *silent dead*. There comes no *voice* from the enslaved. We are left to gather his feelings by imagining what ours would be, were our souls in his soul's stead.

This was precisely his message: *Put yourself in a slave's place. This is really what it's like*. That approach set him apart. As he later explained, "It did not entirely satisfy me to narrate wrongs; I felt like denouncing them." When he did his severest denouncing, he was enthralling. His unique power was his ability to mimic experiences; he made white people feel viscerally what they could barely imagine before. He was both eloquent and ingenious—no one ever addressed slavery with such intimate passion.

After the Nantucket speech, Douglass's new mentor, Garrison, cried out to the crowd, "Have we been listening to a thing, a chattel personal, or a man?" The crowd signified, "A man! A man!" Garrison yelled, "Shall such a man even be sent back to bondage from the free soil of old Massachusetts?" The crowd answered, "No! No!" People went wild, shouting, crying, applauding, shaking Douglass's hand. His career was launched.

Admirably, Douglass never thought, "I'm free now and everybody else has to do *his* share." Instead, he took on the lion's share of changing the system himself. He knew his life was in jeopardy from the moment he stepped up to the speaker's pulpit. But he did not mind watching his back; he was compelled to speak for everyone he left behind in slavery, the abused and tortured and murdered. So when Garrison offered him $450 a year as a traveling speaker for the Massachusetts Anti-Slavery Society, Douglass eagerly became a freedom fighter in the cold war against slavery.

He paid rugged dues. Garrison envisioned that Douglass would serve the cause as "living proof of what freedom meant to the Negro," which white people were not excited to hear. As a result, even though Douglass toured all over the North, from Maine to Ohio, he was met with constant assault. There were "Kill the nigger!" riots at his speeches. He was thrown from stages, beaten, and pushed down stairs. He was harassed in restaurants, hotels, railroad cars. (Douglass would reason with Jim Crow conductors, "If you give me one good reason why I should move, I'll go willingly." When the conductors replied, "Because you are black," he refused to move. When they finally dragged him out, Douglass always took the seat with him in protest.) Finding halls that allowed blacks to speak was nearly impossible. One night he walked around Dorchester, New York, ringing a bell to announce a speech, and then stood by a tree and enthusiastically addressed his five listeners.

Although many voices were raised in the Abolitionist movement, Douglass's was the loudest and most effective. For example, on a brief visit to Rhode Island, his impromptu speech helped defeat a measure to enfranchise poor whites with the vote while denying votes to blacks. He also risked criticizing his own—specifically, free blacks who stayed out of the fray, irresponsibly uninvolved. He reproved them harshly:

> We are one people—one in general complexion, one in common degradation, one in popular estimation. As one rises, all must rise; and as one falls, all must fall . . . Every one of us should be ashamed to consider himself free, while his brother is a slave . . . The wrongs of our brethren should be our constant theme. There should be no time too precious, no calling too holy, no place too sacred, to make room for the cause.

Another courageous decision to lead by example: In 1845, he published his brilliant autobiography, *Narrative*

of the Life of Frederick Douglass. The book described
in unprecedented detail the real people, places, and
events of his twenty years in bondage. He knew it would
identify him as the fugitive Frederick Bailey, but his
primary aim was to give the fullest rendering ever of the
depravity of slavery. In one part, he accused American
Christianity—specifically, slaveholder Christianity—as
the main pillar of slavery. This was the most astute,
scalding, and uncompromisingly courageous attack on
religious duplicity by any public figure in the century:

> . . . I am filled with unutterable loathing when I
> contemplate the religious pomp and show . . .
> which every where surround me. We have man-
> stealers for ministers, women-whippers for mis-
> sionaries, and cradle-plunderers for church
> members. The man who wields the blood-clotted
> cowskin during the week fills the pulpit on Sunday,
> and claims to be a minister of the meek and lowly
> Jesus. The man who robs me of my earnings at the
> end of each week meets me as a class-leader on
> Sunday morning, to show me . . . the path to sal-
> vation. He who sells my sister for the purpose of
> prostitution, stands forth as the pious advocate of
> purity. He who proclaims it a religious duty to read
> the Bible denies me the right of learning to read
> the name of the God who made me. He who is the
> religious advocate of marriage robs whole millions
> of its sacred influence, and leaves them to the rav-
> ages of wholesale pollution. The warm defender of
> the sacredness of the family relation is the same
> that scatters whole families . . . leaving the hut va-
> cant, and the hearth desolate. We see the thief
> preaching against theft, and the adulterer against

adultery. We have men sold to build churches, women sold to support the gospel, and babes sold to purchase Bibles for the *poor heathen! all for the glory of God and the good of souls!* The slave auctioneer's bell and the church-going bell chime in with each other, and the bitter cries of the heartbroken slave are drowned in the religious shouts of his pious master . . . Here we have religion and robbery the allies of each other—devils dressed in angels' robes, and hell presenting the semblance of paradise.

Douglass achieved his goal; the moral power of the book made it a national best-seller. Unfortunately, it also forced him to flee to avoid recapture. He spent the next two years speaking all across the British Isles, where he was astonished to find little obvious prejudice. It took even more courage to return home. But in his farewell speech at London Tavern, March 30, 1847, he expressed unequivocally his commitment, not to Frederick Douglass, but to the greater cause of African-American freedom:

I go, turning my back upon the ease, comfort, and respectability which I might maintain even here, ignorant as I am. Still, I will go back, for the sake of my brethren. I go to suffer with them; to toil with them; to endure insult with them; to lift up my voice in their behalf; to speak and write in their vindication; and struggle in their ranks for that emancipation which shall yet be achieved by the power of truth and of principle for that oppressed people.

Three months earlier, two English supporters had sent Hugh Auld $710.96 to purchase Douglass's freedom. Douglass was grateful; he could now do his work literally unfettered. But he would not acknowledge that he was property to buy or sell. He insisted proudly, "I have as much right to sell Hugh Auld as Hugh Auld had to sell me."

Back home, Douglass practiced what he preached. Moving to Rochester, New York, he started his own Abolitionist paper, *The North Star* (fugitive slaves commonly used the North Star to guide them toward free soil). This established his split from the Garrisonians who were now advocating passive resistance instead of the hard-core political action Douglass desired. He urged black economic and political empowerment: "Every colored mechanic is . . . an elevator of his race. Every house built by black men is a strong tower against the allied hosts of prejudice. . . ."

He did not just address the big issues; he would not tolerate discrimination in *any* arena. In 1850, he orchestrated a boycott to have his own children admitted to the segregated public school in his district rather than the inferior "colored" school farther away. His protest succeeded. The board of education admitted not only Douglass's children, but every Negro child in the district. That was his ultimate plan.

Still he considered himself an advocate for *human rights*, not just African Americans. "I base no man's rights," he liked to remind, "upon his color, and plead no man's rights because of his color. My objection to slavery is not that it sinks the *Negro* to the condition of a brute, but that it sinks a *man* to that condition." He demonstrated this by supporting women's suffrage, op-

posing flogging in the navy, even backing Irish independence.

Following passage of the updated Fugitive Slave Act
of 1850 (allowing slaveholders to aid lawmen anywhere
in the country in the capture of runaway slaves), Douglass became superintendent of the Rochester Underground Railroad, turning his newspaper office into a
"depot" where he engineered illegal escapes. His efforts
were so legendary that he would often find groups of
runaways waiting on his steps when he arrived for work.
Racial divisions were not diminishing, as he had hoped.
As a result, in Rochester on Independence Day 1852,
Douglass delivered his most impassioned speech on how
differently whites and blacks viewed America. The most
memorable portion recalled the failed promises of Washington and Jefferson and, unknowingly of course, antic-
ipated the reproving truths of Martin Luther King and
Malcolm X:

> . . . This Fourth of July is *yours*, not *mine*. *You* may
> rejoice, *I* must mourn. . . . What, to the American
> slave, is your Fourth of July? I answer; a day that
> reveals to him, your celebration is a sham; your
> boasted liberty, an unholy license; your national
> greatness, swelling vanity; your sounds of rejoicing
> are empty and heartless; your denunciations of ty-
> rants, brass-fronted impudence; your shouts of lib-
> erty and equality, hollow mockery; your prayers
> and hymns, your sermons and thanksgivings, with
> all your religious parade, and solemnity, are, to
> him, mere bombast, fraud, deception, impiety, and
> hypocrisy—a thin veil to cover up crimes which
> would disgrace a nation of savages. There is not a
> nation on the earth guilty of practices, more shock-

ing and bloody, than are the people of these United
States, at this very hour.

This was a wake-up call to black people to take bolder
action. He warned repeatedly, "If there is no struggle
there is no progress," and "The limits of tyrants are
prescribed by the endurance of those whom they oppress"—that blacks must be the agents of their own
freedom, just as he himself had done by standing toe to
toe with Edward Covey, demanding, "Enough!" Yet in
August 1859, when fanatical white Abolitionist John
Brown needed a prominent black leader to rally blacks
to join his planned raid on Harpers Ferry, Virginia,
Douglass declined. He shared Brown's fervor and admired him greatly ("I have talked with many men," he
once remarked, "but I remember none who seemed so
excited upon the subject of slavery as he"), but considered the attack on a federal arsenal too provocative and
dangerous. So, in this instance, Douglass demonstrated
his courage through *restraint*. In fact, it was his restraint
that made him so credible with everyone from the common man to President Lincoln—another great man of
restraint.

Douglass's relationship with Lincoln was important
and complex. He knew, long before Lincoln, that the war
was really about coming to terms with the African American. Thus he alternatively distrusted and coaxed Lincoln
to do the right thing. He knew Lincoln was the only
white man in power who could deliver the slaves. But
he also knew that emancipation had long been Lincoln's
ace in the hole. The president's primary aim had always
been to preserve the Union; ending slavery was second-
ary until the war dragged toward its third year, with the
South losing ground but refusing to quit. At that point,

the Emancipation Proclamation became Lincoln's way
of officially warning the South: ''The war *is* about slavery. The Old South is dead.'' But I am convinced that
this decision was influenced by Lincoln's knowledge of
Frederick Douglass's idea of undermining the Southern
war effort by liberating the slaves to destroy the South's
economy, and then enlisting them in the Union Army—a
double deathblow. But only when he saw his reelection
prospects falter did Lincoln reconsider freeing the slaves
to speed an end to the war.

Although Douglass believed in Lincoln's commitment
to freedom for blacks, he goaded him publicly as the
''slow turtle'' in Washington for his reluctance to act,
and was always unsure if Lincoln did right from necessity or choice. He distrusted Lincoln for his inaugural
address promise to *uphold* fugitive slave laws and leave
slavery intact where it was already established. Douglass
also knew that, as early as 1854, Lincoln had considered
the race problem unsolvable and had urged blacks to
voluntarily emigrate to their own colonies in Africa.
Douglass had flirted with colonization when he despaired
of ever seeing full emancipation. He was particularly
concerned after the Dred Scott decision of March 6,
1857, which declared that any Negro descendant of a
slave was not a human being and therefore had no rights
that white men were bound to respect. (Curious irony:
The Dred Scott ruling was rendered by Supreme Court
Chief Justice Roger B. Taney who, decades earlier, had
ruled to free the *Amistad* captives in the government appeal.) But Douglass finally decided against colonization
as just another scheme to avoid the real problem: *slavery.*

In 1861, Douglass was appalled when Lincoln re-
voked General John C. Fremont's order to emancipate

slaves in Missouri, and did the same when General David Hunter freed captured slaves in Florida, Georgia, and South Carolina. Lincoln argued that if he freed the slaves too soon, the Union border states (Delaware, Maryland, Missouri, Kentucky) would join the Confederacy. So his best proposal was graduated emancipation, *over thirty years*, and with government compensation to slave owners. In April 1862, when Lincoln actually ordered compensated emancipation in Washington, D.C., he also withheld approval of measures that would have confiscated—and likely saved the lives of—countless brutalized slaves in captured Southern territory.

All unacceptable policies to Douglass.

So he kept upbraiding the president in speeches, in print, and in a meeting at the White House. In fact, he became one of Lincoln's most persistent gadflies on the issue that was tearing the nation apart.

In early 1863, when Congress finally admitted blacks into the military, the South recoiled at the vision of former slaves killing their masters. So on May 1, 1863, the Confederate Congress formally declared that any captured black soldiers or accomplices would be treated as seditious slaves and punished according to the laws of the state where they were captured. Translation: *"put to death."* And that is exactly what happened, in alarming numbers. Douglass was outraged. He made speeches, wrote letters, ceased his black recruitment efforts. (Two of his sons had been among the first to enlist in the famous Fifty-fourth Massachusetts that Frederick helped form and which acquitted itself nobly in the bloody assault in July 1863 on Fort Wagner.) He met again with Lincoln to urge him to respond quickly and sternly to the Confederate barbarism. Lincoln did; on July 30, 1863, he signed an uncharacteristically ruthless order warning that "for every soldier of the United States killed in violation of the laws of war a rebel soldier shall be executed." While there is no evidence this edict was ever enforced, it was judged to have deterred further Southern reprisals against captured blacks.

Amazingly, nowhere does history acknowledge that the direct pressure applied by Frederick Douglass spurred Lincoln to take this extraordinary action. And I have found no mention in history books of Frederick Douglass's influence on Lincoln's early issuance of the Emancipation Proclamation, followed by the admittance of blacks into the military. All credit is attributed to Lincoln, Great Emancipator. He certainly deserves credit for pulling the trigger, but who loaded and pointed the gun?

In this perspective, President Lincoln may have been the Great Emancipator, but as far as the proclamation was concerned, he was also the *Late* Emancipator. For whatever reasons, he deliberately delayed while black people died. The question is: Would he have taken his time—would the Union have *tolerated* him taking his time—if *white people* were awaiting emancipation? Or if *white people* were being tortured and murdered behind Southern lines?

I also think that Lincoln's hesitancy and indecisiveness on slavery contributed to the South's stubborn, postwar resistance to change. They clung even tighter to the white supremacist view that no matter what laws were passed, or how much society evolved, white people must always keep black people at least one notch below them. It was guaranteed, before the war ended, that despite the outcome, blacks who remained in the South would still be treated like slaves. It was a payback for emancipation and the destruction of their world. The mind-set was: You may *think* you can change the South, but we'll show you that you can't. And this attitude was not hidden—the Alabama Ku Klux Klan openly advertised their goal for the entire postwar South: "... to kill or drive away leading Negroes and only let the humble and submissive remain." This created a ripe atmosphere for the postwar black codes and Jim Crow laws that reversed emancipation by making sure no black person ever reached a position—whether in schools, theaters, trains, restaurants, saloons, hotels, courtrooms, businesses, or anywhere else—as high as the lowest white. In other words, reinstating slavery in everything but name.

Through all this turmoil, there was Douglass, lobbying for the vote for all freedmen, as well as for land. He said the freed Negro needed four things: "the right to the cartridge box, the ballot box, the jury box, and the knowledge box." After the failure of Reconstruction, he made dozens of speeches warning that if blacks were continually defrauded out of participating in their own system of government, they would go outside the system, and then, "Hungry men will eat. Desperate men will commit crime. Outraged men will seek revenge."

His warnings were sadly prophetic, though they went unheeded. Late in life, he was still urging white America to honor the promises of the founding fathers and the Emancipation Proclamation; agitating for the guarantees of the Fourteenth and Fifteenth amendments that were still being denied by custom; still exhorting America—in words forecasting those of Martin Luther King 120 years later—to "make character, and not color, the criterion of respectability."

As elder statesman, Douglass was named Marshal of the District of Columbia, city recorder of deeds, and Minister to Haiti. On February 20, 1895, after giving a speech on women's rights, Frederick Bailey Douglass died—poetically just—of a heart attack. His dream of a unified America was, of course, unrealized. But he lived his paramount thought—that human beings must be free and equal—and through his courage in an era of hate and fear, he inspired others to step forward and help their fellowmen get their just due.

William Lloyd Garrison wrote: "Individual, personal effort is the true foundation of all real prosperity in the social state, and all excellence of character." Well, no American, black or white, has ever brought to a virtuous cause more passionate effort and, certainly, excellence of character than Frederick Douglass.

CHAPTER 5

ESCAPE

Harriet Tubman

I have a friend who teaches grade school outside Atlanta who told me that when she gives tests during Black History Month, her kids know so little about black history that they answer Harriet Tubman for everything. They know she was a slave. They associate her with the Underground Railroad. They know what most people know about Harriet Tubman. But they don't really understand the magnitude of her achievements, or that she was one of a kind.

Like most black youngsters, I first learned about Harriet Tubman in grade school discussions about the Underground Railroad. Until then I didn't know much about African-American history and very little about the realities of slavery. I was aware of the civil rights movement and segregation and that black people were starting to call themselves "black" instead of "Negro." But I really didn't know there *was* a black history. My father's family is from Trinidad so, as a kid, I thought of myself as part of that black culture. My mother is African-American, from Anson County, North Carolina. She grew up under segregation and Jim Crow laws—a history of oppression. But I knew little about that.

I grew up in the Dyckman Street projects in Manhattan where we had a mix of whites, blacks, Puerto Ricans, Cubans, Scandinavians, even a few Russians and Gypsies. The surrounding neighborhoods were Irish and Jewish; the area was like a mini-United Nations. The first time I was made aware of my color was when I saw myself in a Polaroid photo of my third grade class. Besides being the tallest kid in the picture, I was also the darkest. But it wasn't a race issue to me yet; I was just surprised at the contrast. The first time I was affected by race was in seventh grade when my best friend, a white kid named Johnny Harrison, started hanging more with his white friends than with me. So I started hanging with the other two black kids in my class. Nothing was said, but there were hard feelings between us. It led to a two-punch fight, which my punch won. Later, outside school, Johnny called me "nigger" for the first time, and "jungle bunny." I called him "milk bottle"—that was the only thing I could think of. After that, we never spoke again.

Two years later in 1962, my mother sent me off to visit friends in Goldsboro, North Carolina. Riding the Greyhound, as soon as we crossed the bridge into Alexandria, Virginia—not an hour outside *Washington, D.C.*—I started seeing all these COLORED ONLY and WHITE ONLY signs. They were big; these people weren't playing around. And when I saw black people avoiding whites on the street, I realized I wasn't in Kansas anymore. I remember asking someone, "Am I allowed to

Estevanico exploring the Southwest.
THE GRANGER COLLECTION, NEW YORK

Full view of the original John Trumbull painting <u>The Battle of Bunker Hill</u>, depicting Lieutenant Grosvenor shielding his slave Peter Salem after Salem shot British Major John Pitcairn.

THE GRANGER COLLECTION, NEW YORK

The 1845 William Ranney painting of a black bugler shooting a British officer at the Battle of Cowpens, 1781.

Frederick Remington's painting entitled <u>Captain Dodge and His Colored Troops to the Rescue.</u>

James Armistead Lafayette, honored patriot spy.
THE GRANGER COLLECTION, NEW YORK

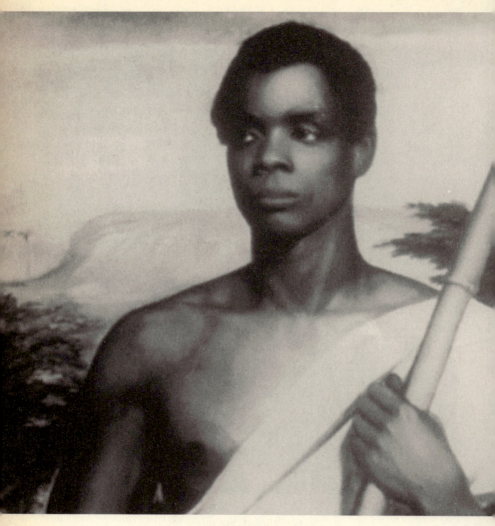

Joseph Cinque.

Crispus Attucks, the first to die at the Boston Massacre, 1770.

Mutiny aboard an eighteenth-century slaver.

Nat Turner urging fellow slaves to rebellion.

Young Frederick
Douglass.
BROWN BROTHERS

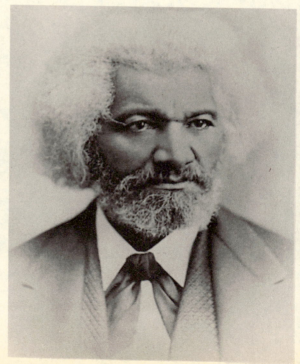

Douglass still
distinguished
in his twilight.
CORBIS/
BETTMANN
ARCHIVES

Harriet Tubman preparing
for another escape.
THE GRANGER COLLECTION,
NEW YORK

Harriet Tubman,
respectable and
free.
THE GRANGER
COLLECTION,
NEW YORK

Deputy U.S. Marshal Bass
Reeves in his prime.
WESTERN HISTORY COLLECTIONS,
UNIVERSITY OF OKLAHOMA LIBRARY

Bass Reeves (front row, far left) and the policemen of Muskogee,
Indian Territory, ca. 1900.
WESTERN HISTORY COLLECTIONS, UNIVERSITY OF OKLAHOMA LIBRARY

Buffalo soldiers charging up San Juan Hill.
NATIONAL ARCHIVES

The Brownsville trial, 1917. Defendants sit cordoned off at upper left.

Largest Murder Trial in the History of the United States.
Scene during Court Martial of 64 members of 24th Infantry U.S.A.
on trial for mutiny and murder of 17 people at Houston Tex. Aug 23, 1917
Trial Held in Gift Chapel, Ft Sam Houston.
Trial Started — Nov 1, 1917 Brig Genl George K. Hunter Presiding.
Col J. A. Hull- Judge Advocate.   Counsel for Defense.
Maj. D. V. Sulphin, Asst.   Maj. Harry S. Grier.
      Prisoners guarded by 19th Infantry Co. "C" Capt. Carl J. Adler
This photo Copyrighted by W. C. Lloyd, San Antonio Tex. Reproduction not allowed

African American soldier coolly oversees
his German prisoners.

Lewis H. Latimer.
SCHOMBURG CENTER FOR
RESEARCH IN BLACK CULTURE,
NEW YORK PUBLIC LIBRARY

Lewis Latimer (front, right) and the original Edison
Pioneers, 1918.
U.S. DEPARTMENT OF THE INTERIOR, NATIONAL PARKS SERVICE

Emmett Till and his mother, Mamie, celebrate Christmas together, December 1954. THE EMMETT TILL FOUNDATION

Mose Wright pointing out Emmett Till's murderers in court.

UPI/CORBIS/ BETTMANN ARCHIVES

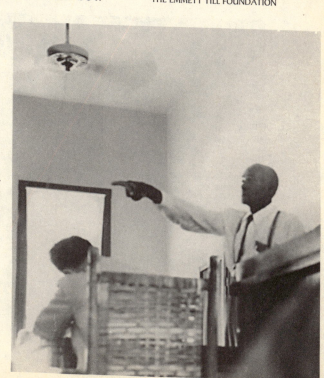

Rosa Parks being fingerprinted by a Montgomery policeman, 1955.   THE GRANGER COLLECTION, NEW YORK

Rosa Parks changes the world.
AP/JOHN DAVID MERCER/MOBILE PRESS REGISTER

walk on the same side of the street as white people?'' I
felt out of my element and I hadn't even left the bus. I
had no idea how to behave.

It was my first taste of Jim Crow and the environment
my mother had grown up in. When I got home we talked
out it. She said she had not been cowed by racism and
I shouldn't be either. She said, ''*Always be proud.*
be intimidated.'' She did everything she could to
but when my father proposed to her, she left to
im in Boston where he was stationed in the
considered it an opportunity to get further
cism than she had ever been before. In fact,
ays been a main theme of black thought:
he discrimination. And that influenced
ding of race issues. For one thing, it
at if you can't help change the prob-
out and fight another day.

Harriet Tubman today, I think
rson who would not be intimi-
ed, as my mother did: *I have*
ded to share her vision with
most powerful voices in
ery.

black in America. Slaves who went with Harriet Tubman understood that capture meant almost certain death. Yet throughout the South, Tubman's name meant the opposite; it meant salvation. They knew she never gave up and, amazingly, never failed.

Her remarkable valor even humbled Frederick Douglass, who understood what it was like to risk his life for others. In an 1868 letter to Tubman, Douglass was effusive in his admiration and praise:

> ... The difference between us is very marked. Most that I have done and suffered in the service of our cause has been public, and I have received much encouragement at every step of the way. You on the other hand have labored in a very private way. I have wrought in the day—you in the night. I have had the applause of the crowd and the satisfaction that comes of being approved by the multitude, while the most that you have done has been witnessed by the few trembling, scarred, foot-sore bondmen and women, whom you have led out the house of bondage. . . . The midnight sky silent stars have been the witnesses of your tion to freedom and of your heroism. Exce John Brown—of sacred memory—I know one who has willingly encountered more p hardships to serve our enslaved people have. Much that you have done would probable to those who do not know you you. . . .

Frederick Douglass delivered inspirati the world spotlight. Harriet Tubman's tions was a six-state corridor north, f

Canada, where she crept under cover of night. Yet her impact was immeasurable. Her existence became a symbol. To the North, she was a constant thorn in the side of the slavocracy; to the South, she was a recurring nightmare—fugitive, felon, raider, spy. To the slaves who told worshipful stories about her, she represented deliverance: a female black Jesus, a black Joan of Arc.

But you can't talk of Harriet Tubman's heroics without revisiting the hell of her world. The slave system in which she grew up was self-contained and self-perpetuating. It operated on deprivation, brutality, fear. Even if you escaped, how far could you get? How would you live? Where could you hide? In the Deep South, you were too far away to even imagine making it North. Unlike everybody else in that society, slaves were instantly identifiable by their color. Even slaves who were hired out to work in the cities had to wear tags identifying themselves by number and trade—NO. 43 PORTER, NO. 1298 SERVANT, NO. 279 CARPENTER. (I always see in these tags the dark shadow of concentration camp tattoos and the Stars of David the Nazis made Jews sew onto their clothes.) Until just before the Civil War, even free blacks were required to carry certificates of freedom at all times. And often they were kidnapped and sold into slavery anyway. Just because they were black.

The most effective tool of the fascist slave master was mind control. The slaves on country plantations and farms were not restricted by walls or bars or gates; they were bound by fear. The typical slave was uneducated and deeply religious. White masters took advantage of this by indoctrinating them on the ''divine right'' of whites to rule, and threatening that disobeying a white master amounted to defying the word of God. Amazingly, this was enough to control most slaves. Add to this an accepted system of totalitarian control, and places like Georgia and Alabama might as well have been czarist Russia. In Lerone Bennett's groundbreaking book on African-American history, *Before the Mayflower*, he describes some of the most demoralizing controls:

> . . . Each slave state had a slave code which was designed to keep slaves ignorant and in awe of white power . . . slaves were forbidden to assemble in groups . . . forbidden to leave plantations without passes . . . could not blow horns, beat drums, or read books. Slave preachers were proscribed . . . and slaves were forbidden to hold religious meetings without white witnesses. Other provisions forbade slaves to raise their hands against whites and gave every white person police power over every black, free or slave. . . . Slave patrols . . . were authorized to make periodic searches of slave cabins and to chastise bondmen found off plantations without passes. . . . The police power of the state, the state militia and the U.S. Army stood behind these totalitarian laws.

White slave masters were not alone in governing their black victims; they had ironclad backup from the legal system. In the Old South, whites were authorized to torture, maim, and murder blacks with impunity. The foundation for this was the early legal codes—rules apart from the Constitution that were applied only to blacks. For example, the original Virginia slave codes dating from 1680 served the entire South for 180 years as a blueprint for the absolute oppression of blacks. Under these shifting codes, resisting a master's orders or running away could be legally punishable by death. Plus, under an earlier (1669) Virginia statute, slave owners could not be prosecuted for the "casuall [sic] killing of slaves." A 1712 South Carolina act sanctioned forty lashes for a first escape attempt; branding of the letter "R" on the right cheek for a second attempt; a severe whipping and the cutting off of an ear for a third; and castration for a fourth. And if the slave should die in the process, the owner could be entitled to compensation from the state. A 1740 act stipulated that nonsubmissive slaves could be apprehended by "any white person"— not just the slave owner; and if, in the process, the slave dared strike a white person, he could be lawfully killed "on the scene"—even if resistance was minimal, or the slave was unarmed, or inflicted no injury. Also at the order of a marshal, any slave could be required "to kill, cut off the ears, or brutally whip a fellow slave." If *that* slave did not comply, he would get twenty lashes on the bare back. In a notable North Carolina decision, *State* v. *Mann*, in 1829 (when Harriet Tubman was a slave of eight or nine years old), the issue was whether it was criminal to subject a slave woman to a "cruel and unreasonable" beating. The court ruled that slaves had *no legal will of their own*, and that the judiciary

> . . . cannot allow the right of the master to be brought into discussion in the courts of justice. The slave . . . must be made sensible that there is no appeal from his master; that his power . . . is conferred by the laws of man at least, if not by the law of God.

In 1860 Kentucky, slaves could be put to death for at least eleven different offenses, six of which were for "crimes" against whites. Georgia statutes offered bounties, not for the return of runaway slaves but for their *ears and scalps.*

Does anyone learn about *that* in school? If you ask any American today "Who do you associate with scalping and mutilation of bodies?" the answer will be: *Indians.* But because a host of recent books and documentaries have exposed the official lies about government orchestration of the eradication of the Native American, they have gained new sympathy. We now know that under government sanction, the white military apparatus systematically exterminated the Native American food supply—the buffalo—and then massacred every Native American they could find off the reservations—man, woman, and child. There were *many* Wounded Knees. If George Armstrong Custer had not been so hasty and vainglorious in 1876, the Battle of Little Big Horn could have been another Wounded Knee.

The point is, the mutilation and murder of blacks was no anomaly. By then—thirteen years after emancipation—whites in power had already had plenty of sanctioned practice torturing and exterminating people of color. Unfortunately, since most eighteenth- and nineteenth-century African Americans ended up slaves—while Indians did not—the prejudice against slaves as inferior chattel, unworthy of sympathy, still lingers. So the same sympathy has not been extended to us.

Slave controls were similar in every Confederate state: no appeal from the master and no legal appeal—in other words, no relief and no help. Some slaves fled anyway, though usually someplace nearby. For example: the infamous Dismal Swamp, a marshy wilderness on the Virginia-North Carolina border. So many slaves fled there, they established a fugitive community known as Maroons (a colloquial translation of the Spanish word *ci-*

marrón, meaning wild). At one point in the 1850s, there were some two thousand fugitive Maroons barely subsisting in shacks in the Dismal Swamp.

The strictures on slaves were so unyielding, blacks that had been freed by their master's will at the master's death could still be held in slavery if the estate had unpaid debts. And even when slaves did go free, if they stayed in the South they had to battle white Southern stereotypes that branded every black as lazy, shiftless, immoral, potentially criminal, and a future ward of the state.

(To appreciate the broad social stigma of black stereotyping, consider the effects today. The predominant images of urban African Americans on TV were, in the past, outrageously demeaning. There was a sea change in the late 1970s and early 1980s with enlightened offerings like *The Cosby Show* and Tim Reid's *Frank's Place*, depicting blacks closer to the norm. All of a sudden, it was no longer just stereotypical blacks laughing and mugging ''Dynomite!'' and making knuckleheads out of themselves; it was characters to whom real black people could relate. And then came black anchors, blacks doing commercials, blacks playing cops and lawyers and average American citizens. On the other hand, the holdout seems to be TV news shows, where the images of blacks are mainly of crime suspects, gangbangers, and general deadbeats. Always the extreme stereotype; rarely the average. The media looks for the most salacious items because that is what drives the sensationalism and, of course, sensationalism boosts ratings. Black criminals are grist for that mill; it has turned into media-driven hysteria and distortion about blacks and crime. I wonder: Is that one reason why a recent study showed that when the number of blacks living in a white neighborhood rises above 8 percent, whites start moving out? Departing whites explained that while they did not consciously keep count of blacks moving in, one day the neighborhood just started "feeling" too black. Which, to many white people, implied gangs, drugs, violent crime: *modern-day* stereotypes that keep blacks and whites separate and unequal.)

Like any prisoners of war, the bravest slaves who stayed in bondage tried to sabotage the system. One way was by conducting what came to be called "day-to-day resistance." They would routinely sabotage tools and farm implements; poison livestock; fake sickness and madness; destroy crops; pretend they could not perform simple tasks. (Since slave owners considered slaves too ignorant or stupid to discipline themselves, that's exactly how savvy, subversive slaves acted.) Beginning with the slave-set fires that terrorized Boston in 1723, fire was a weapon of choice—but also punishable by death. In 1730, slaves in Virginia were so confrontational, the governor ordered all white men to carry pistols to church.

Escape was very difficult. Thousands of slaves escaped north by waterway; some went to Mexico; some to Canada; some to Texas and farther west. But the majority were too afraid to escape. In the 1800s, slaves of the upper South often went North on the Underground Railroad—but that was tougher to accomplish than we have been led to believe. The authorities were backed by stringent fugitive slave laws, and they watched many of the best-known "depots" day and night. It is estimated that only twenty-five hundred a year made it to freedom on the Underground Railroad between 1830 and 1860, and that is probably generous. Because those who did *not* escape numbered nearly four million by 1860.

One theory for the legal system's complicity in controlling slaves was slaveholder fear that as the black population rose, so did the threat of violent revolt. In the 1820s, revolutionary writer and orator David Walker blazed onto the scene as a lone black voice for armed revolt—a forerunner of Mao Tse-tung, some 140 years later. Walker proclaimed that white oppression was violence in itself and therefore deserved a violent response. He urged, ". . . it is no more harm for you to kill a man, who is trying to kill you, than it is for you to take a drink of water when thirsty . . ." Naturally, Walker was a threat to slave owners; armed revolt was their worst nightmare. Which is why it was no surprise that on June 28, 1830, less than a year after Walker issued his 75-page incendiary "Appeal To The COLOURED CITIZENS OF THE WORLD" urging slaves to "slit their oppressors' throats from ear to ear," Walker's body was discovered in the doorway of his secondhand clothing store. The case was never solved; but it was widely believed he was poisoned by his white racist enemies. Their message to the oppressed has always been the same: *If you try to beat the system, we will cut you down.*

The strategy of control was: *Make it as difficult to revolt as possible.* And since blacks were already judged inferior, it was simple to justify every added legal sanction as something "for their own good." In fact, overall, there were very few organized rebellions. And none that succeeded. The first major armed conspiracy was the September 9, 1739 uprising at Stono River, South Carolina. A group of twenty slaves stalked into Charleston, singing, beating drums, and yelling "Liberty!" to attract more slaves. They looted a store, stole gunpowder and guns, and killed two clerks, leaving their severed heads on the steps. When the mob swelled to between sixty and one hundred, they marched ten miles up the main road toward Saint Augustine, burning plantations and killing nineteen more whites. Then they made a fatal mistake: They grouped in a field, expecting more slaves to join them as the word spread. When none showed up, they decided to wait until morning before crossing the Edisto River. But just before dark, a large group of armed white planters surrounded them and a battle ensued in which forty-four slaves were killed. According to a published account, colonists "Cutt [sic] off their heads and set them up at every Mile Post they came to." This was, of course, outright vigilantism: no hearing, no trial.

One black leader who escaped was captured three years later, ironically, by two fugitive slaves. He was tried and promptly hung. On the other hand, in 1740 the South Carolina legislature granted "total immunity to all persons aiding in the suppression of the rebellion." They added that the murder of these slaves was ". . . hereby declared lawful . . . as fully and amply as if such rebellious Negroes had undergone a formal trial and condemnation . . ."

The biggest slave rebellion in American history took place in St. John the Baptist Parish outside New Orleans, in 1811. Up to five hundred slaves organized into military-type squads and marched toward the city, burning plantations and killing three whites. Federal troops and free black units organized by local slaveholders engaged the rebels and killed sixty-six on the spot. Later, sixteen of their leaders were executed. As at Stono River, their heads were "posted" along the road. (Remember, the same gruesome punishment would befall innocent blacks murdered by panicky whites following Nat Turner's rebellion twenty years later. It was a tactic designed to intimidate; white planters knew that religious blacks believed the body must be intact for Judgment Day.)

Stono River, St. John the Baptist, and Nat Turner all became legends. They added up to a daunting history of failure, a confirmation that freedom might always be just out of reach. Nevertheless, every so often a fearless, indomitable slave would plot another revolt.

Two of the most famous were Gabriel Prosser and Denmark Vesey. In 1800, twenty-four-year-old Prosser planned to act out his religious vision of establishing a black state of his own in Virginia, where he was a slave. For six months he noted strategic points in the city of Richmond where his supporters could gain a foothold. He planned a three-pronged attack on the city, one group seizing the arsenal; one the powder house; one sweeping through town, killing white people on the streets. If successful, Prosser would be crowned king of Virginia. But he even planned for failure: Evacuate to the mountains to establish a base from which to conduct guerrilla actions across the state. On the evening of August 30, his "troops"—anywhere from one thousand to three thousand slaves—grabbed their pikes, scythes, hoes, swords, and guns, and prepared to move on Richmond six miles away. But they had been betrayed by two of their own and the governor of Richmond had already stationed troops at the vital points of attack. Then, almost biblically, a torrential rainstorm erupted, flooding key bridges and roads. When the rain subsided, the state struck preemptively, arrested Prosser and thirty-four others, and swiftly convicted and hanged them all. When the rest of the South learned of Prosser's plan, they also found out that except for fate, he would have likely succeeded; because the state had less than five hundred men—only thirty with muskets.

The same year, Charleston carpenter Denmark Vesey, slave to a slave trader for twenty years, purchased his freedom with gambling winnings and started spewing his hatred of slavery to strangers. Twenty-two years later, though admittedly content with his life, he risked all to try to free others, starting with the slaves in Charleston. Like Frederick Douglass, he loathed submissiveness. He was known, for instance, to reproach slaves who bowed to whites. When they replied, ''But I am a slave,'' he would snap, ''You *deserve* to be a slave.'' For months, Vesey and his lieutenants recruited more than 9,000 slaves and freed blacks to join his plot. But a few slaves betrayed the plan and the authorities ended up arresting 130 conspirators. One house slave finally turned in Vesey, and he was convicted and hanged with five of his leaders. Again, the message was clear: *If you try to beat the system, we will cut you down.*

Harriet Tubman's name became important to me as a young adult. Here was this illiterate girl who grew up in slavery, which she called ''the next thing to hell,'' and her only concept of freedom was an overwhelming fear of being carried away by every white man she saw. Yet when she finally escaped in 1849 at about age twenty-nine, she decided to turn around and return to ''hell'' to help her family and others get free. In the annals of slavery, there was no one quite like her.

A few things intrigued me about Harriet Tubman, other than her bravery. One was her use of practical psychology—particularly impressive since she never learned to read or write. Part of her genius was in knowing that her white masters underestimated her. They assumed she was half-witted—mentally impaired. That came out of her first act of open defiance. When she was thirteen, a fellow slave wandered to town from their Maryland farm. An overseer followed the slave, and Harriet followed the overseer. When cornered in a store, the slave started to run. The overseer called to Harriet for help, but she just stepped between them. He then threw a heavy iron weight at the slave, but hit Harriet instead, denting her skull and sending her into a coma. When she recovered, she began having small seizures, or sleeping stupors, in which she literally blanked out several times a day. But when she awoke she was always normal again.

There was no mental impairment. We know that because of her record of returning to slave territory nineteen times and bringing out at least three hundred slaves safely. That took not only exceptional planning, but daring and cunning and intelligent, on-the-spot decision making. For example, she learned the acceptable reasons why slaves might be away from their masters, and whenever possible chose secret routes away from places where no excuse would do. If there was no alternative, and she and her fugitives had to be in hostile towns on the Underground Railroad route, she watched everyone who paid any attention to them. If white people scrutinized them too closely, she would quickly purchase tickets on a train heading south instead of north, so no one would suspect they were runaways. They would regroup later and start north again, hoping to slip through the second time. And they always did.

Ironically, while slave owners misjudged Tubman's intelligence, she kept playing to *their* ignorance and outmaneuvered them. Knowing that slaves were forbidden to communicate while working, she invented an indirect method of sending messages. She figured: Who would pay any notice to an impaired old slave woman singing aloud to herself while walking down a road? So she would disguise herself as an old woman (in her prime as a slave raider, she was only in her thirties) and faking dullness, she would meander a road by the fields, or past the slave cabins, and sing her plans to specific, fore-warned slaves. Shrewdly, she always sang biblical spir-ituals, which no one would suspect as a code. A key one was:

> *I'll meet you in de mornin'*
> *When you reach de promised land,*
> *On de oder side of Jordan,*
> *For I'm bound for de promised land.*

"I'll meet you in the morning" could mean "We go tonight" or "Lie low til tomorrow morning." And "the other side of Jordan" could signify a particular meeting place they all knew: a familiar grove of trees, stream, or barn. After passage of the 1850 Fugitive Slave Law, Tubman moved her home base from Maryland's Eastern Shore to Saint Catherines, Canada. From then on, she switched the "Promised Land" of freedom from free states like Pennsylvania and New York to Canada.

Other evidence of her use of psychology:

• She began her escapes on Saturday night to get a day's head start, since slave owners would not dis-cover the missing until Sunday, the one day they couldn't advertise in the newspaper.

• A legendary Tubman story told of her strolling through the hometown of one of her former masters, disguised as an old woman. Knowing that she might see him, Harriet purchased some live chickens and carried them upside down on rope. Sure enough, there was her old master, walking toward her. To avoid him, she loosened the rope so the birds could run free, and she chased after them over a fence.

• Once a raid got underway, she would brook no delay. If a slave collapsed, got sick, or claimed to be too fatigued to continue, she would point her loaded revolver and warn, "You go on or you die. Dead niggers tell no tales." She almost certainly knew that Gabriel Prosser, Denmark Vesey, and Nat Turner had all been betrayed by their own. Even if not, she was tough and smart enough to know she could not permit a fugitive to turn back and reveal their route. Somehow, her dramatic threats revived the stragglers. Between 1850 and 1860, leading escapes over thousands of treacherous miles, Tubman never left anyone behind.

Another trait that fascinated me was her ability to meticulously plan and execute escapes, despite the fact that slave owners were always on the lookout for her and constantly trying to track her down. John Brown considered Harriet his equal in courage and militancy; he called her "General Tubman" with sincere admiration. In fact, in 1859 Brown enlisted her to recruit slaves for his raid on Harper's Ferry and also to help him map out strategy. If she had not become ill in October 1859, she would have been at the fateful raid—and likely been hung.

Tubman plotted every detail of her raids. To earn the money she knew she would need to finance the escapes, she took work as a cook and housemaid. She acquired

forged papers for runaways and even tincture of opium
to soothe and muffle their sick babies. Though much of
the travel was on foot, she used every mode of transportation at her disposal—horses, wagons, skiffs, boats,
trains, even slave owners' own carriages. (She hid slaves
under vegetables in the carriage and the guards assumed
she was going on an errand for her master.) All planned
in advance. Like the bold, ingenious 1847 rescue of her
own parents, who were too elderly to walk any great
distances. According to a Tubman comrade, Thomas
Garrett, manager of the Wilmington, Delaware, Underground Railroad station:

> She brought away her parents in a singular style.
> They started out with an old horse fitted out in
> primitive style with a straw collar, a pair of old
> chaise wheels, with a board on the axle to sit on,
> another board swung with ropes, fastened to the
> axle, to rest their feet on. She got her parents, who
> were both slaves belonging to different masters, on
> this crude vehicle to the railroad, put them in the
> cars, turned Jehu [a king of Israel noted for his
> furious chariot attacks] herself, and drove to town
> in a style that no other human being ever did before
> or since.

Tubman's uncanny success was galling to slave owners. She was practically a legend throughout the South,
and the more famous she became the more slave owners
beefed up their security. Yet she still batted .1000 against
them.

To me, her most impressive quality was that she in-
tuitively understood the subtle forces she was unleashing
by liberating the strongest slaves, right under slave own-

ers' noses. I believe she instinctively knew that removing slaves would cause economic ruptures; that every escaped slave was another little hemorrhage in the system. She knew that a trained, mature slave was worth between one thousand dollars and two thousand dollars. And that they were the ones constructing the mills; working the harvesting machines; plowing the fields; shodding the horses; picking the cotton; fanning the wheat. They were the *economy*. (This was how American slavery originally evolved from temporary servitude. By 1650, when our rice- and tobacco-based economy expanded and labor grew scarce, planters extended indentured service until all African Americans were declared *durante vita*: servants for life. So at its core, slavery was *economic*: a white-run system of commerce borne on the backs of the strongest blacks.) *They* were the ones Harriet Tubman went after. She selected able-bodied slaves who could run fast and endure hardship, because she knew that by taking *them* away she was removing economic energy and skills from the South.

One yardstick of the damage she caused was the fact that in the late 1850s the South put a *forty-thousand-dollar bounty* on her head. That was an astonishing sum at the time. As far as I know, there was never a higher bounty on any other fugitive slave. That meant that slave owners considered Harriet Tubman more than just an annoying runaway on a moral crusade. The slavocracy *had* no morality. They were not concerned with "We are superior, she is inferior, let's put a reward on her head." That forty grand really meant: This infernal nigger woman is screwing up our farms; she is screwing up our plantations; she is messing with our livelihoods. *She is bad for business. She has to be stopped.*

The truly extraordinary fact about Harriet Tubman is that she was not just a phenomenally successful liberator of slaves. Just before the war, she started speaking publicly at picnics, fairs, and conventions, decrying slavery and promoting women's rights. For an unschooled former slave, someone who did all her talking through action, she certainly took sophisticated stands on the issues of the day. For instance, this homespun speech roundly criticizing President Lincoln for ducking the slavery issue in the early part of the war:

> God's ahead ob Massa Linkum. God won't let Massa Linkum beat de South till he do de right ting. Massa Linkum he great man, and I'se poor nigger; but dis nigger can tell Massa Linkum how to save de money and de young men. He do it by setting de niggers free. S'pose dar was awfu' big snake down dar, on de floor. He bite you. Folks all skeered, cause you die. You send for doctor to cut de bite; but snake he rolled up dar, and while doctor dwine it, he bite you agin. De doctor cut out dat bite; but while he dwine it, de snake he spring up and bite you agin, and so he keep dwine, till you kill him. Dat's what massa Linkum orter know.

What is so astonishing to me is that Harriet Tubman was undaunted by the illiteracy forced on her by slavery. Actually, despite the obvious language barrier, she exhibited a very sophisticated intelligence. Her inability to read, write, or speak the white "king's English" did not deter her from communicating *undetected* coded messages to slaves or refined political analogies to the president of the United States. She may have been ignorant in a literal sense, but she was far from stupid. In fact, she managed to outfox the entire institution of slavery, again and again, in its own backyard. Slavery was stupid: Harriet Tubman was brilliant. *She* helped bring *it* down.

When the war started, instead of dropping out of sight and living more for herself, she decided to parlay her experience as Underground Railroad conductor in the Southern back country into an even more dangerous job: spying and scouting for the Union. She singlehandedly organized a highly efficient intelligence ring of former slaves. Because of her reputation, she was able to recruit slaves from the areas the Union Army wanted to penetrate who thoroughly knew the terrain. She led them out of bondage herself, and they would then consult with Union scouts to map the area, delineating the quickest routes for their troops. These freshly liberated slaves were like surveyors for the Union—advanced intelligence, courtesy of "General" Harriet Tubman. She also dispatched them to bring back intelligence reports of Rebel army and navy defenses, supplies, and even the number of livestock they had for food.

But even that wasn't enough. She actually led commando raids in Georgia and South Carolina with Colonel James Montgomery's Negro brigade, the Second South Carolina Volunteers. Montgomery was an old Kansas friend of John Brown's and a feared Union guerrilla. His favorite tactic was surprise attacks on Southern settlements to free slaves, destroy provisions, and burn lodgings. Harriet Tubman's most notorious raid was on June 2, 1863 when she led Montgomery's brigade up the Combahee River. It made the Boston newspaper *The Commonwealth* on July 10:

Col. Montgomery and his gallant band of 300 black soldiers, under the guidance of a black woman, dashed into the enemy's country, struck a bold and effective blow, destroying millions of dollars worth of commissary stores, cotton, and lordly dwellings, and striking terror into the heart of rebeldom, brought off nearly 800 slaves and thousands of dollars worth of property, without losing a man or receiving a scratch. It was a glorious consummation.

. . . Since the rebellion she has devoted herself to her great work of delivering the bondmen, with an energy and sagacity that cannot be exceeded. Many and many times she has penetrated the enemy's lines and discovered their situation and condition, and escaped without injury, but not without extreme hazard.

Characteristically, Tubman was later proudest not of the raid itself, but the fact that almost every able male slave she helped to free that day enlisted in the Union Army. Yet when the war ended and she put in for a government pension for her three years of service—money she intended not for herself, but to establish schools and homes for freed blacks and their families—the government refused to pay the full debt. But she never quit helping others. Nearing the end of her long life, she sold fruit and begged donations for a "John Brown Home" for indigent blacks, her personal dream for more than fifty years. She eventually earned enough to buy the land and see the foundation laid.

Harriet Tubman died March 10, 1913. She was buried with military honors in Auburn, New York, where she had transformed her own home into a haven for the sick, the elderly, and the poor. Like her remarkable life, the house is now a museum.

CHAPTER 6

RESPECT

Bass Reeves

The first black people I ever saw in a TV western were Ivan Dixon and folksinger Odetta, in an episode of *Have Gun Will Travel*. I was shocked. I thought: "Geez. There might've been a couple of black people in the West."

Then, about ten years ago, I read *Texas* by James Michener and I found out that black soldiers actually patrolled the West. I researched it and found out that after the Civil War, Congress formed six new U.S. Army volunteer regiments to patrol the Great Plains: the all-black Ninth and Tenth Cavalries and Thirty-eighth, Thirty-ninth, Fortieth, and Forty-first Infantries. In 1869, the army consolidated these four into two, the Twenty-fourth and Twenty-fifth Infantries. The black units became known, collectively, as the Buffalo Soldiers. They were sent out to the Plains to accomplish more than the army had ever asked of any military unit in the field:

help build roads and lay railroad track; string telegraph wire; capture cattle rustlers and horse thieves; guard the southern border; protect migrating white settlers; maintain peace between the settlers, cattlemen, hostile Indians defending their homeland, ruthless outlaws, and raiding Mexican bandits.

Even though the Buffalo Soldiers comprised 20 percent of the army of the Plains, I never heard of them as a youngster; never read about them; never saw them on TV or in the movies. As an adult, I read *Under Fire with the Tenth U.S. Cavalry*, and one of its authors, Sergeant Horace W. Bivens, an ex-slave and a Buffalo Soldier marksman, wrote that his unit was once stationed at Fort Apache. I thought, ''Wait a minute. That's Rin Tin Tin territory.'' And I remembered that in the old *Rin Tin Tin* TV show, Lieutenant Masterson, Sergeant O'Hara, Rusty, and everybody else on the post were white. I watched that show for years and I never saw any black faces. That really bothered me—but that was how the history of our country had always been presented to me.

I found out later that the Buffalo Soldiers were significantly involved in historic military events, from the Plains Indian Wars through World War I. Between 1861 and 1890, Kit Carson and Wild Bill Hickok served them as scouts; the famous frontier artist, Frederic Remington, spent part of the summer of 1888 sketching them as they patrolled Arizona. In the desert Southwest and central and northern Plains, they fought hostile Indians, including renegade bands led by legendary warriors like Victorio and Geronimo.

Some historians wrote that these all-black units were sent to the Plains as a deliberate act of segregation because white towns in the East and South did not want blacks stationed near them. That was not entirely true.

Towns in the East and South did not want army posts near them, period, whether manned by blacks *or* whites. The main reason the black units were sent to the West was because that was where they were needed. And they were eager to go because, more than most whites, they needed the security of a steady job. On the other hand, their duty was the toughest the army could offer, in the most remote, uninhabitable terrain, and under primitive conditions. The life was lonely and demanding. They slept on bug-infested, wooden bunks in dusty barracks with no bathtubs. Colds, pneumonia, and other infectious diseases cost more soldiers their lives than shootouts with Indians. To pass the time, Buffalo Soldiers frequently held shooting contests, which was why so many became expert marksmen. The point is, it was not the sort of duty that white soldiers rushed to sign up for.

Of course, all *officers* of black units were white; though most of them considered the assignment a demotion or exile. This attitude was based on the presumption that blacks were incapable of leading, another false stereotype that still lingers today. In spite of all the handicaps, prejudice, and hard duty, the Buffalo Soldiers consistently boasted the army's most disciplined and courageous fighting units, and the lowest desertion and highest reenlistment rates. Ironically, though they were often unwelcome and unappreciated by townspeople nearest their outposts, black soldiers developed a reputation for being the army's finest. An impressed reporter who visited Fort Sill in Indian Territory (the future state of Oklahoma) in the late 1870s referred to them as "active, intelligent, and resolute men." He added that they appeared "rather superior to the average white men recruited in time of peace." The soldiers explained that to him; they said that only "indifferent or inferior whites" enlisted during peacetime.

Occasionally, being black was a hardship, even out in the Plains. In some remote, southwestern towns, where the Buffalo Soldiers protected settlers from renegades, some of these same settlers complained about the presence of blacks. But that happened mostly after the Indian threats had subsided and citizens grew more choosy and sensitive about the color of the soldiers in the nearby forts. It was especially true in Texas, at places like Fort Concho and San Angelo, where the Comanches had once meant business. Those towns grew up servicing the forts until the Comanche threat passed, and then the towns became as hostile to blacks as the pre-Civil War South. So, sometimes, there was just *no* escaping prejudice and hate.

This always seemed bitterly ironic to me. Here were segregated African Americans, perpetual victims of white oppression, helping their own oppressors to eradicate the country's other victimized minority. And yet afterward, as their reward, whites they had protected regarded them as not much better than the Indians they hated almost as much.

It was ironic in another sense; the same Native Americans who fought against the black units named them Buffalo Soldiers, partly because of the resemblance between their hair and the woolly buffalo shag, but mainly in honor of the indomitable spirit of their most sacred animal. And the Indians demonstrated this respect in many ways. For instance, it was said that after the Battle of the Little Big Horn on June 25, 1876, Sitting Bull recognized a dying black soldier and gave him water. He was Isaiah Dorman, the only scout in the fight that day. (A fugitive slave, Dorman had previously lived among the Sioux with his Sioux wife, but left to become an interpreter at frontier forts. He thought it was a step up to be working for the famous General George Armstrong Custer.) After the battle, Sioux women and children mutilated the bodies of all the dead white soldiers to deny them entry into the afterworld. But they left Isaiah Dorman's body untouched. This was confirmed by a Cheyenne warrior who surveyed the battlefield and later described Dorman for posterity: "All of his clothing was gone when I saw him, but he had not been scalped nor cut up like the white men had been." The Native Americans' respect for blacks was so profound, they expressed it even in death.

This respect makes sense when you consider that between the Revolution and the Civil War, African Americans fled to Native American camps in New England, New York, New Jersey, Connecticut, Maryland, Virginia, Delaware, and the Carolinas. In one of the earliest alliances between the two cultures, hundreds of Colonial slaves escaped to the Seminole bands that had broken away from the Creek tribe and taken refuge in Spanish Florida. Native Americans—particularly Seminoles— had an affinity for oppressed blacks because they were both oppressed in the same area by the same racism. So they provided a haven for runaway slaves and incorporated them into their tribes, not only for their special expertise in farming and handling livestock, but also for their useful knowledge of white culture. This alliance was so strong that blacks helped the Seminoles fend off the U.S. Army during the fierce Seminole Wars, spanning from 1816 to 1842. Those battles, aimed at exterminating the Seminoles for refusing to make way for whites and relocate west, ended up costing the government twenty million dollars and the lives of fifteen hun-

dred soldiers. In 1843, the Seminoles—red and black—
were finally forced out to Arkansas and Indian Territory
by President Andrew Jackson's brutal Indian Removal
Policy.

Escape to the frontier might have seemed like a perfect solution for African Americans trying to throw off
slavery and discrimination. But they discovered, like the
Native Americans before them, that white settlers
brought their prejudices with them. A Kansas historian
of the period admitted: "The western settlers did not talk
about the sinfulness of slavery; they despised the Negro." In 1861, a Michigan newspaper editor boasted a
common view of the times: "This government was made
for the benefit of the white race." Not surprisingly,
throughout the nineteenth century heated emotional de-
bates across America centered on the admission of new
states as either slave or free. In 1854, after passage of
Senator Stephen A. Douglas's Kansas-Nebraska Act,
leaving the Kansas slavery question to local residents,
opponents fought a mini-civil war over the issue. On
election day 1855, some five thousand armed Missouri
pro-slavers raided Kansas, took over voting booths, and
cast multiple pro-slavery ballots. When Governor Andrew Reeder protested, he was forced to flee across the
border disguised as a beggar. Meantime, the new ad hoc
government rushed through unconstitutional pro-slavery
laws and declared that any Abolitionist setting foot in
Kansas would be hung.

The conflict was so violent, it became known as
Bleeding Kansas. In Congress, the day after Massachusetts Senator Charles Sumner protested the crimes committed in Kansas, pro-slavery Congressman Preston
Brooks of South Carolina beat him unconscious with a
cane. In 1872, Illinois Senator Lyman Trumbull an-

nounced, "We, the Republican Party, are the white man's party. We are for the free white man, and for making white labor acceptable and honorable, which it can never be when negro slave labor is brought into competition with it." That same year, when presidential candidate and antislavery reformer Horace Greeley issued his famous advice, "Go west, young man," history forgot to mention that he also urged that the western territories must be "reserved for the benefit of the white Caucasian race."

The cards were stacked against African Americans in the West from the start. Yet they came by the hundreds of thousands. And though white history accounts did not record this fact either, blacks were intimately involved in the exploration and settlement of the West. They were involved in every aspect: exploration, law enforcement, mining, tailoring, smithing, tracking, trading, building, soldiering, ranching. Most people still aren't aware of the extent to which African Americans served as cowboys. When Southern whites moved to Texas to try to capitalize on the expanding cattle industry, very few had experience handling cattle. In the South, blacks had not only taken care of the animals but they had also done the same work as slaves on Texas cattle ranches. They knew exactly what to do.

After the annexation of Texas from Mexico in 1845, Hispanics fled central and southern Texas, leaving behind all their cattle except the prime breeding stock. For the next twenty years, these cattle roamed the wide-open prairies freely and reproduced. After the Civil War, poor black Southerners who migrated to Texas to work as cowboys rounded up these vast, roaming herds and learned how to handle them and drive them to Kansas railheads at Dodge City, Wichita, and Abilene. They became so skilled, they were hired repeatedly by ranchers. We know that, after the war, at least five thousand African-American freedmen herded cattle up the Chisholm Trail, the most-traveled route, from southern Texas to Abilene. It is estimated that in the Old West's heyday, blacks made up a quarter of the thirty-five thousand cowboys on the range—and they were regarded as some of the most adept. This was because they had learned to ride, wrangle, and herd from the vaqueros—Mexican ranchers and cowpunchers who first developed the techniques and equipment that white people would later take credit for: everything from branding, roping, and round-ups to the lariat, leather chaps, and spurs. So while the culture always portrayed stereotypes of African-American cowboys as underlings who basically served whites but contributed nothing themselves, the tradition of black cowboys was at least as long-standing as, and maybe more notable than, that of white cowboys.

Of course, while African-American cowboys enjoyed equality on the range—especially on cattle drives when they were assigned the toughest jobs—they were rarely made trail bosses or foremen. In fact, the original term "cow*boy*" referred, contemptuously, to African Americans (and sometimes Hispanics). Whites who worked with cattle always referred to themselves as "cattle-*men*." It is no wonder, then, that in spite of the fact that thousands of African Americans helped develop and settle the frontier, the stereotypical western heroes and heroines promoted in our history books and our culture have all been white: Buffalo Bill, Wild Bill Hickok, Calamity Jane, Kit Carson, Davy Crockett, Pat Garrett, Annie Oakley, Bat Masterson, Wyatt Earp. (Western dime novels about these white protagonists sold five million copies their first five years on the market, 1860–1865.

Edward Z. C. Judson, alias Ned Buntline, wrote two hundred Buffalo Bill novels alone.) And, aside from stigmatized Native Americans, like Sitting Bull, Geronimo, Crazy Horse, and Cochise, our most venerable western villains are all white, too: Billy the Kid, Jesse James, John Wesley Hardin, the Daltons, Ike and Billy Clanton.

For at least a century, the significance of African Americans in the West—heroes and badmen alike—was completely ignored. The motion pictures contributed to this fantasy view of the West. For decades, moviemakers used the western as a forum for portraying false images of not only blacks, who were almost always depicted as servants or slaves, but also the Native American. Depictions of lily-white cowboy heroes who rode to the rescue of other whites under attack by savage "redskins" were very influential in our popular culture. During the forties and fifties especially, western films were often propaganda disguised as entertainment. Their simplistic, slanted images of Native Americans were designed to justify the government's policy of genocide. Kids in the fifties, for example, grew up believing the Sioux were evil Indians who massacred the noble Custer. Neither the history books nor our western movies honestly portrayed the rash glory hound Custer, or the true plight of the persecuted, and mostly peaceful, Sioux. It was Custer who attacked them; they were merely defending themselves and fighting for their existence. Yet as a result of that one Sioux victory—in other words, because Custer got what he *deserved*—the Sioux were permanently demonized in our culture.

The truth was Sioux Chief Red Cloud and most of his tribe were obedient and cooperative with the encroaching white government. Only a small band of renegades split off to fight. Nevertheless, we used the Custer defeat as an excuse to punish the tribe collectively, and destroy their way of life. That was an atrocity committed by American whites in power against people of color, simply because they were people of color; in other words, different from ''us.''

⁕

In 1893, University of Wisconsin historian Frederick Jackson Turner shocked the American Historical Association when he delivered a paper entitled ''The Significance of the Frontier in American History.'' He said the roots of the national character lay not in our European or Colonial heritage, but in the new American frontier that promoted democracy and individualism. Of course, he was not speaking of the same frontier experienced by migrating African Americans; that frontier bristling with the discrimination and hate they had hoped to leave behind. Turner was right: The West did shape our national character. But by the time he delivered his paper, the Old West was dead—along with over 1.2 million Native Americans. In the next seven years, their population in the United States would dwindle to just 300,000. Legal genocide—a fact of white domination that African Americans understood only too well.

So the ''national character'' that Frederick Jackson Turner alluded to in his famous paper was not only rooted in democracy and individualism, but it also grew from white racism, violence, and intolerance.

On the eve of the Civil War, the still virgin frontier comprised everything west of the borders of Minnesota (statehood: 1858), Iowa (1846), Missouri (1821), Arkansas (1836), and Louisiana (1812). To imagine its vastness, consider that as of 1860 none of the following had been admitted yet as states: Oklahoma (1907), Kansas (1861), Nebraska (1867), South Dakota (1889), North Dakota (1889), New Mexico (1912), Colorado (1876), Wyoming (1890), Montana (1889), Arizona (1912), Utah (1896), Idaho (1890), Nevada (1864), Washington (1889). Unlike the prime agricultural grasslands of the Central Plains and Ohio Valley, this was rugged terrain more suited to ranching and mining—and a new American temperament. During the 1850s, ranchers drove enormous cattle herds across the Plains, and the discovery of silver and gold in Colorado, Nevada, Utah, and California drew hundreds of thousands of hopeful prospectors. Cattle centers and mining camps became towns overnight. Following the 1862 Homestead Act—providing 160 acres for settlers who agreed to work the land for five years—the population of the Plains exploded. Overland mail and railroad depots sprang up everywhere and torrents of squatters spilled into Indian Territory.

By 1870, Indian Territory was the most dangerous area of the frontier. It consisted of the government-allotted land spanning most of present-day Oklahoma (Choctaw for "red people"). This no-white-man's-land was ceded to some sixty thousand Native Americans of various tribes who had been forcibly relocated on the pitiful Trail of Tears. (In the winter of 1838, the government uprooted and force-marched thousands of Indians from their homelands in the East and South out to the western Plains. At least four thousand died of starvation, exposure, and disease along the way—which is how the Trail of Tears got its name.) White authorities justified this genocidal policy then—and still justify it today in history books—with every bogus excuse from "manifest destiny" to "progress." The truth is the government knew that a mass march in winter would result in suffering and death; it may even have been part of the plan. Because *no one* came to the aid of those innocent, tormented victims.

Collectively, the surviving, resettled Indians were known as the Five Civilized Tribes: the Cherokee, Chickasaw, Creek, Choctaw, and Seminole. They were considered separate, self-governing nations, so they each maintained their own law enforcement: mainly the Lighthorse mounted police (a name derived from the ponies they rode on patrol). Before the Civil War, the ethnic composition was about 85 percent Native American, 10 percent African American, the rest Caucasian. For a change, whites were in the minority because they were expressly banned in the Territory by federal law. In 1870, there were five all-black towns in Indian Territory (with twenty-three more to come), but not one white man's town. A decade later, at least twenty thousand whites had rushed in to settle—and they were never removed.

A large number of Southern blacks escaped slavery by living with Indians and pretending to be their slaves, and it benefited both the Indians and the blacks. The Indians' idea of slavery was not Simon Legree's; they were happy to have somebody among them who understood white culture and knew how to deal with their system. Other blacks who had served as slaves among the Indians and were freed by the tribes they lived with were rewarded with land. It was legal for Indians to own slaves; so when they accepted treaty land from the government, they had to free their slaves. These blacks were then entitled to land—and that is how African Americans acquired more land of their own in Oklahoma than anyplace else in the country.

While most blacks and Indians coexisted harmoniously in Indian Territory—in fact, often intermarrying—neither trusted white people nor wanted them around. Especially Indians, because this was literally the only place in the country they could call their own. But as in every previous clash between minority cultures and the dominant white culture in America, whites created a chasm between them that could not be broached. According to Art Burton's fascinating book about Indian Territory, *Black, Red, and Deadly*, the unwelcome encroachment of white outlaws seeking refuge in the interior of Indian Territory enhanced the atmosphere of savagery and distrust:

> . . . The white outlaw, completely free of any legal responsibility in this area, ran wild. He abused the Indian women, he stole the Indians' cattle and horses, he commandeered the Indians' food and homes, and he killed any Indian foolish enough to question his right to do these things. Even an organized attempt by a group of Indians to retaliate against the white outlaw was generally doomed to failure because the white outlaw ran in packs, carried generally superior weapons, and was completely ruthless and without pity in a pitched battle. He had nothing to lose by fighting to the death. If an outlaw was captured and expelled from the Indian nations into one of the adjoining states, he was usually arrested for previous crimes committed there, tried, and either promptly hung or sent to prison with a long sentence.
>
> These conditions led the white outlaws to effect a brutal, tough attitude even worse than their own natural, nasty disposition in the belief that fear and intimidation would keep the Indians under their

thumb, and thus insure their position as lord and master of this outlaw paradise.

An inevitable by-product of the sudden inpouring of whites and the collision of cultures was soaring crime. Indian Territory became a sort of petri dish of criminals. This was especially true since there was no organized government deterrent west of Arkansas. Technically, law and order in the Territory was the responsibility of the U.S. Court for the Western District of Arkansas. But there was only one judge and a handful of deputies to enforce the law there, as well as in thirty Arkansas counties. A reporter for the *Western Independent* in Fort Smith, Arkansas, at the edge of Indian Territory, wrote that violent crime was rising so fast, "a regiment of marshalls cannot arrest all the murderers." Muskogee, sixty miles inside Indian Territory, had fifteen unsolved murders within a thirty-mile radius in less than two years. In 1872 alone, under the aegis of corrupt Western District Judge William Story, one hundred Territory murders went unsolved. Story was forced to resign under threat of impeachment for taking bribes.

Crime festered for three more years, until the arrival on May 2, 1875, of the new Western District judge.

By the time thirty-six-year-old Isaac Charles Parker volunteered to President Grant for the thirty-five-hundred-dollar-a-year judgeship, Wild Bill Hickok and Buffalo Bill Cody had already played caricatures of themselves in Buffalo Bill's "fake" Wild West—his famous touring show. Meantime, in the actual Wild West, Indian Territory had become an outlaw's haven. Some of the worst badmen in history had been retreating there for decades—the infamous Cook, Dalton, and Doolin gangs robbed and killed at will across the Territory; the

James brothers considered it their ideal "vacation" spot between stickups. But all that was about to change. Judge Parker was honest, principled, capable, and itching to punish evildoers. He had been a city attorney, presidential elector, and congressional representative. And as a Methodist, he had uncompromising views on punishing criminals. Plus, he sympathized with Indians and blacks—he had been the most active Indian rights advocate on the House Committee on Indian Affairs; and serving on Fort Smith's board of education, he proposed establishment of a school for black children. So if anyone was driven to curb the rampant violence and unlawful encroachment into Indian Territory, it was Judge Isaac Parker.

Operating out of one of the dingy old barracks of Fort Smith (the town was named after its 1817 army post), just a hundred yards from Indian Territory, Parker set up court eight days after arriving. He held court six days a week, into the evenings. Punishment was swift, and between 1875 and 1889 there was no appeal. That was one reason why Parker became the West's most feared judge. In his first eight-week session, he tried 91 defendants. Of 18 charged with murder, 15 were convicted, 6 condemned to hang. They were not notorious killers. They murdered carelessly, for a saddle, or a wallet, or just for fun—typically reckless frontier behavior. Judge Parker decided to hang all 6 simultaneously from a new gallows that he had specially built to hang up to 12. At least 5,000 people attended, twice the population of little Fort Smith. Reporters came from as far away as New York. When word spread about the unorthodox execution, Parker was criticized as inhumane and labeled the "Hanging Judge." (In twenty-one years at Fort Smith, he tried 13,490 cases and won 8,500 convictions. He sentenced

88 men to hang—roughly 1 in 100, not nearly as many as his nickname implied. Only 79 actually hanged: 30 whites, 26 Indians, 23 blacks—so he was also the equal opportunity Hanging Judge.) After those first 6 hangings, Parker's renown was so intimidating that, according to one deputy, "When an attorney started to argue with him, he just pointed his finger at him. The attorney didn't *sit* down, he *fell* down." Offenders coming before the Hanging Judge reacted the same.

There were no guidelines for solving the unique problems presented by hunting outlaws committing crimes in Indian Territory. Here you had disaffected African Americans, Native Americans, and whites, as well as countless interracial groups, all of whom felt oppressed, or persecuted, or dogged by the U.S. government. That was why, according to one historian, the area constituted "a special legal limbo." In fact, Judge Parker often applied whatever law he felt suited the circumstances. His master plan was simple: He would reduce crime in the Territory by conducting the most extensive manhunt in frontier history, bringing to justice *every villain in his jurisdiction.* To accomplish that, he reopened unsolved cases; issued warrants for the most notorious outlaws and gangs known to reside in the Territory; appointed two hundred deputies—far more than in any other jurisdiction—and instructed them to bring in their culprits dead or alive. Of course, this was nearly impossible: How would two hundred deputies cover seventy-four thousand square miles that the outlaws knew like the backs of their hands?

Plus, the job literally didn't pay. There was no salary; for every captured fugitive, deputies earned a two-dollar fee. They received nothing for corpses. Deputies hauling in more than one outlaw at a time had to pay food expenses for anything over their seventy-five-cents-a-day allowance. To make it up, they would often invent fines for misdemeanors and keep the cash. This turned some of them crooked, but as long as they were good with a gun and brave enough to keep working the Territory, minor indiscretions were overlooked.

Hunting criminals in the West was a daunting task, even in the best conditions. In Indian Territory, it was like running an obstacle course, blindfolded and hands tied. Obviously, the work was dangerous; in Judge Parker's two decades as Western District Judge, sixty-five of his deputies were killed on duty. Indian Territory was refuge to more robbers, killers, and thieves than any other area of the country, so it was always a viper's den to deputies. To make things worse, fugitive whites and most Native Americans in the Territory treated Parker's deputies with disdain and impeded their work. Whole towns provided asylum for bandits in return for safety guarantees. Plus, since resisting arrest only brought a year in jail, virtually everyone resisted. And all were armed.

Here is a contemporary report on some of the obstacles Parker's deputies faced:

Some whites gave shelter to outlaws or provided them with supplies or even ammunition. They also warned outlaws of the approach of deputies, who left telltale signs of their presence. As an old-timer later explained: "In those days [our] horses were barefooted. If we discovered a horse's tracks which showed that the horse was shod we knew a United States Marshal was in the neighborhood."

Local hostility presented the deputies with still another problem. To expedite trials at Fort Smith, they usually picked up witnesses at the scene and took them back with them. The witnesses were reluctant both to make the long trip and to run the risk of reprisals. As a trip wore on, the deputies might find it slow going if two dozen or more witnesses chose to balk. Even when they came along willingly, it was no easy matter to get them out of harm's way if a gunfight erupted.

This was why Judge Parker continued to try to find the toughest and shrewdest men to serve his cause.

It might have been his own shrewdest move the day he decided to hire a tall, imposing cowboy by the name of Bass Reeves. Because Reeves would soon be more feared throughout the Territory than even the judge himself.

———

On March 17, 1877, in Washington, D.C., President Rutherford B. Hayes appointed ex-slave Frederick Douglass as the first African-American U.S. marshal. Of course, Douglass was not a law enforcement officer, so it was an honorary political post. Eight years later, when Judge Isaac Parker appointed ex-slave Bass Reeves as the first black deputy U.S. marshal west of the Mississippi, it was the real thing. Unfortunately, no black would ever be appointed marshal in Indian Territory; right through Oklahoma's statehood in 1907, the job was always reserved for whites. But if Judge Parker had been president of the United States at the time, he would have made Bass Reeves the first black U.S. marshal.

In a rare obituary tribute for an African American, a newspaper reporter noted of the recently deceased

Reeves: "In the history of the early days of Eastern Oklahoma the name of Bass Reeves has a place in the front rank among those who cleansed out the old Indian Territory of outlaws and desperados." And though Reeves's astonishing career had no parallel in law enforcement history—including that of the most famous lawman of all, Wyatt Earp—there would be no public acknowledgment of him for sixty-one more years. Not until the 1971 publication of an Oklahoma public school's book, *Black History in Oklahoma*, did America finally learn of the "lawman second to none in the Territory." And how many people read that?

Bass Reeves was born around 1838 in Paris, Texas. As a young man, he was the personal "body servant" of former Confederate Colonel and Grayson County Sheriff George Reeves. Young Bass was unusually bright, strong, skilled with guns, and highly regarded by the colonel and everyone else who knew him. Then a shadowy event changed his life. The most likely version was that during a card game with the colonel, Bass was somehow provoked into knocking him unconscious. He then fled north across Red River into Indian Territory where he remained a fugitive until Emancipation.

While in Indian Territory, the ruggedly handsome six-foot-two, two-hundred-pound Reeves married; settled in tiny Van Buren above Fort Smith; ran a prosperous farm; raised ten children; was so fast and accurate with his Colt pistols and Winchester rifles that he was barred from turkey shoots at local picnics and fairs (it was said "he could shoot the left hind leg off of a contented fly sitting on a mule's ear at a hundred yards and never ruffle a hair"); and, though illiterate, during his extensive travel across Indian Territory he taught himself to speak not only fluent Creek but every language of the Five Civilized Tribes.

In 1875, when Reeves signed on with Judge Parker, Indian Territory was swarming with outlaws who specialized in ducking the law. No matter how proficient you were with a gun, you first had to get close to your man. Since Reeves was devoted to doing the job right, he was more original and relentless than his fellow deputies. It was not unusual for him to depart from Fort Smith on his regular circuit, hunting killers, rapists, bootleggers, and thieves, and return months later with a wagonful of prisoners. During his long, legendary career, his incredible exploits were recounted diligently in area newspapers. Rarely did they say: ''Deputy Marshal Reeves brought in his *man*.'' It was always a *host* of colorful felons—black, white, Indian, male, female— charged with a litany of crimes.

Like this:

Deputy Bass Reeves came in Sunday from an extended trip through the Territory bringing seventeen prisoners, who were registered at the jailer's office as follows: Jonas Stake, Two-a-nuck-ey, one Wiley, (Indians) charged with murder; Chas. Cosy, one Feglin, arson; Ben Bowlegs alias Ben Billy alias Williams, (Indian) John Pickett, larceny; Robert Ken-a-wah, Joseph Dorsey, one Hawkins, Robert Kelly, Wolf alias Ya-gha, Barney alias Hills Harjo, one Winnie, one Siller, one Jennie, (Indians) Adam Brady (negro), introducing and selling whiskey in Territory.

And this:

Bass Reeves, one of the best Marshals on the force, reported at Atoka, Monday, from the Chickasaw, Pottawotamie and Western Creek country with the following prisoners: One Hanna, Creek, murder; Chub Moore, murder; Jedick Jackson, Jno. Bruner, colored, Jim Mack, Chickasaw, for larceny; Jno. Hoyt, Dr. A. Smith, J. M. McConnell, whites, Alex Baker and Daniel Dorsey, Creeks, all for introducing.

And, after false reports that notorious outlaw Ned Christie had killed Reeves in Tahlequah, north of Muskogee, this:

Deputy Marshal Bass Reeves lacks lots of being dead, as was reported recently from Muskogee to the *Dallas News*. He turned up Saturday from the west with two wagon loads of prisoners going to Fort Smith. He had twelve prisoners in all. Eight for whiskey vending, three for larceny and one for murder . . .

These rolls of collared outlaws were, in themselves, revealing narratives on Reeves's extraordinary career in the Territory. When I first read them, I wondered how he managed to round up all these bad men on his own, time after time. And then I discovered just how unique Bass Reeves was. He did not just ride up, pull out his guns, and take the bad guys in. He often had to use subterfuge—something few lawmen did in those days; for example, the use of disguises. No one in law enforcement was more daring or masterly at this ruse. (Izzy Einsten and Moe Smith, a couple of zany federal agents who wore outlandish getups to make over five thousand arrests during Prohibition of the 1920s, come in a close second, and my guess is they knew about Bass Reeves.) One revealing fact that impressed me about Bass Reeves throughout his career was that he stated many times to Judge Parker and fellow deputies that he used disguises to *avoid* shootouts and, therefore, needless violence. This philosophy alone cast him as singular among Wild West lawmen whose common creed—fee or no fee—was something like: *Shoot first and ask no questions.*

Reeves was so adept at operating undercover as a cowboy, tramp, gunslinger, or bandit, stories about his courage and ingenuity spread across the West to friends and foes alike. For instance: The tale of the legendary twenty-eight-mile hike. Sometime in the 1880s, Reeves decided to track two wanted brothers in order to earn a five-thousand-dollar reward. Using his sources, he learned they were holed up in their mother's cabin in southern Indian Territory, near the Texas border. So he formed a small posse, including a cook and wagoner, and they headed south. Eventually, they set up camp twenty-eight miles from the hideout. Reeves later explained he chose this distance so he could study the surrounding land for approach and escape routes, and plan carefully without spooking his prey. He did not want campfires, which could give them away, or chance encounters with the outlaws' allies, who could quickly tip them off. So the twenty-eight miles was not arbitrary; it was key to the element of surprise.

Reeves decided to impersonate a saddle tramp on the lam. So he cut the heels off some old boots and shot three bullet holes in a floppy hat as a disguise. Stuffing his handcuffs, badge, and Colt revolvers under his coat, he started walking to the hideout alone. This was part of the Bass Reeves legend; while most deputies made their

Indian Territory rounds in teams of four or five, Bass Reeves almost always opted for the "lone wolf pursuit" to make the capture. He knew he stood a better chance that way; he would arouse less suspicion on his own. And he knew that Territory outlaws posted lookouts for teams of lawmen on strategic hills. So they would rarely expect anyone to track in alone, especially in disguise.

After hiking the twenty-eight miles and arriving at the mother's cabin, Reeves knocked on the door. When the mother answered, Reeves told her he was a robber running from a posse that had shot the bullet holes in his hat. She believed him and invited him in. While cooking him a meal, she mentioned that her two boys were also on the run and suggested it might be smart if they all protected one another. At dark, someone whistled from across the creek. When the mother went outside, up rode her fugitive sons.

Once inside, they met Reeves, bought his detailed story, and agreed to team up with him for mutual gain. That night, Reeves talked them into sleeping in the same room with him, in case they were rushed by the law. While the unsuspecting brothers slept on the floor, Reeves handcuffed them so expertly they did not awaken. In the morning, the game was up; Reeves ordered them outside. The mother was irate, following them for miles, cursing and screaming at Reeves's back, until she could go no farther. Meantime, he led the outlaws back to his camp where the brothers were shackled to the wagon for the night. Next morning, Reeves led his prisoners, cook, and posse back to Fort Smith. He did not have to wait for the brothers' inevitable conviction to collect his five-thousand-dollar reward—and add another notch to his legend.

Another of his storied undercover jobs happened in

the 1890s when he decided to investigate a robbery in the crude saloon town of Keokuk Falls, one of the most dangerous outposts on the Seminole border of Indian Territory. But he was intrepid; he was widely known as one of the few deputy marshals courageous enough to come through the border towns where disputes were settled on the porches of saloons or by shootouts in the streets. He met with the robbery victim, John F. Brown, Jr., chief of the Seminole Nation, who provided directions to the desperadoes' hideout, an abandoned cabin inside the Creek Nation. When Reeves arrived at the cabin and saw chimney smoke, he concocted a plan: He would return the next day as a tenant farmer and try to draw them outside on a ruse. The following morning, he put on dirty, patched overalls, rented a yoke of old oxen and a rickety wagon and intentionally drove the wagon onto a tree stump in front of the cabin. When the four outlaws came out to run him off, Reeves persuaded them to help. They grudgingly obliged by lifting the wagon free of the stump. But when they finished, they were staring down the barrels of his shiny Colts. Reeves disarmed them without incident—a Bass Reeves trademark because he detested unnecessary violence. Afterward, he chained the four to the wagon; recovered the stolen money from the cabin; then marched them to the county seat at Tecumseh, thirty miles away. They were later convicted and imprisoned.

In 1884, Reeves came the closest to losing his life—and yet still added to his legend. Riding the Seminole whiskey trail with warrants for four badmen, he was intercepted by the three Brunter brothers. They were wanted for robbery and murder and must have known that Reeves would eventually hunt them down. (Outlaws were so intimidated by Reeves's reputation, they often left him printed threats posted to trees on the trail. He knew they meant business; he had escaped assassination by ambush numerous times by adopting the Seminole habit of staying on his horse, even when eating, and *expecting* danger. How do we know these posted outlaw notes were not just some dime novel invention to inflate his own myth? Because when he retired, he kept a dozen of them in his home for posterity. If Bass Reeves was anything, he was *authentic*.)

The Brunters ordered him off his horse at gunpoint, so he had to think fast. He did—by talking about the warrant he had for their arrest and showing it to them and asking what day of the week it was so he could list it on the warrant for the government. This baffled the Brunters; why would Reeves so stupidly seal his fate by confirming he was, in fact, hunting them? Of course, that was the point; Reeves knew this would divert them. It did; because in the split second when they called him crazy and started to laugh, Reeves pulled his revolver and dropped two of them while grabbing the barrel of the third one's gun. The doomed Brunter got off three deflected shots before Reeves killed him with blows to the head from his Colt. Reeves collected no fees for the Brunter brothers, but it was widely known that he was more concerned with serving justice than accumulating cash. Besides, Reeves was so relentless in pursuing fugitives and so devoted to bringing them in alive that by the end of his thirty-two-year career he had arrested over three thousand (killing fourteen—seven more than Wild Bill Hickok—without ever being wounded) and earned more money than any dozen deputies put together.

During that same year, Reeves was involved in an incident later described as ''one of the greatest rifle duels ever to take place in Indian Territory history.'' It was also notable because it revealed how highly regarded Bass Reeves was among even the outlaws he hunted. It developed this way: In 1883, tough-guy Jim Webb was a foreman on an isolated ranch deep inside the Chickasaw Nation. In spring, on a neighboring ranch, a black preacher named Reverend William Steward started a grass fire that spread to Webb's ranch. When Webb confronted the reverend, they quarreled and Webb murdered him. Bass Reeves was given the murder writ. He and a posse man named Floyd Wilson rode out for the arrest.

When they approached the ranch, Reeves disguised himself as an itinerant cowboy looking for work. On the ranch, they found Webb with his friend Frank Smith and asked for some breakfast. Though Webb was suspicious he took them in anyway, but he and Smith held their guns at their sides as a threat. During breakfast, Reeves knew Webb was on to him. When Webb and his pal conversed in the hall, Reeves told Floyd to take care of Smith and he would get Webb. After breakfast, Webb asked Reeves and his posse man to sit on a bench, and then he grilled them. As the tension built, Reeves sensed the flash point. So he lunged for Webb's throat with one hand while pressing his Colt to Webb's face with the other. Webb immediately surrendered.

But Smith backed off and shot twice at Reeves, missing each time. Still clutching Webb's throat, Reeves wheeled and shot Smith in the stomach. He and Webb were cuffed and chained in a wagon for the long trek back to Fort Smith. On the way, Frank Smith died of his wound—they buried him in Tishomingo, the Chickasaw capital. Webb ended up spending a year in jail before being bailed out by two friends, Jim Bywaters and Chris Smith. Of course, he never showed up for trial. So Reeves took a second warrant and again went after

Webb, this time with posse man John Cantrell.

Cantrell found Webb at Bywaters's store in Indian Territory and signaled for Reeves. But when Webb spotted Reeves through the window, he grabbed a rifle and bolted outside for his horse, a hundred yards away. Reeves rode hard and blocked his path, calling for Webb to surrender. Webb took off for cover in the underbrush. Chased by Reeves on his horse, Webb decided to stop and shoot it out. So he crouched and began firing as fast as he could. He had nothing to lose—he knew if he was caught he would hang for Reverend Stewart's murder. A few of Webb's shots came close to finishing Reeves, who even during the fusillade held his fire and repeatedly yelled for Webb to surrender. But that was not to be. Here is Reeves's own account of the soon-to-be-legendary gunfight:

> He stepped out into the open, 500 yards away, and commenced shooting with his Winchester. Before I could drop off my horse his first bullet cut a button off my coat and the second cut my bridle rein in two. I shifted my six shooter and grabbed my Winchester and shot twice. He dropped and when I picked him up I found that my two bullets had struck within a half-inch of each other. He shot four times, and every time he shot he kept running up closer to me. He was 500 yards away from me when I killed him.

But Webb did not die instantly. He was still alive when Jim Bywaters and John Cantrell knelt by his side. Oddly, Webb called for Reeves. So Reeves approached, pointing his Winchester and demanding that Webb toss his pistol away. Webb complied and Reeves kneeled over him. Then Webb made his dying statement (which Bywaters later wrote down):

> Give me your hand, Bass. You are a brave, brave man. I want you to accept my revolver and scabbard as a present, and you must accept them. Take it, for with it I have killed eleven men, four of them in Indian Territory, and I expected you to make the twelfth.

With that, Jim Webb died. Reeves helped bury him and later took his boots and gunbelt to prove the warrant was served. There are two fascinating things about this incident: First, Reeves was not named as Webb's adversary in the newspaper reports. The speculation was interesting. That area of the Territory was dense with racist white Southerners, many of them fugitives like Webb. So the thinking might have been that publicizing a black deputy's killing of a white man might have caused more trouble than it was worth. Around there, Bass Reeves was just another "uppity" nigger that whites were barely willing to tolerate. Second, Jim Webb respected Reeves enormously, even when Reeves was the agent of his death.

Even more infamous criminals respected Bass Reeves. Like Belle Starr. When she married her third husband, Cherokee outlaw Sam Starr, her hideout was some seventy miles west of Fort Smith on the Canadian River near present-day Eufaula, Oklahoma. She worked there as an organizer and fence for bootleggers and thieves, and she was known to bribe snooping deputies with sexual favors in return for immunity. She did not try this with staunch Bass Reeves, who used to stop at her well for water when passing through Indian Territory, hunting

other prey. In 1888, Reeves came through when Belle had guests. She told them he was "one of the few Deputy Marshals I trust," and that although she had fought for the Confederacy, she was a good friend of this special Negro. She referred to him as a fearless, dedicated lawman with a reputation for being tough and mean but always honest, even with bandits. And that was why she considered him "second to none" in the West.

To me, the event in Bass Reeves's life that took the true measure of the man was when he arrested his own son. As far as I know, there was no comparable situation for a lawman in the West. Late in Reeves's career, one of his three sons, Benjamin, was having marital problems because his wife was unhappy that his work kept him from home so much. One night, Benjamin came home to find his wife with another man. He kept his control, forgave her, and took a less demanding job. But she betrayed him again. This time, he flew into a rage, beat the man severely, and murdered his wife. Panicking, Benjamin then fled to Indian Territory.

It was a touchy issue for the Muskogee marshal; he felt another deputy should go after Reeves's son. But despite being shaken, Bass Reeves insisted that it was his responsibility to bring in his son. Sure enough, two weeks later Bass rode in with Benjamin and completed the hardest assignment of his career by turning his son over to the marshal. At trial, Benjamin manfully owned up to his crime and was convicted and sent to the federal prison at Leavenworth, Kansas. Bass stood by him, all the way to the prison doors. For years, Benjamin served as a model prisoner. And though Bass Reeves was too proud to plead for mercy, Muskogee citizens learned from others the details of the circumstances that led Benjamin to commit the uncharacteristic crime. Finally, out of respect for Bass Reeves and based on Benjamin's exemplary behavior in prison, they circulated a petition and pressed for a pardon. It was eventually granted and Benjamin was released—and he later became one of the most popular barbers in Muskogee.

———

This incident exemplifies what I came to admire most about Bass Reeves: his enormous courage to do the right thing. Also the absolute integrity and dedication of his long service: no bribes, nobody bought him off or bargained and skipped—he served them all, including his own son. He was a man of uncompromising principle, something difficult to find, even today, in the character of people in power.

Think of it: Ex-slave goes into Indian Territory without knowing how to read or write; but by learning languages, becomes familiar with the Indians so he can better protect their interests, not just advance himself; ends up first on Judge Parker's list when Parker desperately needs tough, honest marshals to regulate the wildest territory in the history of the country; and eventually becomes not only Parker's most trusted man and the finest ever to work Indian Territory, but by any objective standards, *the single best deputy U.S. marshal who ever lived.*

Circumstances draw people with character forward. Being a slave owner does not make you brave or intelligent, and being a slave does not make you a coward, an animal, or a fool. Bass Reeves's depth of character showed in the way he carried himself. He believed that one man could make a difference, and he lived that way. That is why people were afraid of him just *by reputation.*

Not so much by what he had done as the way he walked and talked. He *looked* like a man you could not fake or bribe or deceive. It was ingrained in his soul that if you were a criminal, and if he crossed your path, you were going in. It was not his six-guns that guaranteed you were going in; it was his character. *But*—and this is another of his admirable traits—*it was his six-guns, too.* He was an expert with the tools of his trade, not an egotistical dilettante, and fearless but also judicious in their use. He constantly said he never shot a man who didn't provoke it. Eyewitness accounts and plentiful other documentation confirm his view. Even a brief reconsideration of the numbers bears it out: in thirty-two years in law enforcement, over three thousand arrests but only fourteen killed—remarkable numbers, especially given the brutal circumstances in the badman's hell called Indian Territory.

In a time that did not encourage blacks to become U.S. marshals, in fact did not encourage blacks to become much of anything, his career was certainly extraordinary and clearly one of a kind.

Judge Isaac Parker died on November 17, 1896, as the frontier was closing forever. In 1898, tribal courts in Indian Territory were abolished. On April 22, 1889, President Benjamin Harrison opened the Oklahoma Territory to white settlement. By that night, over one hundred thousand settlers had staked claims to twelve thousand homesteads. The last Native American refuge was gone. That same year, courts outside Forth Smith were granted jurisdiction over the Territory and Bass Reeves was transferred to Muskogee, a town with large

African-American and Native American populations. Despite the influx of two hundred thousand more whites by the turn of the century and the flaring of racial tensions, Reeves's reputation for principle and fairness preceded him and he continued to be the most respected lawman in the Territory.

Appropriately, his last day as a deputy U.S. marshal was November 16, 1907, the first day of Oklahoma statehood. Now, local courts took over the jurisdiction from the area's federal courts. Sadly, while Bass Reeves's entire professional life flew in the face of white racist stereotypes, and though he represented the highest American ideals, the first Oklahoma legislature quickly passed a series of backward-looking Jim Crow codes, everything from separation of races in railway cars to forbidding interracial marriages. So while Bass Reeves could boast that he was the only deputy U.S. marshal whose career spanned from the start of Judge Parker's court all the way to statehood, he was greatly troubled about the rising racism greeting the new century.

Nevertheless, at seventy, using a cane, he was still patrolling a beat for the Muskogee police force. There were no crimes on his beat right up until November 19, 1909, when he took ill and served his last day. On Wednesday, January 12, 1910, Bass Reeves died—the finest law enforcement officer of a unique era.

An era that, fittingly, died with him.

CHAPTER 7

DEFENSE

Blacks in the military

The military has always occupied a special niche in American society. We give privilege to our fighting men and women because they are willing to sacrifice their lives, or the quality of their lives, for the good of the nation. Foreigners who want to be American citizens can join the army and after one full hitch become citizens. That was what my uncle Willie did; when World War II broke out, he left Antigua and joined the army in the American Virgin Islands, and that earned him his citizenship.

Historically, all the way back to the Revolutionary War, blacks understood they could earn respect in the military that they were denied in society. There was an element of self-esteem involved in joining the armed forces; it represented an oasis of escape from repression and discrimination. But black service in the military also underlined a major contradiction in our attitude toward

equality. Here was a people that always volunteered to
serve the country in times of war only to have the country deny them the equality that was their birthright.
White people today wonder why so many African Americans work for the post office or join the army. The answer is simple: The federal government is required by
law to be an equal opportunity employer. It has traditionally been the one place where an African American
can find a semblance of evenhandedness.

Unfortunately, in its own way, for nearly two hundred
years the military was just as biased and mean-spirited
as society. Up until the late 1960s, the accepted policy
of our armed forces toward African Americans was
something like: *We will employ you if we need you. But
as soon as we don't need you anymore, you're gone.*

Even though African-American soldiers fought nobly
and contributed significantly to winning the Revolutionary War, afterward they were quickly relegated to their
inferior status. Only months after the Battle of Bunker
Hill, General George Washington ordered his recruiters
to decline Continental Army service to Negroes and vag-
abonds. Eventually, protests from African Americans
who had already proven themselves in battle caused
Washington to reverse his decision and authorize limited
black enlistment. But because of repeated Southern protests, he waffled back and forth on the issue throughout
the war. Washington was so unpredictable, he ended up
commanding seven hundred black soldiers himself in the
June 1778 Battle of Monmouth Court House. By war's
end, African Americans had participated in at least fifty
battles, consistently acquitting themselves valiantly.

But it did not count for much. The new U.S. Constitution reemphasized black inferiority by deeming that, for political representation, each slave would only count as three fifths of a human being. A few years later, in 1792, the Militia Act started closing the ranks to blacks again by restricting service in state militias to "each and every free and able-bodied white male citizen of the respective states . . . of the age of eighteen and under the age of forty-five." (Remember: In our first militias, it was the duty of *every* able-bodied man between seventeen and sixty, black or white, to serve. At the time, blacks were not only welcome but they were also encouraged to serve.) In 1798, Secretary of War Henry Knox specifically prohibited "Negroes, Mulattos, and Indians" from joining the marines (a ban that lasted, amazingly, until 1942). That same year, Navy Secretary Benjamin Stoddard barred "Negroes and Mulattos" from the navy, though he excepted Negroes already serving on vessels at sea.

So here was the *real* America, once again slapping blacks in the face: *We don't need you anymore. Go back where you belong.* Until America needed us again . . . to win the War of 1812.

One issue in that brief conflict with Britain was their interference in our merchant trade. But the most sensitive issue was illegal British impressment of American seamen. The British Navy was considered a "floating hell" by its sailors, most of whom were impressed into service against their wills. They were poorly paid and regularly flogged on inadequately equipped ships. They deserted in embarrassing numbers; hundreds joined the U.S. merchant service. To check their losses, the British declared their right to seize and search American merchant ships and to reclaim deserters. When they seized thousands of naturalized Americans along with their own men, President Jefferson protested vehemently, calling the affront a matter of national honor. His protests fell on deaf ears. Illegal searches and impressments continued until 1807 when His Majesty's ship *Leonard* fired on the U.S. Navy frigate *Chesapeake* in Chesapeake Bay because she carried British deserters among her crew. Men of the *Leonard* boarded the *Chesapeake* and dragged four American seamen off the ship—the first direct British attack on a United States military vessel.

The country called for war, but Jefferson exercised restraint. However, he knew war was inevitable. It finally erupted on August 24, 1814, when the British sacked Washington and burned the White House. But the most serious threat came in the South, at Christmastime, when veteran troops under Sir Edward Pakenham, the Duke of Wellington's brother-in-law, landed below New Orleans. In response, militia General Andrew Jackson mustered troops near Crescent City. He planned to go to battle with a motley army composed of Southern frontiersmen and dandies, pirates, Creoles, slaves, and two battalions of six hundred freed blacks. Among the black soldiers were several officers; under Jackson, they would command American troops for the first time in our history. He seemingly relished the participation of blacks so much that, on December 18, he saluted them with this public proclamation:

To the Men of Color: Soldiers! I collected you to arms. I invited you to share in the perils and to divide the glory with your fellow countrymen. I knew that you loved the land of your nativity and that like ourselves you had to defend all that is most dear to you. But you surpass my hopes. I have found in you, united in these qualities, the noble enthusiasm which impels men to great deeds.

But Jackson was not what he seemed. He was shrewd enough to perceive the need for using blacks to help him defeat the superior British in the South (as a student of war, he knew of South Carolina's foolish refusal, under siege in 1780, to arm blacks to help them defend Charleston, which ultimately fell to the British); but he did not personally hold black people in high regard. Of course, that only became obvious after the battle. Beforehand, he had promised his eager slave recruits their freedom in return for their service. He promised the freed blacks the same pay, bounties, and 160-acre land grants he had guaranteed his white soldiers.

When these strange bedfellow soldiers first saw British troops camped at New Orleans, they were awestruck. Across the fields, thousands of Redcoats in shiny steel breastplates, helmets, and silver swords looked like King Arthur's Knights. Curiously, it was not General Jackson but an astute slave named Pompey who bolstered Jackson's ragtag troops. Pompey suggested forming a protective breastwork—a "cotton-bag fort"—by stuffing dirt into cotton sacks and stacking them up like walls. Jackson approved and Pompey supervised construction.

The Battle of New Orleans commenced on January 8, 1815, with three volleys from the British lines at Jackson's men huddled behind their cotton sacks. According to African-American participant and Revolutionary War veteran James Roberts, it was Pompey's "fort" that saved the day. As Pakenham's men tried to yank the sacks outward instead of pushing them toward Jackson's troops, they somehow got "entangled" and became sitting ducks. When Pakenham himself was shot from the wall, the white flag went up and the British retreated. They left behind over seven hundred dead and fourteen hundred wounded. Strangely, while the battle raged, neither Pakenham nor Jackson was aware that an Anglo-American peace treaty had been signed two weeks earlier in Ghent, Belgium, ending the war.

History texts that bothered to record the New Orleans casualties grossly underreported the American totals; for example: ''8 killed, 13 wounded.'' But James Roberts later offered history his more accurate assessment:

> In that battle some sixty or seventy or more of the colored men were killed, of whom no account whatever was ever taken in the details of the war. . . .

Two days later, General Jackson reneged on his promise of freedom for his soldier-slaves. When Roberts pressed him on this, Jackson replied that he did not have the power to free ''another man's property.'' Blacks had heard this lame excuse after the Revolution. Infuriated, Roberts drew his pistol on Jackson and pulled the trigger. But the gun did not go off, because the day after the battle Jackson had confiscated the weapons of all his black troops and secretly ordered their ammunition removed. Another side of the ''Great Democrat'' Andrew Jackson that history overlooked was revealed in a passionate speech he made to white compatriots in a New Orleans tavern after the battle. According to Roberts, who accompanied Jackson that day, the general declared openly:

> Before a slave of mine should go free I would put him in a barn and burn him alive . . . Never arm another set of colored people. We have fooled them

now, but . . . they will not be fooled again with this example before them.

This speech does not appear in any official version of the War of 1812. James Roberts offered a good guess why:

> Such monstrous deception and villainy could not, of course, be allowed to disgrace the pages of history, and blacken the character of a man who wanted the applause and approbation of his country.

Predictably, when the war was over, the promised bounties and 160 acres for Jackson's black troops never materialized. No black units, including the two heroic battalions that assured his key victory at New Orleans, were ever allowed to march in the city's commemorative parades. (True to form, after he was elected president in 1828, Andrew Jackson enforced restrictions against blacks in the military throughout his eight-year reign. It was no coincidence, either, that his first-term vice president was South Carolina's staunchest pro-slaver, Senator John C. Calhoun.)

In February 1820, after defying its own bans on blacks by recruiting them to fight in 1812, the army reverted to its "whites only" policy. The navy caved in to Southern political pressure by fixing black recruitment at less than 5 percent. This was confusing, even to the navy, because it had already violated its own 1798 ban by recruiting blacks so heavily that they comprised about 15 percent of their forces. Plus, black sailors had come through with distinction, time and again. One notable example: In July 1814, when Captain Oliver H. Perry's flagship, USS

Lawrence, was hit at the Battle of Put-in-Bay and started
to burn, black pilot Cyrus Tiffany helped row Perry to
the USS *Niagara*, the new flagship. When the British
spotted their small boat and tried to sink it, Tiffany fear-
lessly draped himself around Perry as a human shield.

However, in return for black contributions in wartime
there were more deceptions and lies. It was the usual
handwriting on the wall: Black patriots, denied access
and recognition in both society and the military, would
still be fighting *two*-front wars. Yet despite the broken
promises, humiliations, and persecution, blacks kept
stepping forward to serve their country, right or wrong.

———∞———

It is hard for me to understand why most Americans
today do not know about the achievements of African
Americans in our wars. But in my travels, I was most
astonished at the ignorance about black contributions in
the Civil War especially. I always thought that was the
one war all Americans knew best. But with the exception
of African-American history curricula, our schools have
seldom taught the whole truth about it, and our historians
have rarely written it. As a result, I don't think the average American knows that:

- without the sacrifices of the 186,000 black combat
  troops in the Union Army and the 29,000 black seamen aboard Union Navy vessels, the North almost
  certainly would have lost the war;

- by war's end, black soldiers comprising about 10 percent of the Union Army had participated in 449 en-
  gagements, including 39 major battles;

- approximately 37,300 black soldiers were killed in the army, a disproportionately high percentage of the Union total;

- 200,000 black civilians joined service and support units;

- 17 black soldiers and 4 black sailors received the Congressional Medal of Honor for their "conspicuous bravery above and beyond the call of duty";

- despite the large number of black participants, the War Department kept black officers at a ridiculous minimum of between 70 and 100—the highest-ranking, a lieutenant colonel, who was a surgeon.

The aversion to black officers characterized the long-standing prejudice underlying the military's policy of keeping blacks out of combat, period. Generally, the thinking was: *Somewhere along the line a black person will be in charge of a white person, and we can't have that.* Two hundred years of white supremacy perpetuated the expectation that if you associated with a black person, you gave him an order and he was supposed to bring you something. But *never* was he supposed to be fighting beside you. Another reason whites were so indecisive on the issue of blacks in the military was that many felt if they were in a black man's shoes, they would want revenge for past offenses; consequently, that was what they were afraid black soldiers might do.

But those fears were unfounded. For example, Frederick Douglass had waited years to break free of slavery's yoke, and yet when he finally escaped, he did not strike back; he did not murder anyone. There was only one Nat Turner in the entire sweep of American history; and he killed one person—a slave owner. His followers did not kill indiscriminately either, they did not harm a single nonslave owner. There were smaller revolts that cost innocent lives. But nowhere in history do we read about repeated black massacres of innocent whites in revenge for hundreds of years of slavery. It never happened. Black people who wanted to fight in wars for their freedom and pride knew this about themselves; they were not Nat Turners nor Denmark Veseys; they did not seek revenge. That was strictly a white man's guilty fear and another excuse to keep the black man down.

Long before the Civil War broke out, Frederick Douglass pressed relentlessly, despite white resistance, for the arming of African-American soldiers. He knew if that happened the war would be over, the South would be crushed, and blacks might have their chance at freedom. He showed he understood the psychology that would propel African Americans to fight for the North when he said:

> Once let the black man get upon his person the brass letters, U.S., let him get an eagle on his button, and a musket on his shoulder and bullets in his pocket, and there is no power on earth which can deny that he has earned the right to citizenship in the United States.

But Lincoln kept ducking the issue, until pressure mounted and he finally proposed his shameful colonization scheme to black leaders. In the summer of 1862, he told them, "It is better for us both . . . to be separated." They rejected his plan angrily.

Meantime, Kansas Senator and Union General James H. Lane, who had previously refused to obey a mandate that soldiers return fugitive slaves to their masters, decided to summon black troops on his own. In August, he formed the First and Second Regiments of the Kansas Colored Volunteers with runaway slaves from Missouri and free Northern blacks. On October 7, they skirmished briefly with Rebel guerrillas in Clay County, Missouri, to become, unofficially, the first Northern black unit to fight for the Union. Three weeks later, still unauthorized, they fought hand to hand with six hundred Rebels on the marshy Osage River in the still obscure Battle of Island Mounds. After the First Regiment ran the enemy off, their bravery was documented by a *New York Times* reporter on the scene. Gradually, as information like this spread in the North, sympathies began to shift.

That summer the war went badly for the Union, forcing Lincoln to acknowledge the inevitable. Accordingly, on July 17, Congress passed the Confiscation Act, repealing the 1792 Militia Act and empowering the president to employ black recruits to suppress the Southern rebellion. The call went out for blacks to enlist to fight not only for their freedom but to prove they deserved it—something no white was expected to do. Immediately, Northern cities were inundated with tens of thousands of eager enlistees. By October, there were nearly forty thousand blacks in uniform—though the army decided they should earn only seven dollars per month instead of the thirteen dollars paid to their white counterparts.

In summer 1863, the Emancipation Proclamation spurred Union General Benjamin Franklin Butler to make a momentous move. A maverick who had agitated for the use of black troops, Butler met with leaders of a New Orleans regiment of fourteen hundred free black soldiers. He did not pull punches; he asked if they were cowards, as many whites believed, or if they would fight. A spokesman replied, "Pardon me, General, but the only cowardly blood we have got in our veins is the white blood." Impressed, Butler started organizing these men into the Louisiana Native Guards—the first official black fighting regiment in the Union Army. The guards were central in the first major battle for black soldiers—the assault on Port Hudson, Louisiana, the last Confederate fortification on the Lower Mississippi. Ironically, this bastion of parapets, rifle pits, and long lines of abatis (barricades of sharpened tree branches) had been built by slave labor. This day, it was supported by twenty siege guns and thirty pieces of field artillery. Nevertheless, the mandate was clear: If Port Hudson fell, so would Vicksburg two hundred miles upriver under siege by Grant. The double victory would cede the Mississippi to the Union and cut the Confederacy in two.

On May 27, 1863, the First and Second Louisiana colored regiments led six charges under a ferocious hail of sharpshooters' lead, artillery shells, canister, and grapeshot. They were repelled but undaunted—wounded blacks repeatedly left the field hospital to rejoin the fight only to be wounded again or killed. Their surgeon said later that he had never seen any soldiers "who, for courage and unflinching bravery, surpass our colored." Even though they were rebuffed and lost six hundred men— a staggering toll—their courage did not go unnoticed. The conservative *New York Times* editorialized that their steadiness and bravery "settles the question that the negro race can fight." Louisiana Guards General Nathaniel

P. Banks wrote Major General Henry W. Halleck, general in chief of the army:

> Their conduct was heroic. No troops could be more determined or more daring. . . . Whatever doubt may have existed before as to the efficiency of organizations of this character, the history of this day proves conclusively . . . that the Government will find in this class of troops effective supporters and defenders.

This kind of bravery among black soldiers was not uncommon. On June 7, 1863, upstream from Vicksburg at Milliken's Bend, 160 white Union soldiers and 840 ex-slaves who were mustered barely two weeks earlier engaged a Confederate force of 2,000 Texans in one of the most savage hand-to-hand fights of the war. When the Texans finally drove the Union force back to the river, they brutally slaughtered some captured blacks before their comrades' eyes. In the Union counterattack, both sides clubbed each other with musket butts and stabbed with bayonets until the Union warship *Choctaw* shelled the Texans into retreat.

The blacks lost almost 40 percent of their men. The Ninth Louisiana alone lost 45 percent (which turned out to be the highest percentage of casualties suffered by any unit in the war). The next day, a correspondent of General Grant's wrote from Milliken's Bend: "The capacity of the Negro to defend his liberty . . . has been put to such a test under our observation as to be beyond further doubt." A Louisiana brigadier general added: "It is impossible for men to show greater bravery than the Negro troops in that fight." A black survivor wrote his aunt from the field: "I never more wish to hear the expression, 'the niggers won't fight.' Come with me 100 yards from where I sit, and I can show you the wounds that cover the bodies of 16 as brave, loyal and patriotic soldiers as ever drew bead on a rebel.'' All three summations were understatements about one of the bloodiest and bravest-fought battles in the annals of American warfare. The truth carried to the Union seat. Assistant Secretary of War Charles A. Dana later announced, ''The bravery of the blacks at Milliken's Bend completely revolutionized the sentiment of the army with regard to the employment of Negro troops.'' So, in one sense, this military loss turned into a significant social triumph.

Even though Frederick Douglass's assessment that blacks were ready to fight was clearly true, it took an added measure of pure courage for blacks to fight in this war. The reason was because the Confederacy had warned that captured black soldiers would be treated as insurrectionists. This encouraged Rebels to commit atrocities under the guise of patriotic duty. The most appalling incident occurred on April 12, 1864, at Fort Pillow in Tennessee. A reckless Rebel force of over 1,500, commanded by Confederate Major General Nathan Bedford Forrest, overwhelmed the Union garrison on the Mississippi, defended by 570 soldiers, nearly half of them black. The Rebs charged, yelling, ''Kill all the niggers!''—and suddenly there was a killing frenzy. After the war, 21 witnesses established for a congressional panel that at least 300 Union troops, mostly black, were ''massacred'' after they surrendered. The testimony of Union Cavalryman William J. Mays was shocking for the day:

Voices were heard upon all sides, crying, ''Give them no quarter; kill them . . . ; it is General For-

rest's orders.'' I saw four white men and at least
twenty-five negroes shot while begging for mercy,
and I saw a negro dragged from a hollow log within
ten feet of where I lay, and as a rebel held him by
the foot another shot him. . . . There were also two
negro women and three little children standing
within twenty-five steps from me, when a rebel
stepped up and . . . shot them all.

When news of the Fort Pillow massacre reached the
troops, blacks fought with intensified emotion. Whole
regiments charged into battle yelling, ''Remember Fort
Pillow!''

Port Hudson and Milliken's Bend were not excep-
tions. Another example: the incredible valor of black soldiers in the pivotal battle of New Market Heights. At
stake was control of the Confederate capital at nearby
Richmond—the Confederacy's last big stand. And here
was General Benjamin Butler again, commanding his
now seasoned black troops of the Army of the Potomac
in what was to be their finest hour. New Market Heights
was the key Confederate position blocking the thresh-
hold to Richmond on the New Market Road. A force of
a thousand Rebels manned an almost impregnable re-
doubt on the Heights, overlooking a swampy creek, a
ravine, and two successive rows of impassable abatis on
its leading slope. Butler, the champion of black soldiers,
had never actually been in battle himself. So when he
learned that a white unit under veteran General W. S.
Hancock had been rebuffed at the Heights, he was eager
to showcase his troops and prove himself at the same
time.

It was his plan for a sneak attack that General Grant
approved for just before dawn on September 29, 1864.

Its success would rest on the performance of the nine black regiments of the Eighteenth Corps USCT (officially, the black regiments were identified as the United States Colored Troops, or USCT), while their white counterparts would attempt to seize the Confederate works at nearby Fort Harrison. At 4:30 A.M., the Third USCT crossed the creek and started up the steep hill toward the first abatis. The Rebels started firing and shouting, ''Come on, darkies, we want your muskets!'' Artillery and grapeshot rained down as the blacks waited for their axmen to chop through the barricade. It cost three sets of axmen before the troops could pour through a narrow opening, only to be stopped by the second abatis fifty yards from the crest. Men were cut down, according to Sergeant Major Christian Fleetwood, ''as hailstones sweep the leaves from the trees,'' while brave new axmen hacked their way through.

Two-thirds of the way up, every white officer was killed in the rush. The only ones left to lead were black corporals and sergeants. In this thirty-minute charge, blacks performed so many acts of heroism it lead to twelve Congressional Medals of Honor. The most memorable may have been when Corporal Miles James of the Thirty-sixth USCT saw his arm shattered by a bullet, tied it bravely to his side, and rallied men around him by loading and firing with his good arm while charging uphill. (Only after the battle was won did he allow a surgeon to amputate.) Once the Rebels were run off the hill, General Butler guided his horse between the bodies of his men. In the narrow lane—maybe eighty feet wide by four hundred yards long—he counted 543 of his gallant black troops. He was so moved he made a solemn oath, which he repeated later to Congress: ''May my right hand forget its cunning, and my tongue cleave to the roof of my mouth, if I ever fail to defend the rights of those men who have given their blood for me and my country this day, and for their race forever.''

A brave, disciplined performance by blacks under fire was significant because it demonstrated that they could do the same in society. Unfortunately, it did not wipe out prejudice. Northern politicians made concessions, not for blacks but instead for the ''wounded pride of the South.'' It was an accepted notion that since the South had lost the war and dropped down a peg in society, the government owed *them* a debt. This paved the way for even greater racial abuses during Reconstruction. (This kind of catering to the South is still an issue in politics. Richard Nixon based his Southern strategy on appealing to white racism; so did George Wallace, David Duke, and, most recently, Pat Buchanan.) Southerners could not acknowledge their diminished status or the notion that an African American was their equal. They also refused to accept that an African American might be in a position to give a white person an order. As I see it, most Northern whites were not anxious to intermingle with blacks either, so they tolerated the resistance of Southern whites, as long as they were not out lynching people. Which, of course, they were; because Southern racists always tested the water to see how excessive they could be in their hatred and oppression of blacks. They adopted the old, arrogant slave owner mentality: *If the North wants to free its own blacks, fine; but we decide what to do with ours*. It was the South's way of extracting payback for being defeated in the war, and having their white supremacy handed back to them on the markers of six hundred thousand graves.

After the Civil War, we no longer needed a big army. Since we were now isolationist in foreign affairs, the only place we needed the military was out on the frontier to protect settlers from Indians. So the army was reduced to 54,000 men. Because of the colored troops' great success in the Civil War, President Andrew Johnson recommended on July 28, 1866 that they be incorporated into the regular army for the first time. The act provided for up to 12,500 men distributed in two black cavalry regiments, the Ninth and Tenth, and four infantry regiments, the Thirty-eighth, Thirty-ninth, Fortieth, and Forty-first. In 1869, the army consolidated these four into two, the Twenty-fourth and Twenty-fifth. These units served out the century at forts along the frontier: Texas to New Mexico in the south; Dakotas to Montana in the north; east to west from Minnesota to Arizona. In harsh, dangerous conditions, they performed a remarkable variety of tasks. They built roads; repaired telegraph wire; escorted cattle herds; fought Indians and bandits; guarded lumber trains and wagon trains; and protected settlers, miners, and surveyors. As a combination army-police force, they were involved in every major army campaign on the frontier.

Despite their legacy of heroism in the Civil War, black soldiers faced the same old prejudices in peacetime. They were commanded only by white officers; they had to overcome white hostility typified by their used equipment and worn-out horses (usually castoffs from the Seventh Cavalry of General George Armstrong Custer); their quarters were so ramshackle and damp, many men caught pneumonia. Colonel Benjamin Grierson, commander of the Tenth, complained but was continually ignored. He insisted, however, that the army address his men as the Tenth Cavalry, not the Colored Cavalry as was the custom. Ironically, some of their Indian counterparts—also oppressed—referred to them scornfully as "black white men."

Between 1870 and 1890, the Ninth and Tenth Cavalries fought sixty battles, including dozens against Geronimo and Victorio. They earned eighteen Medals of Honor, eleven of which were awarded to members of the Ninth (which some white soldiers called the Nigger Ninth). Colonel Grierson praised their "gallant and zealous devotion to duty." Their protection of settlers was legendary. But gratitude was not the rule. While blacks on the Plains risked their lives every day in defense of others, racism and injustice dogged their heels:

- In early 1870, at Jacksboro, Texas (population two hundred; with twenty-seven saloons), the locals enjoyed baiting black troopers when they came to town on leave from nearby Fort McKavett. One afternoon, a white settler named John Jackson murdered Ninth Cavalry Buffalo Soldier, Private Boston Henry, for sport. When two black cavalrymen came to arrest Jackson, he killed them, too. He was tried and found not guilty on all counts by a jury of his white peers.

- In February 1878, Buffalo Soldiers from Fort Concho, Texas, were lured into a shootout with cowboys in the redneck town of San Angelo. Two soldiers were killed and several wounded.

- On January 31, 1881, Private William Watkins of the Tenth Cavalry, Fort Concho, sang and danced for drinks in a San Angelo saloon. When he started to leave, a white gambler named Tom McCarthy insisted he continue. Watkins said politely, "I'm too tired," and McCarthy shot him in the head. The sheriff declared it was "only a minor crime to kill a nigger" in San Angelo, and let McCarthy go. Three days later, a sign was posted in town:

We, the soldiers of the United States Army, do hereby warn cowboys, etc., of San Angelo and vicinity, to recognize our rights of way as just and peaceable men. If we do not receive justice and fair play, which we must have, someone will suffer; if not the guilty, the innocent. It has gone too far; justice or death.

It was signed: "U.S. Soldiers, one and all." Colonel Grierson forced a trial in Austin. But McCarthy was acquitted by the all-white jury. Two companies, one black and one white, marched into San Angelo to arrest the sheriff and commit mayhem. Grierson intervened and confined his troops to Fort Concho for the summer.

On June 14, 1877, Lieutenant Henry Ossian Flipper, son of a Georgia slave, became the first African American to graduate from West Point. During his four years there, cadets rarely spoke to him, yet he maintained his dignity and composure. He recorded this adversity later in his book, *Colored Cadet at West Point*: "I want nothing, not even recognition, unless it be freely given, hence I have not forced myself upon my comrades." After graduation, Second Lieutenant Flipper was assigned frontier duty at Fort Sill, Indian Territory, as the first black officer of the Buffalo Soldiers. There, he was befriended by Captain Nicholas Nolan, the captain's wife, and her sister, Mollie Dwyer, who often accompanied Flipper on horseback rides around the post. But when Flipper was sent to Fort Davis, Texas, in 1880, white

officers disapproved of his continuing friendship there
with Mollie Dwyer.

The new commanding officer, Colonel William R.
Shafter, and other white officers openly resented having
to serve with a black officer. One of Flipper's civilian
friends warned him of a plot to oust him, but he paid no
heed. At twenty-four, he was full of himself as post quartermaster and commissary officer in charge of housing,
food, water, equipment, transportation, financial records,
and the accounting of post funds in the quartermaster's
vault. Then in May 1881, Colonel Shafter mysteriously
ordered Flipper to remove three thousand dollars of post
funds from the vault and store the money in his private
quarters. This worried Flipper because officers he distrusted also had access to the keys.

Sure enough, when Shafter inspected the funds by surprise on July 8, 1881, he discovered $1,440 missing.
Flipper suspected two officers, particularly Lieutenant
Charles Nordstrom, who was in love with Mollie Dwyer
and whom he had recently spotted prowling around his
quarters at night. But Flipper had no proof. And he had
acted indiscreetly himself by permitting his laundress,
Lucy Smith, to store her personal belongings in the same
trunk where he kept the funds. He could not be sure she
wasn't the culprit, so he wrote a personal check to cover
part of the missing funds. He was so well liked in town
that some citizens raised the rest. But Colonel Shafter
brought him up on charges anyway.

Even when Shafter recovered some of the missing
money from Lucy Smith, he continued his prosecution
of Lieutenant Flipper. This prompted Flipper's lawyer to
claim in court that the real issue was not stealing but
''whether it is possible for a colored man to secure and
hold a position as an officer in the army.'' And though

Flipper had clearly been derelict in his duty and un-characteristically careless, the verdict seemed to bear him out. On December 8, 1881, he was found innocent of embezzlement but guilty of "conduct unbecoming an officer and a gentleman." Though this was a misde-meanor (for which Flipper should have been issued a reprimand or assigned extra duty), Shafter recommended the felony penalty of a general court-martial. So on June 30, 1882, despite a personal appeal by Robert Todd Lincoln, son of the former president and then secretary of war, Flipper was dishonorably discharged.

However, he did not fade away in disgrace. He went on to have a remarkable career as a surveyor and civil engineer. Henry Flipper was so highly regarded that be-tween 1893 and 1902, he served as a special land claims agent for the U.S. Justice Department. In that capacity, he was personally responsible for the government's re-claiming hundreds of thousands of acres of valuable land for the public domain. Later, he served as a translator for the Foreign Relations Committee and helped to su-pervise construction of the Alaskan railway system. But while he repeatedly appealed for a new trial to vindicate his name, the army kept turning him down. Until his death at eighty-four in 1940, he had to bear the burden of his disgrace.

In 1972, the army reopened Henry Flipper's case at the urging of a Georgia schoolteacher. After reviewing the trial, the board unanimously reversed the court-martial and, on February 11, 1978, awarded Flipper a posthumous honorable discharge. Shortly thereafter, the governor of Georgia issued a proclamation commending Flipper's devoted service to his country. Today, there is a bust of Henry Flipper in the cadet library at West Point in his honor.

But once again: too little, too late.

Following the Indian Wars, the army downsized again to twenty-five thousand. As African Americans flooded cities for jobs, racism intensified. Especially down South where blacks were disenfranchised through black codes, literacy tests, poll taxes, grandfather clauses, and white primary systems. Congress failed to address the problems. Through segregation of public facilities, blacks in both the North and South experienced the same social evils of pre-Civil War days. The "separate but equal" concept established by the Supreme Court in *Plessy v. Ferguson* (1896) made it possible for a double standard to be applied across the board. By legalizing segregation in society—as long as accommodations were "equal"—it also validated separate units for blacks in the military. Who knows how much this backsliding contributed to the wave of black lynchings that followed—more than one hundred a year through 1904 and double digits for years after that?

Despite the rising climate of hate, blacks were still willing to fight for their country. After the *Maine* exploded in Havana Harbor on February 15, 1898 (22 black sailors among the 250 killed), 16 volunteer African-American regiments were mobilized to fight overseas, the first time blacks would defend America on foreign soil. Among the first were the four black regiments of the West: the Ninth and Tenth Cavalries and Twenty-fourth and Twenty-fifth Infantries. At the time, they were the most famous fighting regiments in the military; they had more than proved their mettle as soldiers and men. For six weeks in May and June, black units camped near racially charged Tampa and Lakeland, Florida, and Chickamauga Park, Georgia. This was also the first time black troops had ever been stationed in the hostile Southeast (in the early 1890s, one company of the Tenth was stationed in Virginia, but was quickly moved west when local whites threatened violence). Tension was so high, regimental officers confiscated black troopers' sidearms to prevent incidents like those out West.

Nevertheless, in Tampa, members of the three-thousand-strong Twenty-fourth and Twenty-fifth Regiments had run-ins with white civilians all over town. In one, a druggist refused to serve them soda water, warning them: "You damned niggers better get out of here . . . or I will kick you black sons of bitches out." Words were exchanged and when he went into his adjoining barbershop and then returned with two pistols, the soldiers shot him to death on the spot. Another incident occurred when a drunken white Ohio volunteer grabbed a two-year-old Negro child from his mother and held him upside down with one hand and spanked him with the other. Then several others used the petrified child as a target while they took shots to see how close they could come without hitting him. One bullet passed through the child's sleeve. But he was unhurt when they returned him to his hysterical mother. Later, in revenge, men from the Twenty-fourth and Twenty-fifth brawled with Ohio volunteers and then rampaged through white businesses in town that refused them service. Since neither the provost guard nor the Tampa police could stop the riot, the Second Georgia Volunteer Infantry obliged by putting twenty-seven black soldiers, and some whites, in the hospital. Next day, *The Atlanta Constitution* editorialized that these events "clearly proved that army discipline has no effect on the Negro." This was the biased version that other newspapers then reported to the nation.

Black soldiers were right to be incensed. These men were going off to fight a war for America—again. Heroes from the frontier who had already risked their lives, riding through sand dunes in 105 degrees, fighting bandits, and hostile marauders from Mexico, and renegade Indians, to try to uphold our Republic. And they end up in Tampa where this ignorant racist feels his integrity is threatened by black men shopping in a "white" store. This incident that has been lost in history is really the whole problem in microcosm: somebody's petty pride and tyranny imposed on somebody else. The way to prevent people from thinking like that is to ensure that everyone lives in an integrated society so we develop a healthy view of people different from ourselves. Had black people ever shopped in that druggist's store before, perhaps he would not have felt so threatened. He would have seen that blacks are people just a little darker than him. And maybe he would not have gone for a gun.

To add to those petty injustices in Tampa, when the black regiments shipped out on June 6, some transports were suddenly segregated: blacks on one side, whites the other; or whites on top decks, blacks below. It was truly absurd aboard Government Transport 14, the ironically named *Concho*, where the Twenty-fifth was segregated from the white Fourteenth Infantry on a damp, unlit, suffocating lower deck, even though they had served in Montana together and liked and respected each other. But even this treatment could not deter the black soldiers from doing in Cuba what they had always done best in battle: Fight bravely, and well, and win.

Ask most Americans what they remember about the Spanish-American War and you will probably hear the

Maine, Teddy Roosevelt, and the Rough Riders taking San Juan Hill. That was all I knew, too. Until I read the accounts of Tenth Cavalry Sergeant Horace W. Bivens in the 1899 book *Under Fire with the Tenth U.S. Cavalry*, which told of forgotten black contributions to our military history. According to Bivens and numerous other eyewitnesses, it was the courage and heroics of the *black* regiments, not Teddy Roosevelt's boys or any other white units, that secured the major victories at Las Guásimas, El Caney, and especially San Juan Hill. Since Horace Bivens's account was so obscure (until 1993, when the University of Colorado Press republished *Under Fire*), history did not record the truth about these battles. The government issued its official propagandist version also in 1899, and that is what people read and believed.

On June 24, 1898, the black Ninth and Tenth Cavalries came to the rescue of Colonel Teddy Roosevelt's First Volunteer Cavalry, or Rough Riders, in the first major action of the war. It happened at a gap in the hills overlooking Santiago called Las Guásimas ("hog nut" trees). The Spanish considered the fight a test of their invaders, and it set the tone of the ten-week war. The volunteer Rough Riders took the lead in the Las Guásimas advance but they were only 250 strong; the other 250 remained on the beach preparing to head to Santiago. They were also inexperienced. Novelist Stephen Crane, serving as war correspondent for the *New York World*, rode with the Rough Riders and found them shockingly careless and naïve. (He wrote later: "They wound along this narrow winding path, babbling joyously, arguing, recounting, and laughing; making more noise than a train going through a tunnel.") Given that their ranks were composed of actors, New York policemen, gamblers, escaped convicts, and wealthy dilettantes who had never been in war, and also that someone had "mislaid" the donkeys transporting their machine guns, it was not surprising they were quickly pinned down on three sides by Spanish snipers in palm trees and by camouflaged sharpshooters. Eventually, they were able to creep up the hill through dense undergrowth, but were unable to charge.

That was when General Wheeler arrived with the First Regular Cavalry Regiment, including the black Buffalo Soldiers. Immediately, the Tenth, under Captain John Bigelow, executed the first charge up the steep hill at the strongest Spanish position, two lines of Spanish soldiers with superior weapons installed in trenches and behind stone walls. Elements of the fearless black Ninth and Tenth Cavalries scurried past the Rough Riders, using their Indian Wars tactics of charging headlong, shooting on the run, then creeping low and patiently picking off their prey. They were so expert at this tactic that many times numerous men's bullets hit the same sharpshooter's head the instant he peeked above a bush. Eventually, Spanish soldiers took to firing blindly over the trench tops without exposing *any* part of themselves. Also, when black soldiers charged, they shouted chilling Comanche war whoops and looked possessed. A Spanish officer later remarked, "What especially terrified our men was the huge American Negroes. We saw their big, black faces through the underbrush, and they looked like devils. They came forward under our fire as if they didn't the least care about it." A white soldier said, "I never saw such fighting as those Tenth Cavalry did. They didn't seem to know what fear was."

According to Sergeant Louis Bowman of the Tenth, without their aid, "the Rough Riders would have been exterminated.'' A white corporal related the death of two white Rough Riders in the battle to an Associated Press reporter this way: ''They were with the Rough Riders and ran into an ambuscade, though they had been warned of the danger. I am not a Negro lover. My father fought with Mosby's Rangers, and I was born in the South, but the Negroes saved that fight, and the day will come when General Shafter [ironically, the man who court-martialed Henry Flipper] will give them credit for their bravery.'' John J. ''Black Jack'' Pershing, a staunch supporter of black troops and a young officer of the Tenth in Cuba (later destined to command all U.S. Army forces in Europe during World War I), insisted that the Buffalo Soldiers' routing of the better-armed Spanish and taking of the blockhouse at Las Guásimas actually won the war.

Nevertheless, despite the fact that the Buffalo Soldiers saved the Rough Riders' lives, and that black Private Augustus Wally won the only Medal of Honor that day, the papers back home reported that the Rough Riders heroically took Las Guásimas.

Next came El Caney, a strategic hill named after its nearby town. At the top, the El Visa stone fort and four blockhouses were defended by five hundred Spaniards. Since it overlooked San Juan Hill, the fort had to be taken first. Of the sixty-six hundred troops assaulting the heights, only the Twenty-fifth Infantry was black (15 percent). Yet, once again, they saved the day. After five hours of no progress under sweeping fire, the men of the Twenty-fifth charged the fort and blockhouses, whooping and shooting. This inspired the white Twelfth Infantry to cover their flank. The most disputed event was when soldiers of the Twenty-fifth stormed the heights and one recovered the Spanish flag, until a white soldier, dressed as an officer of the Twelfth, demanded it. Later, the Twelfth took credit for taking the hill and the flag. But the facts were that the Twelfth came up only after the firing had nearly stopped. And the white soldier who was in the fort first was James Creelman, a Hearst newspaper correspondent who snuck in the back when the Spanish defenders had fled. Private T. C. Butler of the Twenty-fifth was the first *soldier* to enter the fort and find the flag. Mistaking Creelman for an officer, he was obliged to relinquish the regiment's prize. But not before taking the precaution of tearing off an edge for proof. Later testimonies of eyewitnesses, including regimental officers, overwhelmingly supported Private Butler's version.

The worst case of subterfuge was the credit assumed by Teddy Roosevelt for taking San Juan Hill. It just wasn't true. Let me digress. On July 4, 1995, I was in New Mexico with a friend who is an archaeological historian. I had mentioned my interest in the Buffalo Soldiers and he gave me a rare book he had hunted up. It was the official U.S. government account of the Spanish-American War. I took it to my hotel room in Santa Fe and read a summary of the Battle of San Juan Hill and noticed a caption on a photo praising "The Gallant 71st New York Volunteers." This struck me immediately; I knew that the Seventy-first New York Volunteers had *turned and run* in the heat of that battle and were replaced by the black Twenty-fourth Infantry.

What really happened was that when the Seventy-first came out of the jungle growth, low on the hill, into withering fire from the summit, they withdrew back into the woods. This outraged Brigadier General Jacob Ford Kent, former commander of the black Twenty-fourth and now commanding the Seventy-first. He admonished the Seventy-first, "For the love of country, liberty, honor and dignity; in the name of freedom, in the name of God; for the sake of dear mothers and fathers, stand up like men and fight and go to the front." But most cowered in the bushes while others retreated farther away. Kent then ordered Colonel E. H. Liscum to take the lead with the Twenty-fourth. This was corroborated by Tom Horn, a bounty hunter who had fought with the Buffalo Soldiers in the Apache wars and was now with a cavalry detachment in charge of horses. In his own account of his experiences in Cuba, he said he arrived at San Juan Hill with horses for the Seventy-first to ride up the hill when the regiment hid and ran and refused to fight. Obviously, they did not need the horses.

When half the officers were killed or wounded, troops deployed themselves. At first, it was chaos; Roosevelt ended up in charge of not only his own men but also of a sizable group of the Tenth Cavalry who came up in support. He was faced with an unexpected obstacle: the taking of well-fortified Kettle Hill at the base of San Juan Hill. Marksmen of the Ninth and Tenth, under fire from 6 A.M. to 1:30 P.M., wore out the Spanish trenches with small mountain cannons and carbines, allowing the Rough Riders and other units to make their way slowly up the hill. Meanwhile, on the southern slope of San Juan Hill, the Twenty-fourth took the brunt of the fire as they charged the Tenth Spanish Company (wounded Spanish officers later confirmed that the thickest fire was aimed at the black troops) and never wavered. The Tenth took the brunt of fire on Kettle Hill until it was clear, easing the assault on San Juan Hill. When San Juan Hill was finally secure, a wounded white lieutenant pointed out that the Tenth had once again "saved the Rough Riders from destruction" by performing deeds of heroism "which have no parallel in the history of warfare."

For example, Sergeant George Berry, a thirty-year veteran color-bearer for the Tenth, was the first soldier to reach the summit. On his way, he retrieved the discarded banner of the Third Cavalry after its bearer was shot and carried it along with the Tenth's banner all the way to the top under intense fire.

Blacks had again proved their mettle and earned the respect of whites with whom they had fought. A few newspaper accounts like this one carried the truth back home:

> The test of the Negro soldier has been applied, and today the whole world stands amazed at the valor and distinctive bravery shown by the men, who in the face of the most galling fire, rushed onward, while shot and shell tore fearful gaps in their ranks. These men, the Tenth Cavalry, did not stop to ask was it worthwhile to lay down their lives for the honor of the country that has silently allowed her citizens to be killed and maltreated in almost every conceivable way; they did not stop to ask would their dead bring deliverance to their race from mob violence and lynchings. They saw their duty and did it.

When they arrived back in the United States, the black soldiers were honored with scattered luncheons and parades. The Tenth Cavalry marched down Pennsylvania Avenue and were reviewed by President McKinley. But sentiment quickly turned. Although Teddy Roosevelt had been effusive with praise for them while in Cuba, he betrayed the black soldiers at home. While he publicly inflated the miserable performance of his Rough Riders and insisted the Seventy-first New York fought admirably, he criticized black troops for being "peculiarly dependent on their white officers"—an obvious, and completely false, slur. He called the black troops "laggards" who tended to "drift to the rear," and he volunteered a story about having to draw his pistol to keep blacks from running away at San Juan Hill. He had done so but he had misinterpreted the action of the blacks. The men he stopped had been ordered to the rear by a white officer to retrieve ammunition and supplies. It was Roosevelt's racist assumption, at the time, that blacks rushing rearward during a fight must be retreating—even though he, of all people, obviously knew better. Not only that, but by the time he offered up this story for public consumption in the States, he knew the truth. Yet, obviously, he preferred the fabrication.

After the war, five of the men Roosevelt had branded "laggards" won the Congressional Medal of Honor and then returned to an ungrateful, racist society. Roosevelt became governor of New York and president of the United States.

After Cuba, elements of all four black regiments served in the Philippines between 1899 and 1902. They were sent as part of a seventy-thousand-man U.S. force to suppress the independence insurrection of Emilio Aguinaldo. But something unprecedented happened. Most of these soldiers were so disillusioned about the rising prejudice at home, they sympathized with the oppressed Filipinos. One reason was that Filipinos were brown. Another was that the imperialistic Spanish were their slave drivers. So blacks started thinking: "Why are we over here? We should *help* them, not fight them.

They're just like us." They were uneasy about crushing a movement by other "colored people" seeking freedom. And they felt more strongly about it than during the Indian Wars, because the Indians they fought did not care who they killed, including blacks.

These doubts led to an unusually high number of defections. And while almost all the white deserters left the Philippines because of petty discipline problems, most of the black deserters joined the enemy insurgents. Some were eventually hung; one died of disease; many had death sentences commuted, ironically, by President Roosevelt; most ended up serving life at hard labor. (The same phenomenon happened seventy years later in Vietnam where blacks started identifying with the Vietnamese and their struggle against American imperialism. It confused them because here they were fighting for the oppressor again. Didn't Muhammad Ali refuse to be drafted by saying, "Ain't no Vietcong ever called me nigger"? That was a profound statement—it was exactly what black soldiers were thinking in that war. And it was almost surely how they felt in the Philippines.)

On September 25, 1900, the *Cleveland Gazette* ran a letter from Sergeant Patrick Mason, Twenty-fourth Infantry, Philippines, which read in part:

> I have not any fighting to do since I have been here and don't care to do any. I feel sorry for these people and all that have come under the control of the United States. I don't believe they will be justly dealt by. The first thing in the morning is the "Nigger" and the last thing at night is the "Nigger." You have no idea the way these people are treated by the Americans here . . .

What is so interesting is Mason's reference to white Americans calling Filipinos ''niggers'' and his statement that ''you have no idea the way these people are treated *by the Americans here''*—as if he no longer considered himself an American. This brief letter was a little warning of bigger wars to come, at home as well as abroad.

At home, racial bias was simmering. In the army, blacks and whites were increasingly separated. Blacks were much more restricted in their outside contacts with white civilians. The army's attitude mirrored society's; the appreciation and general esprit de corps established over the years by the Buffalo Soldiers had dried up. Now, almost any tense situation between the races became a tinderbox. It finally exploded in August 1906 in Brownsville, Texas—a state that had always been a battleground of prejudice for blacks.

Though 80 percent of Brownsville's seven thousand citizens were Mexican, they were staunchly against the presence of blacks. In spite of protests to their senator, the army sent three companies of the Twenty-fourth Infantry to nearby Fort Brown. Those men immediately encountered conflict in town. It started with three callous incidents: a local custom official pistol-whipped a black soldier for not moving off the sidewalk when his lady friend passed; another custom official shoved a drunken black soldier into the river for refusing to pay a ferry toll; and an unidentified man apparently assaulted a local white woman, but ran when she screamed. The next day, the *Brownsville Daily Herald* ran an inflammatory headline: INFAMOUS OUTRAGE—NEGRO SOLDIER INVADED PRIVATE PREMISES LAST NIGHT AND ATTEMPTED TO SEIZE A WHITE LADY. But they had no corroboration. The next day, the story expanded: Now it was definitely *a black soldier* who grabbed the woman by the hair and dragged her screaming down the street. (What happened to the "private premises" premise?)

Around midnight on August 13, a group of 10 to 20 men fired rifle shots into buildings just outside Fort Brown. They barely missed a woman at home with her five children; wounded a police officer; and killed a white bartender. After the ten-minute spree, the shooters disappeared. No one saw them. Nevertheless, the towns-people concluded that black soldiers were the culprits. Some even called for revenge against "the nigger soldiers." The post, which had been mustered by the alarm and found all 167 men accounted for, insisted civilians were the raiders. Both sides held inquiries. Even though the town had made up its mind beforehand—8 white civilians told the mayor they saw black soldiers shooting, though, in fact, they saw nothing; 1 claimed he could recognize "Negro voices"—it was somehow enough to convince the post commander. He decided his men had planned and executed the raid.

On the strength of this, President Roosevelt ordered the black batallion moved to Fort Reno, Oklahoma, "where there are white troops." Then he issued an ultimatum: If the perpetrators did not appear quickly, all three companies would be dishonorably discharged and barred from reenlistment. When no one stepped forward, government investigators called it a conspiracy of silence. Roosevelt dismissed all 167 soldiers, without a hearing or opportunity to face their accusers. Even the *Army and Navy Journal* said: "The finding against the Negro soldiers is based upon the testimony of white men, given under circumstances that deprive it of all value as legal evidence." No one cared. All 167 careers were ruined based on hearsay and racist innuendo.

Everyone knew that if these were white companies, they would still be in service.

Thanks to Ohio Senator Joseph Foraker, a special board of inquiry was formed in 1908. Although key doubts were raised, the board made no decision. A year later, Foraker arranged for an army rehearing. But the fix was in; five generals took testimony from eighty-two soldiers, yet ignored seventy others who applied to be heard. They only accepted evidence pointing to guilt. On April 6, 1910, the generals rendered their illogical decision: Everyone was guilty except fourteen men, who would qualify for reenlistment. A confused *New York World* reporter wrote: "As the report reads, nobody is guilty; therefore everybody is guilty; and everybody being guilty, nobody is innocent, unless it be presumably the fourteen men recommended for re-enlistment. How could they escape being guilty when the entire battalion is guilty . . . ?"

It was blind prejudice—nothing to do with the facts or justice. So 167 innocent lives were ruined, basically because they were black. It took until 1970 for somebody to redress the wrong. After Augustus Hawkins, an African-American congressman from California, read a book entitled *The Brownsville Raid* by John D. Weaver, he spurred a Defense Department review of the case. On April 28, 1972—sixty-six years after the event—the secretary of the army admitted "egregious errors" and issued honorable discharges to all 167 soldiers. Only one was still alive. Dorsie Willis, eighty-six, who'd spent his life after the discharge sweeping floors and shining shoes, remarked, "That dishonorable discharge kept me from improving my station. Only God knows what it did to others." He might have added: *God and the white men who fired the shots.*

By 1917, sanctioned racism had reduced opportunities
for African Americans so severely, they were isolated
from whites, as in the past. When World War I rolled
around, the army weighed the same old "color question": *What should we do with our blacks? Should we
let them fight? If they fight, should we stick them in separate units?* The drift was familiar: *If we let blacks serve,
we have to keep them away from whites.* It was like time
was moving backward.

Eventually, the army formed two African-American
divisions—the Ninety-second (365th, 366th, 367th,
368th Regiments) and Ninety-third (369th, 370th, 371st,
372nd), comprised of some 40,000 troops. They joined
the Allied Expeditionary Force (AEF) in France in
1917–1918. Altogether, the army conscripted about
370,000 African Americans for service (of the more than
2 million who enlisted), including more than 1,200 officers commissioned to lead in combat for the first time.
The Ninety-second saw almost no action under AEF
command; they were mainly used in the war's last assault on the Hindenburg line. It was not their fault. The
AEF did all it could to keep blacks out of the war entirely; and its officers were mostly Southern whites who
resented having to serve with black draftees and routinely undermined the black soldiers' morale. No wonder. Our Virginian President Woodrow Wilson was back
home insisting that the new D. W. Griffith movie, *Birth
of a Nation*, with its overtly racist depictions of ignorant,
cowardly blacks, was "history written in lightning."
And when the Ninety-third was transferred to the French
command, W. E. B. Du Bois, founder of the original Na-

tional Association for the Advancement of Colored People (NAACP), uncovered a document entitled "Secret
Information Concerning Black American Troops." It
was actually an AEF profile masquerading as a French
guide to "understanding" American blacks. In part, it
warned:

> ... Although a citizen of the United States, the
> black man is regarded by white Americans as an
> inferior being. . . . The black is constantly being
> censured for his tendency toward undue familiarity.
> The vices of the Negro are a constant menace to
> the American who has to repress them strongly. . . .
> We must prevent the rise of any pronounced degree
> of intimacy between French officers and black of-
> ficers. We must not eat with them or seek to talk
> with them outside of the arrangements of military
> service.

This was such an amateurish attempt to bias the
French against the imagined "vices of the Negro," it
read like something by the pre-Civil War bigot George
Fitzhugh. In any case, the strategy failed miserably. The
Ninety-third performed so valiantly in the field and be-
haved so graciously as people, the French treated them
like kings. Many wanted to remain after the war. One
officer wrote home: "I have never before experienced
what it meant really to be free, to taste real liberty—in
a phrase, 'to be a man.' "

The Ninety-third delivered no less remarkably in battle than so many other black soldiers before them. The
369th was so brilliant, it received more citations than
any other regiment in the AEF. They were the first
American unit to reach the Rhine and "fought for 191

consecutive days without losing a trench, giving an inch or surrendering a prisoner.'' Throughout American military history, no other combat unit ever fought so long nonstop. It earned 170 individual soldiers, as well as the 369th *as a unit*, France's highest military award, the Croix de Guerre. The 370th and 371st also received the Croix. This was an unprecedented gesture of honor, by *any* army's standards.

But it would not change the bias on the American side. A typical example: Despite 6,000 black casualties in America's ''War for Democracy,'' after the armistice an American officer denied an African-American unit access to the home-bound *Virginia* and substituted a white unit in its place. The home front had been worse, all throughout the war, and it would be the same upon return. The Houston riot was a stark reminder. In July 1917, the 645-member Twenty-fourth Infantry arrived for duty in Houston, Texas. Immediately, there were confrontations with civilians. These men were proud fighting veterans; they refused to abide segregated streetcars, cafes, or even drinking fountains. Fights broke out repeatedly. On August 23, the lid blew off when a member of the Twenty-fourth came to the aid of a black woman being beaten by a white policeman. The officer assaulted the soldier and fired shots that missed him as he fled. But rumors spread at the fort that one of their own had been shot dead by a racist cop.

That night, disobeying orders to stay on the base, some two hundred soldiers of the Twenty-fourth raided the armory for guns and headed to Houston, bent on revenge. They roamed the streets, shooting into stores and intimidating pedestrians. Finally, a melee erupted in which twenty-one whites were injured, and sixteen white civilians (including four policemen) and four black sol-

diers were killed. After an investigation, fifty-four soldiers were court-martialed for mutiny and murder;
forty-one were sentenced to life at hard labor; thirteen
were condemned to hang. Later came sixteen more death
sentences (all but six were eventually commuted to life).
It was like Nat Turner's rebellion all over again. It inspired the War Department to concoct plans to maintain
black troops in small concentrations through the coming
war; and the publicity called into question the integrity
for which black soldiers had fought so heroically since
the Revolutionary War.

Not surprisingly, between World Wars I and II the
army practically decertified its traditional black units.
The majority of officers returned to civilian life because
they saw that advancement was unlikely for blacks. By
the 1930s, a planned decline in black recruitment meant
that only one in thirty soldiers was black—even though
blacks made up 10 percent of the population. The Buffalo Soldiers were hit hard. Out of the four regiments,
only the Twenty-fifth Infantry, isolated at Fort Hu-
achuca, Arizona, was provided any combat training.
Everyone else was relegated to service duties. The Tenth
lost its combat identity when the army transformed them
into horse groomers for white officers and cadets. They
had not been on maneuvers in three years. In 1934, General Douglas MacArthur, chief of staff, denied that black
regiments were being turned into service units. He
claimed the issue was a ''lack of appropriations.'' The
adjutant general's lame reply to an irate NAACP inquiry
was that all cavalrymen must care for horses, and ''the
men of the 10th Cavalry have acquired an enviable reputation in the care of horses.'' As though it was an honor
instead of an obvious demotion.

World War II saw one major political breakthrough

for blacks: the appointment of Colonel Benjamin O. Davis as the nation's first African-American general. Much of the rest was downhill. Over 1 million African Americans (including a large contingent of women: 4,000 enlisted and 120 officers in the segregated Women's Army Corps) were drafted during the war. But 90 percent were assigned to service or labor jobs, and those who did see combat waited four years and served in segregated units until manpower shortages forced blacks into all-white units as emergency replacements. By June 1944, only 134,000 African Americans were serving in Europe, and just one unit, Benjamin O. Davis's Ninety-ninth Pursuit Squadron, saw combat.

But once *in* combat, successes were notable. Between 1944 and 1945, the 333rd Field Artillery Battalion served with distinction in General George S. Patton's Third Army in France, and the 969th Field Artillery Battalion and 614th Tank Destroyer Battalion became the first black combat units on the ground to receive the prestigious Presidential Citation, the nation's highest military honor. Even the black noncombatant Fifty-sixth Ordnance Company distinguished itself in combat by defeating a unit of Hitler's elite Waffen SS troops, killing thirty-six and taking twelve prisoners. That unexpected battle earned them the slightly sarcastic nickname of the "Fighting Fifty-sixth." The all-black 761st Tank Battalion—soon nicknamed the "Black Panthers"—finally got to fight when the Germans damaged all our frontline tank battalions in the Battle of the Bulge. The only fresh unit left, the 761st, comprised of 27 officers and 529 enlisted men, was languishing at Camp Hood, Texas, where it was scheduled to spend the war because of racist quotas. But General Patton had seen these troops train in 1942 and remembered thinking they were the best tankers he had ever seen. So he requested them in November 1944 and gave them key assignments on the front line at the Bulge. They were so inspired that they repeatedly tore up their counterparts in the feared German panzer platoons. In April 1945, they even initiated the liberation of the Buchenwald and Dachau concentration camps. (Ironically, camp inmates were so astonished at their first sight of black people that they thought all Americans were black.) The unit saw combat every day to the end of the war and acquitted itself nobly in battles with the finest German combat troops and tankers in five European nations. In fact, the 761st singlehandedly made the army's policy of no blacks in combat look ludicrous and absurd.

The reactivated Ninety-second Infantry Division also distinguished itself, a delayed triumph after being held back in World War I. Among its more than 7,000 decorations were 3 Distinguished Service Crosses, 16 Legion of Merit awards, 95 Silver Stars, 753 Bronze Stars, and 1,377 Purple Hearts. The famous Tuskegee Airmen of the 332nd Fighter Group performed so outstandingly (1,578 missions; 400 enemy kills, a record 13 in one day, plus a destroyer; 900 medals) that the air force reversed its segregation policies.

Ultimately, it was the amazing courage and devotion of African-American soldiers in all our wars that prompted President Harry Truman to finally abolish segregation in the armed forces in 1948. But it was not until President John F. Kennedy issued an executive order instituting affirmative action in the armed forces on July 26, 1963—193 years after the death of Crispus Attucks—that American military segregation policies were finally finished off. Just in time to lay the pathway for the crowning success: President George Bush's 1989 appointment of General Colin L. Powell as America's first African-American chairman of the Joint Chiefs of Staff— the nation's highest military post.

Crispus Attucks, rest in peace.

CHAPTER 8

DISCOVERY

Lewis H. Latimer

The period between 1840 and 1900 was one of extraordinary expansion for the United States—territorially, economically, and especially industrially. During President James K. Polk's administration alone (1844–1848), the government acquired over a million square miles of new terrain. This extended our western boundaries from the Louisiana Purchase line (roughly from present-day northwest Montana to Louisiana) all the way to the Pacific Ocean. In July 1845, journalist John L. O'Sullivan coined the phrase "manifest destiny" in news articles on U.S. expansionism. He implied that with recent expansion into Oregon and the Southwest, and the annexation of Texas, America was destined to control the North American continent. Constant growth and change was the spirit of the times.

In 1860, only 20 percent of the nation's population lived in or around cities—some six million people. But over the next sixty years, as cities became commercial centers, the numbers jumped to 51 percent, or fifty-three million people. America started to transform more dramatically from an agrarian society to a modern, consumer society. Dramatic population shifts and the rapid rise of industrialization inspired technical advances aimed at making life and work simpler for everyone. Innovation was the name of the game. As an illustration, in 1830 there were only 544 inventions patented in the United States. By 1860, the number shot above 4,000. Between 1870 and 1910, about 1 million patents were registered with the U.S. Patent Office.

Inventors became increasingly important. Charles Goodyear, a New England hardware merchant, invented the rubber treatment process of vulcanization in 1839 when he accidentally dropped a mass of rubber and sulphur on his hot stove and it didn't melt. Samuel F. B. Morse, an artist interested in science, revolutionized communications in 1844 when he announced Polk's presidential nomination over his electric telegraph wire from Baltimore to Washington. By 1848, every state east of the Mississippi, except Florida, was connected by telegraph lines. Thirteen years later, the entire country was hooked up along fifty thousand miles of wire. In 1866, Cyrus W. Field completed a project he started before the Civil War by successfully laying a transatlantic cable between America and Europe. In 1876, just seven years after completion of our first transcontinental railroad, Alexander Graham Bell invented a practical telephone. By the 1890s American Telephone & Telegraph—representing Bell's interests—had installed nearly half a million of his telephones across the country.

One of the most momentous inventions of modern times was Thomas Alva Edison's electric light. It revolutionized almost every aspect of civilized existence. And yet while most people think of the famous white ''Wizard of Menlo Park'' as the man who lit up the world, almost no one knows it was an African American who showed him how to keep it lit.

⁂

Like most heroes of color, African-American inventors and scientists were systematically ignored by mainstream history or otherwise swindled out of their legacies. Since no patents were issued to African Americans until 1863, uncounted inventions by slaves ended up patented by whites. It was like not being able to own land, or vote, or amass any personal wealth or power. Another weapon in the white supremacist armory designed to suppress the African American.

During the last quarter of the nineteenth century, when a flurry of astonishing inventions literally changed the world, almost nothing changed in white America's treatment of blacks. Citizenship was eventually granted, grudgingly, but equality was constantly denied. Blacks were not encouraged to compete, in any field, with whites. And because of the abuses of slavery and the failures of Reconstruction, even though education was high on the African-American priority list, blacks were discouraged from self-improvement at every turn. In spite of these obstacles, black pioneers of invention developed innovations that still rank among the most significant in history.

Lewis Howard Latimer is a prime example.

Here is a man who made vital contributions to the work of three of the greatest scientific inventors in American history: Alexander Graham Bell, Hiram S.

Maxim, and Thomas Alva Edison. He was someone who played critical roles in the development of two of the most important inventions of modern times: the telephone and the incandescent light bulb. Yet few people know anything about Lewis Latimer today, because he did not make it into the history books.

Before Lewis was born, his father's life and inadvertent association with great American heroes, like Frederick Douglass, Charles Lenox Remond, and William Lloyd Garrison, changed history. If the courage to go against the grain to make a mark on the world can be inherited, then certainly Lewis Latimer acquired it from his father. George Latimer became famous for something he would not do. As a young man, this Virginia son of a white slave owner's brother and his slave mistress decided not to endure the brutality of his miserable master, James B. Gray. Since married slaves were not allowed to live together, and because George and his pregnant wife Rebecca wanted their child born free, they decided to escape. So, on October 4, 1842, riding boats north, they alternately hid in steerage and posed as a slaveholder and servant. But even when they arrived in the free state of Massachusetts, they knew they were in perpetual danger of being recaptured as fugitive slaves.

Less than two weeks later, the Latimers were spotted in Boston by a former employee of James Gray, who showed up on October 18 to reclaim his "property." The police promptly arrested George Latimer without a warrant and jailed him, illegally, without filing charges. Meantime, Abolitionists safely hid Rebecca away. When word spread that Gray intended to sneak George Latimer back to Virginia the next day, three distinguished white lawyers, including Abolitionist Samuel Sewell, founder of the New England Anti-Slavery Society (1831), took

George's case, gratis. There was such a public outcry, a meeting was held on October 30 in Boston's famous Faneuil Hall. (By then, Faneuil was known as the cradle of liberty. Crispus Attucks had lain in state there after the Boston Massacre, and the patriots met there to protest British rule.) As one of the meeting's secretaries, Charles Lenox Remond, the first African-American Abolitionist orator, recorded a resolution to raise money for George Latimer's release.

Protests mounted nationwide. William Lloyd Garrison defended George Latimer in *The Liberator* and published a supportive letter from Frederick Douglass—the first words Douglass ever published. When contemporary poet John Greenleaf Whittier glorified Latimer in a poem entitled ''Virginia to Massachusetts,'' the case became a cause célèbre.

In November, despite a Supreme Court ruling permitting Gray custody, Abolitionist Reverend Samuel Caldwell purchased George Latimer for four hundred dollars and set him free. Unfortunately, George and Rebecca had become so famous, they had to keep on the move to avoid recapture. Public outcry arose again; 110,000 Bostonians signed what came to be known as the Latimer petitions to thwart the fugitive slave laws. These petitions led to the Massachusetts Personal Liberty Law prohibiting state officials from paticipating in fugitive slave hunts. There was a ripple effect; the Latimer case would eventually influence passage of two pro-slavery measures: the 1850 Fugitive Slave Act, charging ordinary citizens with the duty of aiding in the capture of runaway slaves, and the 1857 Dred Scott ruling that slaves taken temporarily to free states were not entitled to freedom.

Four years later, on September 4, 1848, as George and

Rebecca Latimer continued to struggle for freedom, their fourth child, Lewis, was born. Social conditions were still so hostile for African Americans, one of the Latimer's neighbors provided their home as a depot for the Underground Railroad. Money was another problem; young Lewis had to work instead of play with other kids. He helped in his father's barbershop, sold newspapers (ironically, including *The Liberator*), and worked nights helping George moonlight as a paperhanger. When Lewis was ten, George left home and never returned; no one knew why. But George stayed nearby and intermittently checked in with his family, leading to speculation that he left because he knew if he was recaptured, the whole family would be sent back to slavery along with him.

Lewis had done well in the Phillips Grammar School (his favorite subjects were reading, writing, and art), although he missed too many days because he had to work. With George gone, he finally had to quit school to help support the family full-time. So at thirteen, he hired on as an errand boy in a law office. Three years later, with slavery abolished and his brothers in the armed forces, Latimer entered the navy. At just sixteen, he served as a "landsman" (mainly a cabin boy) on the Union escort gunboat USS *Massasoit*. He saw battle numerous times and served out the war until his honorable discharge on July 3, 1865.

When he returned home, he was disappointed to find racism still going strong, even in antislavery Boston. In fact, enforced prejudice prevented him from earning a working wage. On a tip from an African-American office girl, he found a job with Crosby and Gould, patent solicitors who needed an office boy with an interest in drawing. Fascinated with the draftsmen's patent drawings, Lewis studied their techniques and spent his three-dollar-a-week wages on secondhand tools and used copies of the books the draftsmen used at work. With only occasional tutoring and little formal education, he mastered the highly technical process on his own. He was so gifted, Crosby and Gould promoted him to junior draftsman. Eventually, he became chief draftsman at twenty dollars a week (the white draftsmen still earned twenty-five dollars), supervising the production of models that accompanied patent applications to the U.S. Patent Office.

In his spare time, Lewis cooked up contraptions of his own. On February 10, 1874, at just twenty-six, he was issued his first patent with fellow inventor W. C. Brown, for an improvement of the water closet for railway cars. The clever invention—a pivoted bottom—opened and closed with the raising and lowering of the toilet seat cover. About the same time, Lewis met Alexander Graham Bell, who had been teaching his father's visible speech method (an alphabet of sounds made by the vocal cords, invented to teach deaf people to "talk" to each other), along with sign language, at the Boston School for the Deaf. In 1875, when Bell was not teaching or lecturing at Boston University, he was busy trying to perfect an electronic device for transmitting the sound of the human voice. On June 2, 1875, he perfected the first practical telephone. Now he needed a patent.

Though Bell had lawyers in Washington to file for his patents, he hired the local firm of Crosby and Gould to prepare his most important blueprints. Bell personally evaluated their draftsmen. And though Lewis Latimer's only experience with electrical devices was drawings he had made for patents on railroad crossing signals, Bell selected him to draw the sketches and blueprints for one of the world's most significant inventions. Patent No. 174,465, based on the critically precise drawings of Lewis Latimer, was issued on March 7, 1876. However, today, when we read about the white British subject Alexander Graham Bell and his revolutionary telephone, nowhere do we also find the name of his key draftsman, the African-American son of slaves Lewis Howard Latimer.

—⦅∞⦆—

In 1879, when the world was lit by flickering oil and gas lamps (the word "bulb" was not yet in use), Thomas Alva Edison invented the incandescent electric lamp. The process of producing and sustaining incandescence—electrically heating a wire or filament to make it glow—was complex and impractical. For fifty years, inventors worldwide had failed to develop an inexpensive, long-lasting filament. Arc lighting, in which a spark made a luminous arc between two terminals, had been discovered in 1802 by Humphrey Davy, who used charcoal connected to a battery to produce a flickering four-inch arc of light. It competed successfully with gas lighting, but was much more costly. And the carbon in charcoal got consumed when it burned. In 1873 in St. Petersburg's Admiralty Dockyard, inventor Alexandre de Lodyguine installed two hundred incandescent lamps, which utilized graphite filaments immersed in nitrogen gas to slow consumption. But these filaments still incinerated too fast. Fellow inventor, Russian Paul Jablochkoff, improved on this with multiple carbon rods that replaced each other as they burned out. Other experiments followed; but incandescent lamps remained too costly for commercial use.

Between 1809 and 1878, at least twenty different types of incandescent lamps were invented. In 1860, a British druggist named Joseph Swan seemed to have the solution when he incandesced a thin strip of carbonized cardboard. But he failed to perfect the vacuum to keep the carbon from disintegrating. Afterward, nearly every major inventor tested filaments made of platinum, the metal with the highest melting point. But without a regulator to control the electrical current, the heat consumed the platinum.

Thomas Edison was obsessed with developing a commercial electric lamp. He experimented with every filament material he could find, from bristol board to Japanese bamboo to exotic plants from the Amazon. (He tested over six thousand different types of vegetation.) In 1879, with new vacuum pumps that reduced the rate of burn, Edison finally succeded with carbonized thread as the most workable filament for the electric lamp. But he knew it would need improvement. So the greatest inventor of all time constantly worried that somebody else would eventually develop a better filament and reap the glory and rewards.

During 1879, Lewis Latimer was out of work. On advice from his sister in Bridgeport, Connecticut, he and his wife moved there and he ended up working as a paperhanger. When he was commissioned to make a routine drawing for a small machine shop, he had no way of knowing that this simple assignment would turn into the seminal event of his career. While Lewis was creating this drawing, Hiram S. Maxim entered the shop and observed him at work. Maxim, chief electrician for the United States Electric Lighting Company, was impressed. "I have never seen a colored man making drawings," he admitted. "Where did you learn?" Latimer said Crosby and Gould. Pay dirt: Maxim once worked for them himself and always admired the excellent work of their draftsmen. So he hired Latimer on the spot as his assistant manager and personal secretary.

This was a godsend. Latimer knew that Maxim was a prolific inventor who had competed with Edison for the development of an incandescent lamp. He had worked extensively with arc lighting, too; and by 1883, he would have thirty-nine patents for electric lighting innovations, including two for an incandescent lamp using carbon strips as filaments. (Maxim's other major inventions would eventually include a steam-powered airplane, a self-regulating electrical generator, and his most famous, the machine gun.)

Since Latimer had been studying the electric light business, he appreciated the promise of working for an electric industry giant like Hiram S. Maxim. In fact, while in Maxim's employ Latimer learned almost everything he needed to know about electric lighting. Both men were especially interested in the incandescent lamp; despite Edison's 1879 patent, incandescent filaments still burned too fast and were too expensive to replace. That was why new electric companies kept sprouting up around the country. Each hoped to be the first to develop and market a long-lasting filament that could light up ordinary people's homes. This was Lewis Latimer's dream, too; so he conducted hundreds of painstaking experiments on his own, testing for the perfect filament that had eluded everyone, including the famous patent holder of the electric lamp himself.

Finally, Lewis discovered how to develop an inexpensive filament that lasted. It was a matter of stuffing fibrous materials, like paper or thin strips of wood, inside tiny cardboard "envelopes," which were then electrically heated in a vacuum. Latimer prevented the materials from sticking to the cardboard by coating it with nonsticky substances, or draping the strips in tissue paper. The key was that while others had tested similar materials, their carbon burned erratically, or shattered the glass bulbs, or incinerated under the intense heat while Latimer's ingenious "envelope" burned evenly every time, and over extended periods. And they could be replaced for pennies.

While history does not record Lewis Latimer's amazing breakthrough, it does record that on February 19, 1881, he became the only person to apply for a patent on "The Process for Manufacturing Carbons." Numerous other historical documents, as well as actual models he created for the patent approval process, establish undeniably that it was Lewis Latimer's inexpensive method of producing carbon filaments that transformed the industry by making electric lamps commercially viable. His patent was issued almost a year later on January 17, 1882, after passing rigorous comparison tests against all comparable inventions, including those of the world-renowned Edison and Maxim.

Nevertheless, since Edison held the 1879 patent on the first "successful" incandescent lamp, it was not surprising that the world—with help from a supportive press—associated Thomas Edison with Latimer's invention, too. There were other factors. This was an era in which African Americans were still regarded as unworthy and inferior to whites, especially intellectually. Therefore, the achievements of African Americans were rarely publicized. And strange as this practice might sound today, inventors who worked for large companies routinely transferred credit for their inventions to their employer. For example, in 1881, while awaiting the filament processing patent, Latimer teamed with fellow inventor Joseph V. Nichols on a patent for an improvement of Edison's incandescent lamp. The simple, yet momentous, application read, in part:

> Our invention relates to electric lamps in which the light is produced by the incandescence of a continuous strip of carbon secured to metallic wires and enclosed in a hermetically sealed and thoroughly exhausted transparent receiver; and it relates more especially to the method of mounting the carbons or connecting them with wires.

This understated "method of mounting carbons" was more critical than it sounded here; the new process significantly extended the life of carbon filaments. But when this major patent was issued on September 13, 1881, Latimer ceded the credit to Hiram Maxim.

However, there were repeated abuses of this kind of trust, especially against black inventors. Maxim and others frequently jumped the gun by taking credit that had not yet been granted to them. For instance, later in 1881, when Latimer and John Tregoning patented a "Globe Supporter," a new base for electric lamps (original models are still on display at the Smithsonian Institute in Washington, D.C.), Maxim publicly named the invention after himself, calling it the Maxim Electric Lamp. Yet Latimer had not yet granted him permission to take credit for the invention, never mind to willfully deceive the public by naming it falsely.

The sad fact was that, back then, employers like Maxim not only stole credit for other people's inventions, but they also stole the profits.

Throughout the 1880s, though Lewis Latimer remained obscure to the public whose lives he had improved, he was regarded as a rising star by people in the electric lighting industry. On behalf of Maxim's company, he had already supervised the installation of electric lights in business offices, commercial buildings, and railroad stations. And he was the supervisor of the installation and operation of America's first electric plants and street lights in New York City and Philadelphia. In addition, in 1881, when he was sent to Montreal, Canada, to fit railroad stations with electric and arc lighting, he was so adept at his business that he taught himself to speak French well enough to write out the crucial technical instructions for his workmen. Decades later, he wrote of this proudly, though typically modestly, in his private journal:

> This was my mighty lesson. My day was spent climbing telegraph poles and locating arc lamps on them with the assistance of my laborers who seemed much impressed with my effort to speak their native language.

In the spring of 1882, Maxim sent Latimer to London, England, to establish the first lamp factory for the British Maxim-Weston Electric Light Company. Latimer was the only man in Maxim's employ who understood all aspects of the manufacturing process—no mean feat, especially for an African American with barely a grade school education. Immediately, however, Lewis faced a familiar dilemma that surprised and disgusted him. The problem was that British businessmen could not abide taking "orders" from an "employee," especially a man of color. Their assumption that black people were workers, not executives, made cooperation that much harder. Although Lewis was repulsed and deeply offended, his journal reflections on the insensitive attitudes of these bigoted Brits is almost genteel:

> . . . The prevailing motif seemed to be humility of the workmen and the attitude that nothing that I can do can repay you for permitting me to earn an honest living. My assistant and myself were in hot water from the first moment to the end of my engagement, and as we were incapable of assuming a humility we could not feel, there was a continued effort to discount us and to that end the leading men would ask us about some process and failing to perform it would write to the U.S. saying that we did not understand our business . . . In nine months time we had the factory in running order . . . and as our easy independence was setting a bad example to the other workmen, we were released from our contract and permitted to return to the U.S.

Not long after Latimer's return, Maxim published an autobiography in which he made no mention of Lewis Latimer. Maybe this, together with Maxim's repeated infringements on Latimer's patents, prompted him to resign in 1883. He almost certainly read the damning charges against Maxim that another inventor, Professor William Sawyer, gave a newspaper around this time: "I know Mr. Maxim very well, and while he is beyond doubt one of the best mechanical engineers in this country, I have no hesitation in saying that in his last attempt at electric lighting he has made a wholesale appropriation of other people's property.'' Sawyer was alluding to Maxim's outright infringements of patents belonging to both Edison and Latimer. But the public, which had never heard of Lewis Latimer, assumed that Sawyer meant Edison. Another ''infringement'' on Latimer— this time on his professional pride.

Unfortunately, when Lewis Latimer resigned from Maxim's company, the country was mired in a deep depression. Jobs were scarce, especially for black people. Then in 1884, he managed two short stints in New York, one with the Olmstead Electric Lighting Company in Brooklyn, and another with the Acme Electric Light Company of Manhattan. Thomas Edison had long been aware of Latimer, particularly through Edison's fierce competition with Maxim to perfect the incandescent lamp. So it made sense when Edison finally hired Latimer to work as an engineering draftsman for the Edison Electric Light Company—Maxim's biggest rival in the field.

In 1886, Edison formed a legal department and appointed Latimer his chief patent expert. His main job was to protect Edison from patent infringements and lawsuits charging the same against Edison. (Latimer spent an inordinate amount of time just fending off Maxim's suits.) Another aspect of Lewis's work was serving as Edison's expert witness in legal proceedings where millions of dollars were at stake. Ironically, though Latimer never received his due for his own scientific achievements, he was recognized for decades as the architect of Edison's major legal triumphs. So he not only helped Edison earn millions in the industry, he also prevented him from *losing* millions in court.

(One other fascinating irony: Despite Lewis Latimer's uncanny legal expertise, Edison twice lost suits to African-American inventor Granville T. Woods. Woods's 150 patents within thirty years, 35 in the electrical business, earned him the nickname of "The Black Edison." In 1881, he established the Woods Electric Company of Cincinnati to manufacture electrical, telegraph, and telephone equipment. In 1884, he patented the steam boiler furnace and formed the Woods Railway Telegraph Company. His work was so impressive, a Cincinnati newspaper called him "the world's greatest electrician." Woods was well known in the industry for his railroad induction telegraph, which helped railroads avoid accidents. In 1890, he invented the so-called third rail, which was immediately adopted throughout New York's train system, causing the white locomotive engineers it had replaced to riot. In 1901, he sold this invention to Edison's General Electric Company; the third rail was so cutting edge, it is still widely in use today. In 1902, Woods invented the electromagnetic railway brake and sold the patent to the powerful Westinghouse Air Brake Company. Woods was so exceptional at his craft that after his second triumph over Edison in court, Edison offered him a consultant job, allegedly for ten thousand dollars a year, then a princely sum. Woods flatly refused. Perhaps that is another reason we do not find Granville T. Woods's name in our history texts today.)

While working for Edison in the 1880s, Lewis Latimer continued to secure patents for his own inventions. He came up with the safety elevator (which he guaranteed against free fall); electrical fireworks; an apparatus for cooling and disinfecting that was mainly designed to sanitize the air in hospitals and community sickrooms; a simple, inexpensive locking rack for holding hats, coats, and umbrellas, used widely in hotels and restaurants; and a book supporter to arrange books and keep them from falling over on shelves, especially useful in libraries.

In 1890, he achieved another remarkable first. As a tribute to Edison, he wrote the first known and most complete textbook on electrical lighting. The 140-page book was titled *Incandescent Electric Lighting: A Practical Description of the Edison System*, and it was illustrated with Latimer's own drawings. Engineers started calling it the electrical bible.

―――∞∞――――

Lewis Latimer's activism in support of African-American rights is even less known than his scientific contributions. Since the 1870s, he had worked tirelessly with civil rights organizations and spoke out often against racism. He kept up a correspondence with Frederick Douglass, at least through 1894. One of Latimer's lifelong friends was Richard Theodore Greener, scholar, lawyer, diplomat, and the first African American to graduate from Harvard University. Greener shared Latimer's activist passion. He once debated Frederick Douglass in 1879 at Saratoga Springs, New York, on the subject of former slaves migrating to Kansas and other points west, and purchasing the cheap tracts of land to work for themselves. While Douglass opposed the so-called great exodus, Greener, as national secretary of the Emigration Aid Society, strongly favored it as a positive effort to attain black self-sufficiency.

In 1894, Greener invited Latimer to Detroit for the National Conference of Colored Men, but Latimer had to decline. Instead, he wrote a passionate statement of his feelings about the plight of African Americans, which partially said:

I am heart and soul in the movement, because:

(1) it is necessary that we should show the people of this country that we who have by our martyrdom under the lash; by our heroism on the battlefield; by our Christian forbearance beneath an overwhelming burden of injustice; and by our submission to the laws of the native lands, proven worthy citizens of our common country.

(2) Because there is no separation of the colored Americans from those of the white American, and it is our duty to show our country, and . . . the world that we are looking to the interests of the country at large, when we protest against the crime and injustice meted out to any class or conditions of our citizens.

(3) Because the community which permits a crime against its humblest member to go unpunished is nursing into life and strength a power which will ultimately threaten its own existence.

(4) Because our history conclusively proves that the attempt to degrade any portion, class, or race of our common people has always been fraught with more danger to the oppressor than the oppressed.

(5) Because an evenhanded justice to all, under and through the law, is the only safe course to pursue, for where might makes right, brute strength

will supersede intelligence in the control of our communities. . . .

But Latimer didn't just care about black people, he cared about all people. In 1906, he taught classes in English and mechanical drawing at the Henry Street Settlement in New York. It was founded by Lillian Wald in 1893 to provide recreation, health care, and job training for immigrants of all races and nationalities (though, at the time, most immigrants there were European Jews). As a child of slaves, it was easy for Latimer to identify with the plight of persecuted people. Maybe that was one reason he never turned down a request from the Henry Street Settlement. Another was certainly that he never forgot—and liked to recall—his parents' story about how William Lloyd Garrison and his busy Abolitionist friends found the time to save their lives and help them gain their freedom. It was a lifelong reminder to Lewis that a little help can go a long way.

On January 24, 1918, Lewis Howard Latimer received his most cherished honor when he was named a charter member of the Edison Pioneers. The distinguished group was composed of twenty-eight men who helped Thomas Edison usher in the age of electricity, pre-1885. Latimer, of course, was the only African-American Pioneer—the proudest distinction of his life. In the 1918 official photograph of this group, seventy-year-old Latimer faces the camera squarely, dignified and exalted, and precisely where he belongs: in the very front seat.

⸻

Lewis Latimer died at home in 1928 at the age of eighty. Obituaries and notices appeared in newspapers across the country. A statement issued at the time of Latimer's death by William Miron Meadowcroft, the Edison Pioneers historian, declared:

> We hardly mourn his inevitable going so much as we rejoice in pleasant memory at having been associated with him in a great work for all people under a great man. Broadmindedness, versatility in the accomplishment of things intellectual and cultural . . . were characteristic of him, and his genial presence will be missed from our gatherings . . . Mr. Latimer was a full member and an esteemed one, of the EDISON PIONEERS.

Over the next forty years, Latimer's name and accomplishments faded. On May 10, 1968, they were briefly revived when a public school in Brooklyn, New York, was dedicated as The Lewis H. Latimer School. In the 1970s, The Henry Ford Museum in Dearborn, Michigan, held exhibitions featuring his life and work. He was saluted again at the Edison National Historic Site in West Orange, New Jersey, during Black History Month in 1984, as well as in ''The Black Scientists and Inventors'' traveling exhibit prepared in 1988 by the Museum of Science and History in Chicago. Press coverage of all these events was negligible, and Latimer is still ignored in mainstream history books.

I know of two major motion pictures that dealt with Thomas Edison's life and career: MGM's 1939 *Young Tom Edison*, starring Mickey Rooney, and the 1940 film *Edison, the Man*, featuring Spencer Tracy. Of course, neither touches on Lewis Latimer; I doubt if any of the writers knew who he was. But Edison's biographers must have been aware of Latimer's role. Yet no biography of Edison that I have read credits Lewis Latimer as an essential player on Edison's team, including three of the most acclaimed: Robert Conot's *A Streak of Luck* (1979); Martin Melosi's *Thomas A. Edison and the Modernization of America* (1990; part of the reputable Library of American Biography series); and Neil Baldwin's 1995 *Edison: Inventing the Century*. Conot's book was hailed as "brilliant" and "the first genuine biography of Edison." Nevertheless, in the six consecutive chapters extensively detailing Edison's quest to perfect the incandescent lamp, there is not a single reference to Lewis Latimer. Nor does his name appear in the index, or the special Reference Guide in the appendices that meticulously list Edison's most significant associates, partners, friends, and employees. Latimer's name is also conspicuously absent in Melosi's book, even though Melosi devotes an entire chapter to the incandescent lamp issue. But the most egregious, to me, is Neil Baldwin's book, because it is the most recent and most exhaustively researched Edison biography to date. (It merited a full-page analysis in *The New York Times Book Review*, boasting that:". . . Baldwin has written a solidly researched book that relies on a wealth of scholarly sources together with his own careful reading of Edison's private papers. . . .") Yet somehow, despite pointing out that Edison relied heavily on carefully selected assistants, Baldwin fails to mention Lewis Latimer, even in passing. I don't know if it is significant, but I believe it is no coincidence that none of these books was written by an African American.

Maybe nothing can do justice to Lewis Howard Latimer's depth of courage and accomplishment. He was not a world explorer, a soldier in war, a rebellious slave, a rugged cowboy. He fought his way up from nothing, nurtured his impressive native intelligence, and, during a time when blacks were not known for their intellectual achievements, wound up rubbing shoulders with the greatest scientific minds of his time—maybe of all time. He knew he was their equal, and they knew it, too.

So maybe it is enough to say that he believed, and his life epitomized, the notion he recorded in an essay he wrote to inspire others: *"We create our future, by well improving present opportunities: however few and small they be."* Here is an African American whose opportunities in life, at the start, could not have been fewer and smaller, but who had the courage and character to follow his gifts, and light up the world with his genius and heart.

CHAPTER 9

CHANGE

Rosa Parks

Southern white supremacists called it black Monday. And it was, for *them*. Because on Monday, May 17, 1954, thanks to the brilliant advocacy of NAACP chief counsel, Thurgood Marshall (destined to become the first African-American Supreme Court justice in 1967), the Supreme Court ruled for the plaintiffs in *Brown* v. *Board of Education of Topeka*. *Brown* was actually five consolidated cases from around the country, each challenging the constitutionality of segregation in public schools. The Court's historic 9 to 0 ruling that separate public educational facilities were "inherently unequal" and that segregation had a detrimental effect on black children sounded the death knell for segregation in America.

The case was named for Oliver Brown because his name appeared at the top of the alphabetical list of petitioners. He had filed on behalf of his eight-year-old daughter, Linda, who was denied entrance to an all-white elementary school just blocks from her home in Topeka, Kansas. She was a perfect symbol of an innocent victim; her name became associated with victory for generations of disenfranchised African Americans. And even though the Court delayed a year before issuing guidelines to desegregate "with all deliberate speed," the decision undermined the 1896 *Plessy* v. *Ferguson* ruling that justified separate accommodations in public transportation as long as those accommodations were "equal." In other words, *Brown* was finally showing segregation the door.

But as President Kennedy once said, "Law alone cannot make men see right." In fact, *Brown* was not only bitterly resisted in the South, but it also caused a backlash of burnings, beatings, and lynchings. In Mississippi, the most segregated state, the Ku Klux Klan increased violence against blacks; Klans in other states quickly followed suit. They had support from newly formed White Citizens Councils, which civil rights leaders called white-collar Klans. Their stated purpose was "to make it difficult, if not impossible, for any Negro who advocates desegregation to find and hold a job, get credit, or renew a mortgage"—economic terrorism. They never said *how* they would accomplish it; they just made it clear they were ready for war.

In 1955, the first salvos were fired at Reverend George W. Lee and Lamar Smith, NAACP organizers who were registering black voters in Mississippi. On May 13, Reverend Lee was ambushed and killed; Smith was murdered two months later. Loose-lipped whites boasted that the two men were killed because they refused to quit their voter registration work. But African Americans knew why they were *really* killed; they were casualties of the same racist war against blacks that Southerners had waged right through Emancipation. One Southern resistance leader, Mississippi Circuit Judge Tom Brady, eloquently stated the white supremacist resistance to *Brown* and desegregation when he declared, ''We say to the Supreme Court and to the northern world, 'You shall not make us drink from this cup.' '' What he meant was: *We will destroy anyone who gets in our way.*

Apparently, young Emmett Till got in their way.

At only fourteen, he was too young to vote and had no idea what *Brown* v. *Board of Education of Topeka* meant. To Southern racists, he was just another ''uppity nigger'' sticking his nose where it didn't belong. But what those people did not count on was that Emmett Till would become even more symbolic than little Linda Brown. In fact, *this* black child would become the catalyst of a civil rights revolution that would tear the nation apart and alter our race relations forever.

⸺⸻⸺

Emmett Till had badgered his mom to let him go to Money, Mississippi, to visit his cousins, just as they had visited him in Chicago. But his Mississippi-born mom resisted; she knew he did not understand the dangers. He had experienced segregation by attending an all-black elementary school, but he knew nothing about segregation *Southern style*.

Before Emmett and several cousins boarded the Illinois Central (where, ironically, they had to ride in the colored section), Mamie Till Bradley drilled her son on how to act down South: Say ''Yes, sir'' and ''No, sir.'' Never look a white person straight in the eyes. Mind the COLORED ONLY and WHITE ONLY signs. And especially: ''If you have to get on your knees and bow when a white person goes past, do it willingly.''

Arriving in Money on August 20, Emmett and his cousins stayed with his great-uncle, Mose Wright, a sharecropper and part-time preacher. For a week, Emmett was the talk of the town, especially among the black kids. Despite a stuttering problem caused by a mild case of polio at age five, he was prankish and bold. He laughed at the way Southern blacks deferred to whites; in Chicago, it wasn't that way. To impress his new pals, he boasted all week about a white girl he knew in Chicago, and showed everyone her photo. On Wednesday, August 28, Emmett and eight cousins drove Mose Wright's old Ford to Bryant's Grocery and Meat Market. They met up with some local kids and fooled around outside. Emmett flashed the photo of the white girl again, bragging that she was his girlfriend. One kid said, ''Hey, there's a white girl in that store there. I bet you won't go in there and talk to her.'' Emmett took the dare.

Inside, he apparently brought candy to the counter to pay the darkly attractive clerk, Carolyn Bryant. She claimed later that he acted brashly and said ''Bye, baby'' on his way out. Carolyn's husband, Roy, had been away hauling shrimp from Louisiana to Texas; but when he returned, he heard the story about a northern black boy ''sassing'' his wife. Three days later, several men, including Roy Bryant and his half-brother, J. W. Milam, entered Mose Wright's shack at 2 A.M. with pistols drawn. Bryant demanded ''the nigger who done the talkin'.'' Mose tried to talk him out of it, until one of them asked how old he was. Wright said sixty-four. ''If you cause any trouble,'' he warned, ''you'll never live to be sixty-five.'' Then Emmett showed himself and they dragged him outside.

The next morning, Emmett's Chicago cousin Curtis

Jones called the sheriff, who picked up Bryant and Milam and charged them with kidnapping. Five days later, a white teenager fishing the Tallahatchie River found Emmett's corpse tangled on a river root. A cotton gin fan was lashed to his neck with barbed wire; an eye was gouged out; his skull was crushed on one side. The body was so deformed, Mose Wright could only identify it from an initialed ring. The charge was now amended to murder.

Surprisingly, the trial was set for September 19, just two weeks after Emmett Till was buried in Chicago. By then, the story had gone national and outraged people everywhere. Hundreds of journalists descended on the segregated courthouse in rural Sumner (where a town square sign bragged: A GOOD PLACE TO RAISE A BOY); the pressure for justice was turned up high.

Though Judge Curtis Swango refused to let Carolyn Bryant testify and inflame the jury, she had already spread the word that Emmett had grabbed her hand in the store and said he'd been with white women before. Four white witnesses testified that Emmett gave Carolyn a wolf whistle when he came out of the store. (Emmett's mother still insists today that was probably just Emmett trying to overcome his stammering by following her advice to ''whistle and blow it out.'') Neither Roy Bryant nor J. W. Milam testified; the entire defense was comprised of testimony by six character witnesses.

None of Emmett Till's cousins testified, either. Curtis Jones's mother forbid him to return to Mississippi because, like the other moms, she was afraid her son might be lynched like Emmett Till. However, Mose Wright did something almost unheard of in the South at the time. In the face of threats against himself and his family, he defied the unwritten Southern prohibition on blacks testifying against whites in court. When asked to identify the men he saw dragging Emmett away, he stood up straight and pointed at Bryant and then Milam, and said emphatically, *"Thar he."* It was one of the rarest and most dramatic moments in the history of the New South: a black man publicly accusing whites of murder. Wright said later, "I could feel the blood boil in hundreds of white people as they sat glaring in the courtroom."

After his courageous stand, three other black witnesses came forward. The most compelling was a young field hand named Willie Reed. He claimed he saw Emmett Till at 6 A.M. the morning of his disappearance, in the back of a pickup truck with two blacks and four whites, one of whom was J. W. Milam. After the truck drove to a shed on the plantation where Reed worked, he heard a beating being administered inside, and a boy's agonized cries, "Mama! Lord have mercy! Lord have mercy!" Later, he saw Milam and others hauling out something wrapped in a tarpaulin and driving away. Later still, Reed saw Milam wash away what appeared to be blood from the bed of the truck.

On September 23, 1955, the all-white jury deliberated just over an hour. Jury foreman J. W. Shaw announced "not guilty" at 5:43 P.M. Afterward, he confided disdainfully to a reporter that it only took so long to reach the verdict because they had all paused to "drink a pop." The case against Milam and Bryant was dead, but the moment the verdict was read, the civil rights movement was born.

There were protest rallies all across the country. NAACP leader Roy Wilkins spoke angrily in Harlem. He said, "Mississippi has decided to maintain white supremacy, by murdering children. The killer of the boy felt free to lynch because there is, in the entire state, no restraining influence of decency, not in the state capital, among the daily newspapers, the clergy, not among any segment of the so-called lettered citizens.'' Meantime, Mamie Bradley lectured across the country, referring to Emmett as a ''little nobody who shook up the world.''

The protests had little effect in Mississippi. An all-white grand jury failed to indict Milam and Bryant on the obvious kidnapping charges. Mose Wright, who had testified at that trial, too, left the state immediately for Chicago. He was aided by the new field secretary for the Mississippi NAACP, Medgar Evers, who would himself be murdered—shot in the back—on June 11, 1963. Admitted racist, Byron de la Beckwith, was arrested because the murder weapon belonged to him; his fingerprints were on the telescopic sight; and he had asked cab drivers for directions to Evers's house the night of the murder. Nevertheless, the trial ended in a hung jury and de la Beckwith went free. New evidence surfaced in 1994 and he was finally retried and convicted. He was sentenced to life in prison. (It was an improvement; it only took Mississippi thirty years and eight months to mete out justice in that case.)

Two months after the Emmett Till murder trial, Roy Bryant and J. W. Milam accepted four thousand dollars from *Look* to tell their version of the story. They arrogantly admitted to white Alabama journalist William Bradford Huie that they had kidnapped and beat Emmett Till, only to scare him—which is what they claimed at trial. But immune now from further prosecution, they went further; they admitted that when Emmett would not apologize or beg for mercy, they felt they had to kill him. They even described the murder: After beating Emmett in the shed, they drove him to the river, made him strip, and used wire to tie a seventy-five-pound cotton gin around his neck. Milam asked, "You still as good as I am?" When Emmett replied, "Yeah," they shot him in the head and threw him in the river.

"What else could we do?" Milam rationalized. "He was hopeless. He thought he was as good as any white man. I'm no bully. I never hurt a nigger in my life. I like niggers, in their place. I know how to work 'em. But I just decided it was time a few people got put on notice."

In the late sixties, when I was at UCLA, I read an amazing book that affected me profoundly. It was Anne Moody's autobiography *Coming of Age in Mississippi*. Moody was fourteen when Emmett Till was lynched. His murder was so savage, it petrified her. This passage about it in her autobiography has never left me:

> Before Emmett Till's murder, I had known the fear of hunger, hell and the Devil. But now there was a new fear known to me—the fear of being killed just because I was black. This was the worst of my fears. I knew once I got food, the fear of starving to death would leave. I also was told that if I were a good girl, I wouldn't have to fear the Devil or hell. But I didn't know what one had to do or not do as a Negro not to be killed. Probably just being a Negro period was enough, I thought.

I remember when I first read this, it gave me chills. I felt like I was living inside Anne Moody's skin. It made me recall, vividly, how Emmett Till's lynching affected *me* when it happened. And I starting feeling uneasy all over again. I was eight years old when I saw a photo of Emmett's body in *Jet* magazine. It made me sick. His face was distorted, gruesomely bloated. I had no idea what happened to him, but my parents discussed it at length; and the *Jet* photo left an indelible image I could never forget.

But that was the point; Emmett's mother had insisted on an open casket and a public viewing because she wanted people to see what senseless racism had done to her child. The day of his funeral, she was addressing the *world* when she asked reporters: ''Have you ever sent a loved son on vacation and had him returned in a pine box so horribly battered and waterlogged that someone needs to tell you this sickening sight is your son—lynched?''

That was *her* way of putting people on notice.

And it worked. Thousands of Chicagoans viewed Emmett's body that day and millions saw the grisly photo from *Jet*. (In 1955 black newspapers, like the *Chicago Defender, Amsterdam News, Pittsburgh Courier*, and *Baltimore Afro-American*, and magazines, like *Jet* and *Ebony*, were among more than two hundred black publications reaching African Americans.)

The murder shocked me; I began thinking of myself as a black person for the first time, not just a person. And I grew more distrustful and wary. I remember thinking: *They killed him because of his color*. In a way, I lost my childish innocence. I felt like I was living in Transylvania; all of a sudden, the color of my skin represented a danger. From then on, I was always aware, like Anne Moody, that I could be hurt or even killed just for being black.

Pretty soon, my relationships started changing in school. For example, I remember that the day we had to rearrange our desks in sixth grade, I was out of the class-room. When I came back, my desk was the only one set apart. One of the kids said, "Yeah, he's *segregated!*" And everyone thought it was funny, except me and the only other black kid in the class. I think the reason I remember that innocuous incident is because it was part of an aftershock from Emmett Till.

The same apprehensions kept bubbling up all through my adolescence. When I was at parties with my parents, there were often discussions about black-white relations, and I started to listen. I remember a man from the Cape Verde Islands who lived in New England and was mar-ried to my mom's best friend. He had what people back then called black consciousness. He would speak in terms of "The Black Man"; around 1960, that was a *flamethrower*. Lightning in the sky: *The Black Man.*

As an adult looking back, it always intrigued me how Emmett Till's murder became so momentous. Of the thousands of black lynchings in this country since Eman-cipation, his was the one that racists could not sweep under the rug; Mamie Bradley had seen to that. Author Clenora Hudson-Weems, a professor at the University of Missouri-Columbia who wrote *Emmett Till: Sacrificial Lamb of the Civil Rights Movement*, said about Emmett's photo, "His bloated face was the ugliness of American racism staring us right in the eye." That was how I ex-perienced it; and how millions of other African Ameri-cans experienced it, too.

Certainly, Rosa Parks. Because when *her* opportunity came up, *she* put some people on notice. And like Em-mett Till, she changed all of our lives.

Just after 5 P.M. on December 1, 1955, forty-two-year-old Rosa Parks concluded her day as a seamstress in the men's alteration shop of the Fair Department Store in Montgomery, Alabama. Rosa was weary—her neck and shoulders ached; her feet were sore. She just wanted to get back to her little home at 634 Cleveland Court and relax before having dinner with her husband. She could not have known that instead of getting her home on the west side of town, her Cleveland Avenue bus was transporting her straight into history.

After leaving work, Rosa strolled to Lee's Cut Rate store to buy pain pills for her shoulders and neck. Then she returned to wait for the bus, as always, at historic Court Square. The square was a reminder of the Old South racism on which Montgomery was founded. Slaves had once been auctioned there; in 1861, at the Exchange Hotel bordering the Square, secessionist leader William Lowndes Yancey inaugurated Jefferson Davis as president of the Confederate States, claiming, ''The man and the hour have met''; it was at the square, too, where Yancy declared Montgomery the first capital of the New South and the cradle of the Confederacy.

Rosa rarely thought about that. To her, Court Square was now just part of the bus-stop landscape. And she barely noticed anymore the familiar Christmas banner proclaiming PEACE ON EARTH, GOOD WILL TOWARD MEN; though the irony of that message was a constant rebuke to African Americans in Montgomery, where white racism and segregation were still the rule ninety-two years after Emancipation. Still, the only thing on Rosa Parks's mind that gloomy Thursday was finding a seat.

Rosa was a slight, bespectacled, soft-spoken woman, well known and respected in the black community. As a longtime secretary in the local NAACP chapter and a dedicated volunteer with the association's youth council, she knew the political scene, but was certainly no activist. (The biracial NAACP was established in 1909 to achieve equal citizenship for all Americans by peacefully opposing discrimination. It was formed in response to the increasing number of race riots, not just in the South but in places like Abraham Lincoln's hometown of Springfield, Illinois, where, in 1908, forty-six blacks were killed and over two thousand fled the city.) In fact, Rosa was so shy and reserved as to be almost invisible; she barely raised her voice, much less confrontational issues.

Rosa let the first bus pass because it was too crowded and she wanted to be as comfortable as possible. The second bus looked more inviting. After paying the ten-cent fare, she headed for the one vacant seat left, in the fifth row. This was the first row of the middle section known as "no man's land," customarily open to blacks if no whites were standing. Rosa took this seat on the aisle and thought nothing of it.

Residents knew by heart the segregation law cited in chapter 6, section 11 of the city code; and there were printed reminders in every bus, reserving the front four rows for WHITES ONLY. The official policy assigned blacks to the rear, based on the number of blacks and whites on the bus at any given time. As more whites boarded, the imaginary color line was supposed to shift farther back, with blacks nearest the line expected to give up their seats. But drivers made it understood that whites must *never* stand. Blacks also understood that if a white person sat beside a black person, the black had to stand because city regulations prohibited public integration. (In 1955, Montgomery's bus law was already outdated compared to those in other Southern cities. For example, Baton Rouge, Louisiana, passed an ordinance in 1953 abolishing whites-only sections and establishing first-come, first-serve seating—though blacks still had to ride in the rear.) The Montgomery bus system was so corrupt, blacks complained often that it was the city's worst arena of racial abuse.

That was nothing new. From the turn of the century, the city's transportation system had been the focus of intense racial strife. In 1900, segregation was instituted on all streetcars. But a surprisingly effective black boycott resulted in an amendment to the Jim Crow law, stipulating that no black person had to give up a seat in the white section unless another was available in the black section. The problem was that bigoted white drivers ignored the amendment. In 1906, the white city fathers went the other way, mandating separate buses for blacks and whites. By 1955, city buses were the chief mode of transportation for thousands of African Americans traveling to their mostly domestic jobs in the white sections of town. Yet white drivers still baited blacks with racial epithets. Another intimidation tactic was forcing blacks to pay at the front and then reboard at the rear. (It was not uncommon for sadistic drivers to drive away before blacks could reboard.) By the midfifties, these drivers had been granted a sort of "special deputy" status by police, empowering them to enforce the segregation law and even arrest violators themselves.

Rosa Parks knew the drill. When she sat in the fifth row that night, she also knew her rights. At the next two stops, whites got on and started filling the reserved seats. At the Empire Theater stop, more whites crowded on, leaving one white man standing. That prompted veteran driver James F. Blake to yell back to the four blacks in the fifth row, "All right, you niggers. I want those seats." No one moved. Maybe it was because the demand was so unreasonable: Why should four black people, including three women, have to stand in the unreserved section just so one white person could sit?

Blake was irate. He warned, "Y'all better make it light on yourselves and let me have those seats." When the man next to Rosa stood up, she just shifted her legs to let him pass. The two women opposite her got up, too. But Rosa slid over to the window seat, unwilling to budge. (White reporters would later insist that her reaction that night was due more to fatigue than courage; but nothing was further from the truth. She had decided firmly that she would not only not move *then*, but that she would never again move in that situation.)

It isn't hard to understand why she "suddenly" decided to resist. It really wasn't so sudden. Never mind her devoted work for the NAACP, Rosa was aware, as a citizen, that in the last twelve months alone three African-American females had been arrested for the same offense. One incident made the newspapers in March; it even happened on the same bus line. Of four black passengers asked to surrender their seats in no-man's land, two refused—an elderly woman and fifteen-year-old Claudette Colvin. "I done paid my dime," Colvin had said. "I ain't got no reason to move." The elderly woman got off the bus before police arrived. Colvin refused to move, so police dragged her, fighting and crying, to the squad car, where she was rudely handcuffed. That brought protests from the black community: Was it really necessary to manhandle and handcuff a fifteen-year-old girl, especially since she had acted within her rights?

Colvin was charged with violating the city segregation

law, disorderly conduct, and assault. With the NAACP
defending her, she was convicted but fined only for assault, the most absurd of the three trumped-up charges.
It was a shrewd ruling; it sent a tough message to blacks
while avoiding an NAACP appeal of a clearly unconstitutional law. Afterward, E. D. Nixon, former Pullman
porter and president of the local NAACP chapter, met
with the indignant young Colvin to determine if she
might make a strong plaintiff in a test case. But she had
recently become pregnant, which spelled trouble; Nixon
knew that Montgomery's church-going blacks would not
rally behind an immature, unwed, teenaged mother who
was also prone to using profanity. She would have problems, too, with the biased white press. So he advised
black community leaders: "She is not the kind we can
win a case with."

Rosa Parks was intimately involved with the case; she
was still disgusted by the outcome. She felt the same
about another recent incident. In October, a white
woman on the Highland Avenue bus had asked the
driver to force eighteen-year-old Mary Louise Smith to
give up her seat for her. When Smith refused, she was
arrested, convicted, and fined nine dollars under the segregation law. She might have been ideal for a test case,
except that her father was a known alcoholic. Nixon
ruled her out as another bad risk.

Rosa was also distressed over another bus outrage.
After a heated exchange on a city bus between a white
driver and an infirm black passenger, the driver had
dropped him off, returned shortly, found him at the same
stop, and beat the disabled man with a metal coin
changer. The NAACP brought suit; predictably, the ail-
ing black man was convicted instead of his brutal, racist
attacker. Well aware of this in her own present dilemma,

Rosa knew there might be more in store for *her* right now than just an arrest.

Something more personal was troubling her, too: James Blake was the same driver who humiliated her once before. In 1943, after she had paid at the front of his crowded bus, he asked her to get off and reboard at the rear. When she refused, Blake evicted her. She never forgot the indignity; it was on her mind when Blake snarled the word "nigger" a moment earlier, and hovered over her now, threatening, "Look, woman. I told you I wanted the seat. Are you gonna stand up?"

So Rosa said, "No, I'm not."

"Well, if you don't stand up," Blake threatened, "I'm gonna have to call the police to come and arrest you."

This was usually all it took. But Rosa did not flinch. The words came rolling off her tongue: "Well then, you may do that." In this simple act of defiance, obscure, nonconfrontational Rosa Parks became one of our greatest African-American heroines. Here was a quiet, courteous, law-abiding woman, seeking only a comfortable ride home; yet in another of those accidents of fate that draw forth character, she decided to challenge not only the law and history, but racism itself.

Even then, her voice was so soft that Blake could barely hear her. He chewed it over and stomped off the bus for the corner phone. While she waited calmly, others piled off. Rosa thought about her childhood, when she had to walk to a ramshackle, one-room, all-black school in rural Montgomery while white kids rode buses to their brand-new school a few blocks away. She never forgot those buses; they symbolized a separate world for whites that was always closed to blacks. And here she was, so many years later, still fighting for a seat on a Montgomery bus.

When the police finally arrived, Rosa was still by the window, cradling her Lee's Cut Rate bag and her purse. One policeman asked if she had understood the driver's request. She coolly said yes.

He could not understand her stubbornness. "Then why didn't you get up?"

"I didn't think I should have to. Why do you push us around?"

That caught him by surprise. He just shrugged. "I don't know. But the law is the law, and you are under arrest."

What happened to Rosa Parks struck a deep chord in the black community. Maybe it was because Rosa was so well known and respected, particularly among NAACP members and other activists; or just the years of senseless abuse overflowing; or the frustration rising again over the Colvin and Smith incidents; or that blacks still fumed about the NAACP leaders killed in Mississippi, the last one just fifteen days earlier; or unspent rage over poor Emmett Till. Most likely it was a combination. Regardless, things started happening that had never happened here before. Things that made African Americans feel hopeful for a change.

Friday morning, December 2, E. D. Nixon phoned Martin Luther King, Jr., the little-known twenty-six-year-old new pastor of the Dexter Avenue Baptist Church. Nixon said, excitedly, "We got it! We got our case!" Naturally, he meant his secretary, Rosa Parks. That evening, Nixon told Rosa herself, "We can go to the Supreme Court with this." Rosa consulted first with her husband, Raymond, and her mother. Both were against it. "The white folks will kill you, Rosa," Raymond pleaded with her. But Rosa made up her mind to cooperate. She told Nixon, "If you think it will mean something to Montgomery and do some good, I'll be happy to go along with it." Her second act of selfless bravery, this time on behalf of everyone else.

At 5 A.M. the next morning, Nixon phoned Reverend Ralph Abernathy (from 1950 to 1961 pastor of Montgomery's historic First Baptist Church) to tell him the news. He and Nixon started planning a strategy meeting with civil and religious community leaders.

Meantime, late Thursday night, Fred Gray got involved. Gray, Rosa's young African-American lawyer (who had previously agreed to represent Claudette Colvin, if her case went further), phoned his friend Jo Ann Robinson, an English professor at Alabama State. As an organizer and president of a three-hundred-member civil rights protest group called the Women's Political Council, Robinson had represented both Claudette Colvin and Mary Louise Smith in unofficial talks with city and bus officials to try to defuse those disputes. She agreed now to help Nixon and Gray support Rosa Parks. Immediately, she called her activist friends and suggested a bus boycott. She knew the statistics: forty thousand blacks rode city buses every workday, compared to twelve thousand whites. A boycott could break the system and paralyze the city. Her friends agreed enthusiastically that Rosa Parks was just the right person to rally behind.

The idea to boycott was not new. Vernon Johns had attempted to start one himself one day on a Montgomery bus. Until he was replaced by Martin Luther King, Jr., Vernon Johns was the fiery, black activist pastor of the

Dexter Avenue Baptist Church. He was fearless of white authority, especially over the Jim Crow codes he detested so fiercely. In Ralph Abernathy's autobiography *And the Walls Came Tumbling Down*, Abernathy relates a story that Johns told him in 1950. Apparently, Johns, then in his sixties and frail, boarded a Montgomery bus and accidentally dropped the dime fare near the driver's feet. "Uncle," the driver threatened, "get down and pick up that dime and put it in the box." Johns snapped back, "I've surrendered the dime. If you want it, all you have to do is bend down and pick it up." The driver was surprised. He ordered Johns to pick up the dime or get thrown off the bus. Johns calmly turned to the busful of black passengers and suggested they all get off with him, in protest. But no one moved; they were too afraid. Later, when telling Abernathy this story, Johns concluded disgustedly, "Even God can't free people who behave like that."

The problem at that late hour on Thursday night was how to get the word out quickly to mobilize the black community, most of whom were still reluctant. Plus, few had access to newspapers and radios. Robinson concocted an ingenious plan: If she had a flier, it could be reproduced and distributed across town in hours. So she quickly created one that read:

This is for Monday, Dec. 5, 1955—Another Negro woman has been arrested and thrown into jail because she refused to get up out of her seat on the bus for a white person to sit down.

It is the second time since the Claudette Colvin case that a Negro woman has been arrested for the same thing. This has to be stopped.

Negroes have rights, too, for if Negroes did not

ride the buses, they could not operate. Three-fourths of the riders are Negroes, yet we are arrested, or have to stand over empty seats. If we do not do something to stop these arrests, they will continue. The next time it may be you, or your daughter, or mother.

This woman's case will come up Monday. We are therefore asking every Negro to stay off the buses Monday in protest of the arrest and trial. Don't ride the buses to work, to town, to school, or anywhere on Monday.

You can afford to stay out of school for one day. If you work, take a cab, or walk. But please, children and grown-ups, don't ride the bus at all on Monday. Please stay off all the buses Monday.

Robinson cut stencils and took them, secretly, to her college. Using an Alabama State mimeograph machine, she stayed up until dawn running 35 reams of paper to produce a total of 52,500 fliers. (She took a huge risk. If officials had learned she had used taxpayer-supported facilities to engineer a boycott against the segregation law, funding for the college could have been withdrawn. At the very least, Robinson would have been fired.) The next morning, Robinson recruited students, church volunteers, and Women's Political Council members to distribute the fliers in schools, churches, bars, stores, and private homes throughout Montgomery.

Though King, Nixon, Gray, and even Robinson expected perhaps a 40 percent to 60 percent response, they were astonished to discover, early Friday morning, that virtually 100 percent of blacks had boycotted the buses. They ran nearly empty all day. (King would later recall, ''They knew why they walked, and the knowledge was evident in the way they carried themselves. And as I watched them, I knew that there is nothing more majestic than the determined courage of individuals willing to suffer and sacrifice for their freedom and dignity.'')

That same morning, the most courageous of these individuals, Rosa Parks, entered the courthouse to the rousing cheers of five hundred supporters outside. Inside, she was convicted of violating a state segregation law (not the city law, according to the original charge) and fined fourteen dollars for disobeying the segregation law. Fred Gray filed an appeal and paid a one-hundred-dollar bond for her release. When E. D. Nixon emerged outside without Parks, who was busy signing paperwork, her supporters screamed at the police guards armed with sawed-off shotguns, ''If you don't bring her out in a few minutes, we're going in after her!'' Nixon was amazed. He said later, ''It was the first time I had seen so much courage among our people.''

That evening, King and Abernathy drove to the special boycott meeting at Holt Street Baptist Church. When they arrived within three blocks of the church and saw hundreds of cars occupying every available space, their first impression was that someone important had died, most likely the deacon. They were flabbergasted at the enormous crowds lining the lawns and filling the alleys and streets. It took them at least fifteen minutes to shoulder through an estimated four thousand people, who cheered them in the churchyard like military liberators. Inside, the church had been jammed to the rafters for over an hour, well over its normal thousand-person capacity. There had never been such an inspired turnout of African Americans committed to a common cause—and it had all come about because of Rosa Parks.

No one knew what to expect. Least of all young Mar-

tin Luther King, who had been selected only that morning as president of the new Montgomery Improvement
Association, which had been invented by Nixon and Abernathy as the official boycott organization. King had
just twenty minutes to prepare the keynote speech. He
did not know then that this speech would be the most
important of his life, and one of the most significant in
American civil rights history. After the singing of the
opening hymn, "Onward Christian Soldiers," King
stood at the pulpit and silence descended. The moment
was at hand, and he rose, passionately, to meet it. He
told the audience they were there for "serious business."
Then he recounted the history of strife in the Montgomery bus situation, invoking Rosa Parks's ordeal:

> Mrs. Rosa Parks is a fine person. And since it had
> to happen I'm happy it happened to a person like
> Mrs. Parks, for nobody can doubt the boundless
> outreach of her integrity. Nobody can doubt the
> height of her character, nobody can doubt the depth
> of her Christian commitment and devotion to the
> teachings of Jesus . . . And just because she refused
> to get up, she was arrested . . .

Next, King addressed the injustice of bigotry, raising
his rhetoric to an evangelical pitch:

> . . . You know, my friends, there comes a time
> when people get tired of being trampled over by
> the iron feet of oppression . . . tired of being flung
> across the abyss of humiliation where they expe-
> rience the bleakness of nagging despair. There
> comes a time when people get tired of being
> pushed out of the glittering sunlight of life's July

and left standing amidst the piercing chill of an Alpine November.

He was setting the tone for the whole civil rights movement by urging drastic, but nonviolent, action so that Montgomery's blacks could always hold the moral high ground:

> . . . Now let us say that we are not here advocating violence. We have overcome that. I want it known throughout Montgomery and throughout this nation that we are a Christian people. . . . The only weapon we have in our hands this evening is the weapon of protest. . . . My friends, don't let any-body make us feel that we ought to be compared in our actions with the Ku Klux Klan or the White Citizens Councils. There will be no crosses burned at any bus stops in Montgomery. There will be no white persons pulled out of their homes and taken out to some distant road and murdered. There will be nobody among us who will stand up and defy the Constitution of this nation. We only assemble here because of our desire to see right exist.

In closing, King tried to prepare his people for a long road ahead. He advised them to work together, if not for themselves, then for the sake of future generations. He urged them to pursue "persuasion," "coercion," and "legislation," so that even if they should fail today, history would still acknowledge the righteousness of their cause:

> Right here in Montgomery when the history books are written in the future, somebody will have to

say, "There lived a race of people, fleecy locks and black complexion . . . who had the moral courage to stand up for their rights. And thereby they injected a new meaning into the veins of history and of civilization." And we're gonna do that. God grant that we will do it before it's too late.

It was not too late; the timing was right. After King concluded, everyone seemed drained. In this lull, Reverend Abernathy outlined the association's three basic demands for changes in the city's bus system: courteous treatment of blacks on all city buses; first-come, first-served seating, with whites sitting in front and blacks in the rear; and the hiring of black drivers on all-black routes.

An end to segregation was not a demand; that would be challenged in court. The cheers inside the church and out in the street, where thousands heard everything over loudspeakers, were thunderous. It was like the war had already been won. "The fear left that had shackled us across the years," Abernathy would later remark.

The Montgomery bus boycott that everyone, even the boycotters themselves, expected to last a few weeks, dragged on month after month. Two mass meetings were held every week to raise everyone's spirits and collect contributions. (Money was raised every way imaginable: One of King's ideas was for people to donate a third of their Christmas gift money to charity, a third to their own accounts, and a third to the MIA boycott fund.) Some 350 car pools provided a phenomenal 20,000 rides a day, even though police repeatedly harassed drivers with citations for fabricated violations. No one was immune from predicaments. Jo Ann Robinson, a careful, meticulous driver, was issued 17 tickets the first few months. Martin Luther King's first arrest was for "speeding thirty miles an hour in a twenty-five zone"; and since he thought the city jail was downtown, he assumed he was about to be lynched when he realized he was being driven out into the country and when they passed under an unfamiliar bridge. Then he saw the sign reading MONTGOMERY JAIL. He was actually glad, at that moment, to go to jail.

The boycott was starting to affect the Montgomery bus line. It was losing twenty-two cents a mile transporting only handfuls of whites around the city. Meantime, most whites stuck to driving their cars to work, a privilege that few were willing to sacrifice just to undermine the boycott. So the bus line started eliminating routes. But even that wasn't enough. The impatient parent company in Chicago ordered the fare doubled to twenty cents to stave off bankruptcy.

Then came the threatening calls, hate letters, and violence.

On January 30, 1956, a bomb exploded on Martin Luther King's porch, but no one was hurt. When he was informed while preaching a sermon at the First Baptist Church, King took a moment to remind churchgoers about nonviolence. He said, "An eye for an eye and a tooth for a tooth will only end up in a blind generation and a toothless people." When he arrived home, King encountered an irate crowd of blacks that was losing control. One man challenged a policeman with a .38; others threatened with broken bottles. King got their attention with an impromptu speech. He told everyone to refrain from violence. He told them to meet hate with love and do what Jesus advised: Love your enemies. Miraculously, the edge was off and the crowd dispersed. One policeman admitted later to a reporter, "I was terrified. I owe my life to that nigger preacher, and so do all the other white people that were there.''

On February 1, a dynamite bomb detonated on E. D. Nixon's lawn. A few days later, white students at the University of Alabama rioted to protest the court-ordered admission of Autherine Lucy, the school's first Negro student. When whites attempted to murder Lucy, the university expelled *her*; they said it was for her own protection. Yet they did nothing to the out-of-control white students. Days after that, White Citizens Councils of Mississippi and Alabama held a joint segregation rally at the Montgomery Coliseum that drew ten thousand. It was said to be the largest hate rally in a century. The featured speaker was Mississippi Senator James Eastland, a notorious white supremacist. As he criticized the boycott, the NAACP, and Martin Luther King, thousands of copies of this handbill were circulated:

When in the course of human events it becomes necessary to abolish the Negro race, proper methods should be used. Among these are guns, bow and arrows, sling shots and knives. We hold these truths to be self-evident that all whites are created equal with certain rights, among these are life, liberty and the pursuit of dead niggers. In every stage of the bus boycott we have been oppressed and degraded because of black, slimy, juicy, unbearably stinking niggers. The conduct should not be dwelt upon because behind them they have an ancestral background of Pygmies, Head hunters, snot suckers . . . If we don't stop these African flesh eaters, we will soon wake up and find Reverend King in the white house.

On February 21, an all-white grand jury indicted eighty-nine black Montgomery leaders under a forgotten antilabor law prohibiting boycotts. In Martin Luther King's sham show-trial on March 21, he was quickly convicted and fined five hundred dollars plus court costs. It was no coincidence that King was the only one convicted. On the other hand, the judge said he had spared King a harsher sentence because he had been urging nonviolence. It made no sense.

The story of Rosa Parks, Martin Luther King, and the Montgomery boycott was now major national news. But supporters in Montgomery were weary and ready to quit. Then, on Tuesday, November 13, 1956, the Supreme Court finally came through with a monumental victory: It declared Alabama's bus segregation laws unconstitutional. When the mandate reached Montgomery on December 20, blacks boarded buses again for the first time in 382 days. And while the boycott begun by Rosa Parks's indignation did not change how most Southern whites viewed blacks, it dramatically changed the way Southern blacks perceived themselves. More and more of them could now identify with Rosa Parks: proud Americans who could make a difference with a simple gesture of courage and pride.

———◦◦◦———

When I think of Rosa Parks now, I think of the power of an individual act of courage. I am reminded again that when one individual takes a stand, even though the motive in that person's mind might not be heroic at the time, it can affect the lives of other people. Joseph Cinque's revolt resulted in the wider application of the habeas corpus concept of justice. He did not intend that;

it happened as an offshoot of his personal act of courage. It was another example of the idea that if you do stand up, good things can happen. You may not know what those good things are for years, or maybe ever, but they can happen. To me, that is what Rosa Parks's heroism was all about. Here was an inconspicuous, private woman, minding her own business, when lightning struck. I believe the lightning struck *this* particular woman because she had the courage and dignity to command respect, even over the seemingly trivial issue of a seat on a bus.

In November 1995, eighty-two-year-old Rosa Parks was interviewed on the forty-first anniversary of the Supreme Court ruling banning bus segregation in Alabama. She told reporters, with the same modest pride she exhibited back then, ''I was willing to risk whatever happened to me to let everyone know that this treatment of our people had been going on much too long.''

If anyone epitomizes Jackie Robinson's inspiring statement that ''a life is not important except in the impact it has on other lives,'' it is Rosa Parks. If she had given in just one more time on that bus in 1955, if she had not taken a stand for all of ''our people'' by keeping her seat, imagine how much poorer a place our world would be today.

BIBLIOGRAPHY

Ralph David Abernathy, *And the Walls Came Tumbling Down*, New York: Harper & Row Publishers, 1989.

Neil Baldwin, *Edison: Inventing the Century*, New York: Hyperion, 1995.

Lerone Bennett, Jr., *Before the Mayflower: A History of Black America*, 5th revised ed., New York: Penguin Books, 1982.

————, *Wade in the Water: Great Moments in Black History*, Chicago: Johnson Publishing Company, Inc., 1979.

Taylor Branch, *Parting the Waters: America in the King Years, 1954–63*, New York: Simon & Schuster, 1988.

Arthur T. Burton, *Black, Red, and Deadly*, Austin, TX: Eakin Press, 1991.

Álvar Núñez Cabeza de Vaca, *The Account: Álvar Núñez Cabeza de Vaca's Relación*, Houston: Arte Público Press, 1993.

Clayborne Carson, David J. Garrow, Gerald Gill, Vincent Harding, and Darlene Clark Hine, *The Eyes on the Prize Civil Rights Reader*, New York: Penguin Books, 1991.

Herschel V. Cashin et al., *Under Fire with the Tenth U.S. Cavalry* (originally published 1899), Niwot, CO: University Press of Colorado, 1993.

Robert Conot, *A Streak of Luck*, New York: Bantam Books, 1980.

Dudley Taylor Cornish, *The Sable Arm: Black Troops in the Union Army, 1861–1865*, Lawrence, KS: University Press of Kansas, 1987.

Jay David and Elaine Crane, *The Black Soldier*, New York: William Morrow, 1971.

Burke Davis, *Black Heroes of the American Revolution*, New York: Harcourt Brace Jovanovich, 1976.

Marvin E. Fletcher, *The Black Soldier and Officer in the United*

States Army: 1891–1917, Columbia, MO: University of Missouri Press, 1974.

Philip S. Foner, *Blacks in the American Revolution*, Westport, CT: Greenwood Press, 1975.

Howard Jones, *Mutiny on the Amistad: The Saga of a Slave Revolt and Its Impact on American Abolition, Law, & Diplomacy*, Oxford: Oxford University Press, 1988.

William Loren Katz, *The Black West*, Seattle: Open Hand Publishing Inc., 1987.

William H. Leckie, *The Buffalo Soldiers*, Stillwater, OK: University of Oklahoma Press, 1967.

James McPherson, *The Negro's Civil War*, New York: Ballantine Books, 1991.

Martin V. Melosi, *Thomas A. Edison and the Modernization of America*, Oscar Handlin, ed., New York: HarperCollins, 1990.

Russell B. Nye, *William Lloyd Garrison and the Humanitarian Reformers*, Boston: Little, Brown, 1955.

Bill O'Neal, *Fighting Men of the Indian Wars*, Stillwater, OK: Barbed Wire Press, 1991.

Stephen B. Oates, *Let the Trumpet Sound: The Life of Martin Luther King, Jr.*, New York: New American Library, 1982.

Lou Potter with William Miles and Nina Rosenblum, *Liberators*, New York: Harcourt Brace Jovanovich, 1992.

Douglas Preston, *Cities of Gold*, New York: Simon & Schuster, 1992.

Benjamin Quarles, *The Negro in the Civil War*, Boston: Little, Brown, 1953.

———, *The Negro in the Making of America*, revised ed., New York: Collier Books, 1973.

Ivan Van Sertima, *Blacks in Science*, New Brunswick, CT: Transaction Books, 1986.

———, *They Came Before Columbus*, New York: Random House, 1976.

Edward Van Zile Scott, *Unwept, Unhonored, Unsung: Black American Soldiers & the Spanish-American War* (unpublished proof), Montgomery, AL: The Black Belt Press, 1955.

The Editors of Time-Life Books, *African Americans—Voices of Triumph: Perseverance*, Alexandria, VA: Time-Life Books, 1993.

Glennette Tilley Turner, *Lewis Howard Latimer*, Englewood Cliffs, NJ: Silver Burdett Press, 1991.

Juan Williams (with the *Eyes on the Prize* Production Team), *Eyes on the Prize: America's Civil Rights Years, 1954–1965* (companion volume to the PBS television series), New York: Viking Penguin, 1987.

Roberta Hughes Wright, *The Birth of the Montgomery Bus Boycott*, Southfield, MI: Charro Press, Inc., 1991.

INDEX